The *Complete*
BARTENDER'S
GUIDE

A FIREFLY BOOK

Published by Firefly Books Ltd. 2003

First printing

Publisher Cataloguing-in-Publication Data (U.S.)
(Library of Congress Standards)

Spence, Jordan.
    The complete bartender's guide / Jordan Spence _1st ed.
[400] p. : col. photos. ; cm.
Includes index.
Summary: Cocktail sourcebook including recipes, serving suggestions, tasting notes, brief histories of spirits, essentials for a well-stocked bar, and a directory of the world's top 500 cocktail bars.
ISBN 1-55297-643-2 (pbk.)
1. Bartending. 2. Cocktails. 3. Liquors. I. Title.
641.8/74 21   TX951.S64 2003

National Library of Canada Cataloguing in Publication Data

Spence, Jordan
    The complete bartender's guide / Jordan Spence.

Includes index.
ISBN 1-55297-643-2

    1. Cocktails. 2. Liquors. 3. Bars (Drinking establishments)--Directories. I. Title.

TX951.S66 2003   641.8'74   C2003-903498-4

Published in the United States in 2003 by
Firefly Books (U.S.) Inc.
P.O. Box 1338, Ellicott Station
Buffalo, New York 14205

Published in Canada in 2003 by
Firefly Books Ltd.
3680 Victoria Park Avenue
Toronto, Ontario, M2H 3K1

Project editor: Martin Corteel
Editorial assistant: David Ballheimer
Project art direction: Darren Jordan
Design: David Mitchell, Pipsqueak Media
Picture research: Marc Glanville
Production: Lisa French

Printed in China

The *Complete*
BARTENDER'S
GUIDE

Jordan Spence

FIREFLY BOOKS

Contents

Right: Vodka Martini with a twist of lemon

Introduction

Cocktails are cool once again. The very word "cocktail" conjures up an image of a glass with an elegant stem, chilled to the perfect temperature and filled with a shimmering pale-colored liquid. It is a timeless work of art when created with the skill of a genuine bartender, not a mixologist.

Of cursory glances, social chit-chat, cocktail party LBDs worn with *Sex and the City* stilettos, shining with diamante clips, waiters in white jackets proferring trays of fancy finger food, instantly at your beck and call. Such fantasies of a world apart from the everyday! The cocktail encapsulates all of these fantasies.

Having stepped out of the speakeasy culture into the mainstream around the 1950s, cocktails cruised along through the 1980s and 1990s, and shook themselves into the 21st century with classics such as the Sidecar still in demand. As for the Martini, it has been reinvented countless times in recent years, and one begins to wonder when a Martini is not a Martini! Certainly the discussions as to what makes the prefect dry Martini still fill the cigar smoke–filled air in bars around the world.

When created thoughtfully, a cocktail can bring a range of taste sensations to your palate; it can stimulate taste memories of a flavor savored long ago, bringing a lump to the throat. Open a bottle of vintage champagne and all the aromas of a far-flung foreign field fill the nose as you sniff the contents. Open a bottle of pure vodka made by a boutique company such as Ketel One or Grey Goose, and a host of flavors will waft by. Like a fine wine, a balanced cocktail satisfies the senses: taste, aroma, color and sight, each discovered sip by sip.

Drink wisely. And remember, there is no cure for a hangover. Cheers!

Mardi Gras: Every night is party night on New Orleans' Bourbon Street, famous for its bars and jazz

A–Z of Cocktails

Some cocktails appear in two categories and they are listed with both page references here.

Cocktail Recipes

Isn't it interesting how the spirits are raised whenever the invitation slides through the mail slot? "Come over for cocktails. 7 p.m. Saturday." It must be the expectation of the taste of exotic things to come that causes the heart to flutter and the lips to pucker up.

Give 10 people a large bottle of vodka, a selection of mixers, a cocktail shaker and bags of ice and it is guaranteed that within minutes someone will claim they can make the best Daiquiri this side of Cuba – and would you like to try one?

This section is for those who love the cocktail, and to allow them to make and serve a cocktail in the right manner. Not for them the bottles or sachets of premixed horrors sold as Margaritas or Moscow Mules. A handmade cocktail, stirred, mixed or shaken, is a work of art descended from a great tradition.

These recipes are the real thing, a selection of classic and modern cocktails as they were meant to be mixed and served. There are also modifications to recipes acknowledged as the original; sometimes the additional ingredients are an improvement, created by a bartender who wasn't satisfied with the taste of the original. It is only through experimentation that we can seek perfection.

Whether you are a whiskey lover, or a vodka-on-the-rocks fanatic, you will be pleasantly surprised at the selection of recipes here. There are sweet, sour, creamy, frozen, purely spirit, and bubbly recipes in this section, served in a selection of glasses: highball, tumbler, old-fashioned, margarita, champagne flute, liqueur and shot glasses. However, it is the elegant martini (cocktail) glass that best serves most recipes. It's the taste and color of what lies inside its sleek shape that matters.

Drink me: A kaleidoscope of color, a smorgasbord of taste, what more needs to be said about a cocktail?

Vodka Cocktails

Without vodka there would be no Cosmopolitan, Apple Martini or Bloody Mary. Its first appearance in America came in the 1950s when it was mixed with ginger beer, thus creating the Moscow Mule, which was served in a copper mug. Vodka is a great mixer, doesn't color the drink or taste strong on the breath. New vodkas are not as tasteless as they once were. Here is a selection of vivacious vodka cocktails from all over the world, including the **Black Russian**, **Key West Cooler** and **Mandarin Blossom**.

This selection includes flavored vodkas.

57 T-Bird

1 oz. (30 ml) vodka
²/₃ oz. (20 ml) amaretto
²/₃ oz. (20 ml) melon liqueur
²/₃ oz. (20 ml) peach schnapps
1²/₃ oz. (50 ml) freshly squeezed orange juice

Shake all the ingredients. Strain into an old-fashioned glass filled with ice cubes.

Absolut Hero

1 oz. (30 ml) blackcurrant vodka
1 oz. (30 ml) lemon vodka
1 oz. (30 ml) melon liqueur
²/₃ oz. (20 ml) freshly squeezed lime juice
²/₃ oz. (20 ml) egg white
soda water to fill
lime wedge as garnish

Shake all the ingredients, except soda water. Strain into a highball glass with ice. Fill with soda. Stir. Garnish with a lime wedge.

Aqueduct

3 oz. (90 ml) vodka
¹/₂ oz. (15 ml) triple sec
¹/₂ oz. (15 ml) apricot brandy
¹/₂ oz. (15 ml) fresh lime juice

Shake all the liquids together, then strain into a martini glass and serve.

Adios Mother

1 oz. (30 ml) vodka
1 oz. (30 ml) white rum
¹/₂ oz. (15 ml) lemon juice
¹/₂ oz. (15 ml) melon liqueur
dash of triple sec
dash of blue curaçao
3 tsp. (15 ml) superfine sugar

Shake all ingredients and strain into a highball glass with ice.

Alexander the Great

2 oz. (60 ml) vodka
1 oz. (30 ml) coffee liqueur
1 oz. (30 ml) white crème de cacao
1 oz. (30 ml) light cream
coffee beans as garnish
chocolate flakes as garnish

Shake all the liquid ingredients together and strain into a martini glass. Garnish with the coffee beans and chocolate flakes, and serve.

Anglo Angel

1 oz. (30 ml) vodka
1 oz. (30 ml) Mandarine Napoléon brandy
1 oz. (30 ml) mandarin juice
2 dashes Angostura bitters
lime spiral as garnish

Shake all the ingredients. Strain into a cocktail glass. Add a lime spiral.

Appease Me

1 oz. (30 ml) vodka
1 oz. (30 ml) mango liqueur
2 oz. (60 ml) orange juice
²/₃ oz. (20 ml) advocaat
1 oz. (30 ml) light cream
2 slices mango
orange slice as garnish

Blend all ingredients with ice. Pour into a highball glass. Garnish with a slice of orange and serve with a straw.

Apple Martini

2 oz. (60 ml) vodka
²/₃ oz. (20 ml) apple sour liqueur
¹/₃ oz. (10 ml) Cointreau

Shake all the ingredients. Strain into a chilled cocktail glass.

Après Ski

1 oz. (30 ml) crème de menthe
¹/₂ oz. (15 ml) Pernod
¹/₂ oz. (15 ml) vodka
lemonade to fill

Pour the crème de menthe, Pernod and vodka over ice cubes in a highball glass. Top up with lemonade and serve.

Aquamarine

1 oz. (30 ml) vodka
²/₃ oz. (20 ml) peach schnapps
¹/₃ oz. (10 ml) blue curaçao
¹/₃ oz. (10 ml) Cointreau
3 oz. (90 ml) apple juice

Shake all the ingredients. Strain into an old-fashioned glass with ice.

Aviation 2

2 oz. (60 ml) vodka
1 oz. (30 ml) maraschino liqueur
²/₃ oz. (20 ml) freshly squeezed lemon juice
maraschino cherry
twist of lemon as garnish

Shake all the ingredients. Strain into a cocktail glass. Drop a maraschino cherry in the drink and a twist of lemon.

Bali Trader

2 oz. (60 ml) vodka
²/₃ oz. (20 ml) green banana liqueur
²/₃ oz. (20 ml) pineapple juice

Shake all the ingredients. Strain into a cocktail glass.

Ballet Russe

1 oz. (30 ml) Smirnoff vodka
¹/₂ oz. (15 ml) crème de cassis
¹/₂ oz. (15 ml) fresh lime juice
¹/₂ oz. (15 ml) lemon juice

Shake all ingredients with ice. Strain into a cocktail glass.

Banana Peel

2 oz. (60 ml) vodka
2 oz. (60 ml) banana liqueur
1 oz. (30 ml) orange juice

Shake all ingredients and strain into an old-fashioned glass.

Bikini

2 oz. (60 ml) vodka
1 oz. (30 ml) white rum
4 oz. (120 ml) half-and-half or milk
¹/₂ oz. (15 ml) gomme syrup

Shake the ingredients together, then strain into a highball glass and serve.

Black Magic

2 oz. (60 ml) vodka
1 oz. (30 ml) Kahlua
dash of lemon juice
twist of lemon to serve

Stir all the ingredients together, then pour into an ice-filled old-fashioned glass. Serve with the lemon twist.

Black Magic (alt)

1 oz. (30 ml) vodka
$^2/_3$ oz. (20 ml) Kahlua
dash of freshly squeezed lemon juice
8 oz. (240 ml) cold coffee

Pour ingredients into an old-fashioned glass filled with ice. Stir.

Black Maria

1 oz. (30 ml) vodka
1 oz. (30 ml) dark rum
4 oz. (120 ml) cold coffee

Shake all the ingredients together, then strain into an ice-filled old-fashioned glass and serve.

Black Russian

1 oz. (30 ml) vodka
$^2/_3$ oz. (20 ml) Kahlua

Pour the vodka, then the Kahlua into an old-fashioned glass straight up or over crushed ice, then serve.

Blood Shot

1 oz. (30 ml) vodka
½ oz. (15 ml) lemon juice
2 oz. (60 ml) condensed consommé
½ oz. (15 ml) tomato soup
dash of ketchup
½ oz. (15 ml) Worcestershire sauce
celery salt as garnish
cucumber slice as garnish

Shake all ingredients and strain into a cocktail glass. Garnish with a sprinkle of celery salt and a slice of cucumber.

Bloody Caesar Shooter

1 clam
1 oz. (30 ml) vodka
1 oz. (30 ml) tomato juice
2 drops Worcestershire sauce
2 drops Tabasco
½ tsp. (2 ml) horseradish purée
1 pinch celery salt

Put the clam in the bottom of the shot glass, then shake the rest of the ingredients together in a shaker. Strain into the glass and serve.

Blowout

1 oz. (30 ml) vodka
1 oz. (30 ml) triple sec
dash of orange juice
dash of Bacardi white rum
dash of lemon-lime soda

Shake all the ingredients, except for the lemon-lime soda, with ice and strain into a cocktail glass. Add lemon-lime soda. Stir, then serve.

Blue Dove

1 oz. (30 ml) vodka
1 oz. (30 ml) blue curaçao
lemonade to fill
whipped cream

Pour the blue curaçao and vodka over ice in a highball glass. Then stir, and top up with lemonade. Float whipped cream on the top and serve.

Blue Mandarin

2 oz. (60 ml) Absolut Mandarin vodka
1 oz. (30 ml) blue curaçao
3 oz. (90 ml) sour mix
lemon slice as garnish

Shake all the ingredients with ice and strain into a chilled cocktail glass. Garnish with a slice of lemon.

Blue Martini

2 oz. (60 ml) vodka
$^{1}/_{3}$ oz. (10 ml) blue curaçao
$^{1}/_{3}$ oz. (10 ml) freshly squeezed lemon juice
8 fresh blueberries

Add blueberries to a shaker. Muddle. Add remaining ingredients. Shake. Strain into a cocktail glass.

Blue Orchid

2 oz. (60 ml) Absolut Citron vodka
dash of blue curaçao
dash of sour mix
dash of lime juice
dash of triple sec
lemon twist as garnish

Shake all the ingredients with ice. Strain into a chilled cocktail glass. Garnish with a twist of lemon.

Bongo Lemon Crush

3 oz. (90 ml) lemon vodka
4 lemon wedges
2 tsp. (10 ml) superfine sugar

Muddle the lemon wedges and the sugar in a mixing glass. Add the vodka to muddled mixture and stir. Strain into an old-fashioned glass filled with crushed ice.

Bonza Monza

1 oz. (30 ml) vodka
²/₃ oz. (20 ml) crème de cassis
2 oz. (60 ml) grapefruit juice

Pour ingredients into an old-fashioned glass full of crushed ice and stir.

Boston Bullet (all)

2 oz. (60 ml) chilled dry vodka
spray of dry vermouth from an atomizer
green olive stuffed with an almond to serve

Pour the vodka into a chilled martini glass with a spray of dry vermouth. Add the olive and serve.

Breakfast Bar

2 oz. (60 ml) vodka
handful cherry tomatoes
1 leaf fresh basil
pinch ground coriander
pinch celery salt
chopped chives
pinch ground pepper

Blend all the ingredients together, then strain into an ice-filled highball glass.

Bullshot

1²/₃ oz. (50 ml) vodka
5 oz. (150 ml) beef bouillon
dash of freshly squeezed lemon juice
2–3 dashes Worcestershire sauce
celery salt
Tabasco sauce
black pepper

Shake bouillon, lemon juice, Tabasco and Worcestershire sauces with vodka.
Strain into a highball glass full of ice cubes. Add celery salt and black pepper.
Serve with a stirrer.

Caesar

2 oz. (60 ml) Absolut Pepper vodka
Clamato juice
Worcestershire sauce
horseradish sauce
white pepper
celery salt
splash of fino sherry
splash of orange juice
Tabasco sauce to taste

Pour the vodka over ice in a highball glass. In a pitcher, combine the other
ingredients, then add mix to the vodka and ice, and stir.

Caipirovska

2 oz. (60 ml) vodka
1 lime, diced
dash of freshly squeezed lime juice
2 tsp. (10 ml) superfine sugar

Muddle diced lime and sugar in an old-fashioned glass. Add vodka and lime
juice. Fill glass with crushed ice, stir, and serve with a straw.

Cajun Martini (alt)

2 oz. (60 ml) chilled vodka
spray of dry vermouth from an atomizer
jalapeno chilli to serve

Pour the vodka into a chilled martini glass with a spray of dry vermouth. Add the chilli and serve.

Cape Codder

1½ oz. (45 ml) vodka
3 oz. (90 ml) cranberry juice
1 wedge of lime

Pour vodka and cranberry juice into a highball glass over ice. Stir well, add the lime and serve.

Cargo

2 oz. (60 ml) vodka
1 oz. (30 ml) white crème de menthe
2 fresh mint leaves

Rub the rim of an old-fashioned glass with one of the mint leaves. Pour the crème de menthe and vodka over ice cubes into the glass. Garnish with the other leaf and serve.

Chambord Kamikaze

3 oz. (90 ml) vodka
½ oz. (15 ml) Cointreau
½ oz. (15 ml) lemon juice
½ oz. (15 ml) simple syrup
½ oz. (15 ml) Chambord
½ lime, sliced
lime slice to garnish

Place all ingredients (including the sliced lime) in a large shaker with ice. Shake violently. Strain and pour into a cocktail glass. Garnish with a slice of lime.

Chartreuse Dragon

2 oz. (60 ml) vodka
2 oz. (60 ml) lychee juice
²/₃ oz. (20 ml) green Chartreuse
¹/₃ oz. (10 ml) blue curaçao
dash of freshly squeezed lime juice
lemon-lime soda to fill

Shake all ingredients, except lemon-lime soda. Strain into a highball glass full of ice cubes. Fill with lemon-lime soda. Stir.

Chee Chee

1 oz. (30 ml) vodka
1 oz. (30 ml) pineapple juice
1 oz. (30 ml) coconut milk
pineapple wedge as garnish

Shake all ingredients and strain into a cocktail glass. Garnish with a pineapple wedge.

Cherry Blossom Martini

2 oz. (60 ml) vodka
¹/₂ oz. (15 ml) black forest cherry liqueur
¹/₂ oz. (15 ml) triple sec
dash of Rose's Lime Juice
cherry blossom as garnish

Shake all the ingredients with ice and strain into a martini glass. Garnish with a cherry blossom on top.

Chi Chi

2 oz. (60 ml) vodka
1 oz. (30 ml) coconut cream
3 oz. (90 ml) pineapple juice

Blend all the ingredients together and pour into a large goblet.

Chiquita

2 oz. (60 ml) vodka
1/3 oz. (10 ml) banana liqueur
1/3 oz. (10 ml) lime juice
1/2 banana, sliced
pinch of superfine sugar

Shake all ingredients and strain into a cocktail glass. Garnish with a slice of banana.

Chocolate Martini

2 oz. (60 ml) vodka
1/2 oz. (15 ml) crème de cacao

Pour ingredients into shaker filled with ice then pour into martini glass.

Chocolate Mint Martini

2 oz. (60 ml) vodka
1 oz. (30 ml) white crème de cacao
dash of white crème de menthe

Pour ingredients into a mixing glass with ice and stir. Strain into a cocktail glass.

Cliffhanger

2 oz. (60 ml) pepper vodka
1 oz. (30 ml) Cointreau
2/3 oz. (20 ml) lime cordial
lime twist as garnish

Shake all the ingredients. Strain into a cocktail glass. Add a twist of lime.

Cobbler

1 tsp. (5 ml) powdered sugar
1 oz. (30 ml) soda water
2 oz. (60 ml) vodka or any spirit
seasonal fruit as garnish

In an old-fashioned glass, dissolve the sugar in the soda water, then fill the glass with ice. Stir in the spirit, garnish with the fruit and serve.

Cool Martini

2 oz. (60 ml) vodka
²/₃ oz. (20 ml) apple juice
¹/₂ oz. (15 ml) Cointreau
¹/₂ oz. (15 ml) freshly squeezed lemon juice

Shake all the ingredients. Strain into a cocktail glass.

Copenhagen

2 oz. (60 ml) vodka
¹/₂ oz. (15 ml) aquavit
slivered blanched almonds as garnish

Shake and strain into a cocktail glass and garnish with almonds.

Cordless Screwdriver

1 oz. (30 ml) chilled vodka
1 orange wedge
sugar

Coat the orange wedge in the sugar and pour the vodka into a shot glass.
Drink the vodka, then eat the orange.

Cosmopolitan 2

1 oz. (30 ml) vodka
¹/₂ oz. (15 ml) triple sec
¹/₂ oz. (15 ml) cranberry juice
juice of 1 lime
flamed orange peel to garnish

Shake all the ingredients, then strain into a chilled cocktail glass and serve
with the flaming garnish.

Croc Cooler

1 oz. (30 ml) lemon-flavored vodka
1 oz. (30 ml) Midori
¹/₂ oz. (15 ml) Cointreau
2 oz. (60 ml) sour mix

Pour the ingredients into a highball glass filled with ice. Stir, and serve with a straw.

Cyber Punch

1 oz. (30 ml) vodka
1 oz. (30 ml) gin
1 oz. (30 ml) white rum
1 oz. (30 ml) triple sec
$^1/_2$ oz. (15 ml) beer
1 oz. (30 ml) lemon juice
1 tsp. (5 ml) superfine sugar
dash of grenadine

Pour all ingredients into a highball glass and stir. Serve with a stirrer and a straw.

Czarina

2 oz. (60 ml) vodka
1 oz. (30 ml) apricot brandy
$^1/_2$ oz. (15 ml) dry vermouth
dash of Angostura bitters

Stir all the liquids together. Strain into martini glass and serve.

Deep Freeze

1 oz. (30 ml) peppermint schnapps
$^1/_2$ oz. (15 ml) vodka

Pour in a chilled shot glass or on the rocks in an old-fashioned glass. Stir. Serve.

Demon Possession

1 oz. (30 ml) citrus vodka
1 oz. (30 ml) light rum
dash of blue curaçao
lemon-lime soda
maraschino cherry as garnish

Shake all ingredients with ice. Strain into chilled highball glass filled with crushed ice and garnish with a maraschino cherry.

Derby Punch

2 oz. (60 ml) vodka
2 oz. (60 ml) gin
2 oz. (60 ml) white rum
2 oz. (60 ml) Sauza silver tequila
$^1/_2$ oz. (15 ml) triple sec
1 oz. (30 ml) pineapple juice
dash of cranberry juice
lemon-lime soda to fill
maraschino cherry as garnish

Shake all ingredients, except lemon-lime soda, and strain into a highball glass
with ice. Top up with lemon-lime soda. Garnish with a cherry.

Detroit Martini

2 oz. (60 ml) vodka
$^2/_3$ oz. (20 ml) gomme syrup
mint leaves

Shake all the ingredients. Strain into a cocktail glass.

Diplomat

2 oz. (60 ml) vodka
3 oz. (90 ml) pineapple juice
2 oz. (60 ml) Midori
$^1/_2$ oz. (15 ml) lemon juice

Shake all ingredients and strain into a highball glass filled with ice. Serve
with a straw.

Dirty Jane

1 oz. (30 ml) Ketel One vodka
1 oz. (30 ml) liquid from pickled green tomatoes
thin wedge of a pickled green tomato as a garnish

Pour the vodka and pickling liquid into a shaker with ice and shake. Strain into
a cocktail glass and garnish with a tomato wedge.

Dock of the Bay

1 oz. (30 ml) vodka
²/₃ oz. (20 ml) schnapps
3 oz. (90 ml) cranberry juice
2 oz. (60 ml) pineapple juice
lime wedge as garnish

Shake all the ingredients. Strain into a highball glass full of ice cubes. Add a lime wedge.

Double Vision

1 oz. (30 ml) lemon vodka
1 oz. (30 ml) blackcurrant vodka
4 dashes Angostura bitters
1 oz. (30 ml) apple juice

Shake all the ingredients. Strain into a cocktail glass.

Dragon Fly

2 oz. (60 ml) vodka
²/₃ oz. (20 ml) melon liqueur
dash of freshly squeezed lime juice
1 oz. (30 ml) apple juice

Shake all the ingredients. Strain into a cocktail glass.

Dyevtchka

1 oz. (30 ml) vodka
1 oz. (30 ml) Cointreau
½ oz. (15 ml) fresh lime juice
½ oz. (15 ml) fresh lemon juice
½ oz. (15 ml) pineapple juice
pineapple wedge as garnish
maraschino cherry as garnish

Shake ingredients with ice and strain into an old-fashioned glass. Garnish with a pineapple wedge and maraschino cherry.

Eight Mile Creek Cosmo

2 oz. (60 ml) Absolut Mandarin vodka
1 oz. (30 ml) fresh lime juice
1 oz. (30 ml) triple sec
1 oz. (30 ml) passion fruit purée
lemon twist as garnish

Shake with ice, strain and serve in martini glass with a lemon twist.

Evita

1 oz. (30 ml) vodka
1 oz. (30 ml) melon liqueur
2 oz. (60 ml) freshly squeezed orange juice
1 oz. (30 ml) freshly squeezed lime juice
dash of gomme syrup

Shake all the ingredients. Strain into an old-fashioned glass with ice.

Flirt

1 oz. (30 ml) vodka
1 oz. (15 ml) black sambuca
2 oz. (60 ml) cranberry juice

Shake all the ingredients. Strain into a cocktail glass.

Fortunella

1 oz. (30 ml) Ketel One vodka
³/₄ oz. (22 ml) Bombay Sapphire gin
³/₄ oz. (22 ml) Caravella
splash Cointreau
splash Campari
1 tsp. (5 ml) candied kumquat nectar
twist of lemon as garnish
twist of kumquat as garnish

Coat a shaker with the Cointreau and Campari and discard the excess. Add the remaining liquid ingredients, shake, then strain into a cocktail glass and garnish with the twists of lemon and kumquat.

Forward Pass

1 oz. (30 ml) vodka
1 oz. (30 ml) Cointreau
1 oz. (30 ml) dry vermouth
1 oz. (30 ml) fresh lemon juice

Shake ingredients with ice and strain into a cocktail glass.

French 76

$^3/_4$ oz. (22 ml) vodka
$^1/_4$ oz. (8 ml) lemon juice
dash of gomme syrup
dash of grenadine
champagne to fill

Shake the first four ingredients together, strain into a champagne flute, and top up with champagne.

French Kiss 1

1 oz. (30 ml) vodka
1 oz. (30 ml) crème de mure
$^1/_2$ oz. (15 ml) white crème de cacao
1 oz. (30 ml) heavy cream

Mix the ingredients together in a shaker, then strain into a martini glass.

French Martini 1

2 oz. (60 ml) vodka
dash of Chambord liqueur
dash of pineapple juice

Shake all the ingredients together and strain into a cocktail glass.

French Martini 2

1 oz. (30 ml) vodka
$^1/_3$ oz. (10 ml) Chambord liqueur
dash of pineapple juice
dash of apple cider
pinch fleurs de sel
thinly sliced green apples

Line a cocktail glass with green apples, with the skins coated with fleurs de sel. Shake the vodka, Chambord and juice with ice. Chill and strain into the cocktail glass. Shake the cider until it foams and pour on top.

French Martini 3

3 oz. (90 ml) vodka
1 oz. (30 ml) raspberry liqueur
3 oz. (90 ml) pineapple juice
pineapple slice as garnish

Shake ingredients with ice, strain and serve in a cocktail glass. Garnish with a slice of pineapple.

Fruit Passion

1 oz. (30 ml) vodka
1 oz. (30 ml) rum
pineapple juice
$^1/_2$ oz. (15 ml) passion fruit pulp
pineapple wedge as garnish

Half-fill a highball glass with ice and pour in the vodka, rum and passion fruit pulp. Top up with the pineapple juice. Garnish with a pineapple wedge.

Fuel for Thought

1 oz. (30 ml) lemon vodka
$^1/_3$ oz. (10 ml) blue curaçao
dash of sour mix
dash of pineapple juice
maraschino cherry as garnish

Shake all ingredients with ice and strain into a cocktail glass. Garnish with a cherry.

Giada

1 oz. (30 ml) vodka
½ oz. (15 ml) Campari
½ oz. (15 ml) Galliano
dash of pineapple juice

Shake all the ingredients together, then strain into a martini glass and serve.

Gimlet

2 oz. (60 ml) vodka or gin
1 oz. (30 ml) lime cordial
wedge of lime to garnish

Over ice, pour the vodka or gin and lime cordial into an old-fashioned glass and serve with the lime wedge.

Ginger Martini

2 oz. (60 ml) vodka
freshly grated ginger
dash of gomme syrup
orange zest
slice of fresh ginger as garnish

Shake ingredients with ice. Strain into a chilled cocktail glass. Garnish with a slice of fresh ginger.

Godmother

2 oz. (60 ml) vodka
1 oz. (30 ml) amaretto

Pour the vodka and amaretto into an ice-filled old-fashioned glass and serve.

Goose Bumps

1 oz. (30 ml) vodka
1 oz. (30 ml) red cherry purée
dash of cherry liqueur
champagne to fill

Pour vodka, cherry purée and cherry liqueur into a champagne glass. Stir, then top up with champagne.

Green Dinosaur

⅔ oz. (20 ml) vodka
⅔ oz. (20 ml) gold tequila
⅔ oz. (20 ml) light rum
⅔ oz. (20 ml) gin
⅔ oz. (20 ml) triple sec
1 oz. (30 ml) freshly squeezed lime juice
dash of gomme syrup
dash of melon liqueur

Pour ingredients, except melon liqueur, into a shaker. Shake, then pour into a highball glass full of ice. Float the melon liqueur over the top.

Green Tea Martini

2 oz. (60 ml) lemon vodka
1½ oz. (45 ml) green tea, pre-steeped
dash of triple sec
squeeze lemon
lemon twist as garnish

Pour vodka, green tea and triple sec into a shaker with ice. Add a squeeze of lemon and shake. Strain into a chilled cocktail glass and add a twist of lemon.

Hair Raiser

2 oz. (60 ml) 100 proof vodka
1½ oz. (45 ml) rye whiskey
½ oz. (15 ml) fresh lemon juice

Mix together the vodka, whiskey and lemon juice in a shaker. Strain into a martini glass and serve.

Harvey Wallbanger

2 oz. (60 ml) vodka
5 oz. (150 ml) freshly squeezed orange juice
1 oz. (30 ml) Galliano
slice of orange

Pour vodka and orange juice into a highball glass full of ice and stir. Float Galliano on top. Garnish with a slice of orange and serve with a stirrer.

Hot Ice

1 oz. (30 ml) pepper vodka
½ oz. (15 ml) blue curaçao
½ oz. (15 ml) pineapple juice
lemon-lime soda to fill

Shake the first three ingredients with ice and strain into a highball glass with ice. Top with lemon-lime soda.

Iceberg

2 oz. (60 ml) vodka
dash of Pernod

Stir the vodka and Pernod together, then pour into an ice-filled old-fashioned glass and serve.

Imagine!

2 oz. (60 ml) vodka
2 oz. (60 ml) clear apple juice
pulp of one passionfruit
ginger ale to fill

Scoop out the passionfruit pulp and put into a shaker with crushed ice. Add vodka and apple juice. Shake. Pour into a highball glass full of ice. Fill with ginger ale. Stir.

Joe Collins

2 oz. (60 ml) vodka
1 oz. (30 ml) lemon juice
1 tsp. (5 ml) superfine sugar
dash of Angostura bitters (optional)
soda water to fill

Place the first three ingredients in a tall glass half-filled with ice, and stir to mix. Top up with soda. Add bitters if wanted. Stir gently.

Joe Fizz

2 oz. (60 ml) vodka
1 oz. (30 ml) lemon juice
1 tsp. (5 ml) superfine sugar
dash of Angostura bitters (optional)
soda water to fill

Shake and strain into a tall glass, and top up with soda.

Joe Sour

2 oz. (60 ml) vodka
³/₄ oz. (22 ml) lemon juice
1/2 tsp. (2 ml) superfine sugar

Shake and strain into a sour glass.

Kamikaze

1 oz. (30 ml) vodka
1 oz. (30 ml) freshly squeezed lime juice
1 oz. (30 ml) triple sec

Shake all the ingredients together, then strain into a shot glass.

Key West Cooler

¹/₂ oz. (15 ml) vodka
¹/₂ oz. (15 ml) peach liqueur
¹/₂ oz. (15 ml) Midori
¹/₂ oz. (15 ml) Malibu
2 oz. (60 ml) cranberry juice
2 oz. (60 ml) orange juice
orange slice as garnish

Fill a highball glass with ice and add the vodka, then peach liqueur, Midori
and Malibu. Add the cranberry and orange juices. Stir well. Garnish with a
slice of orange.

Kurrant Affair

1 oz. (30 ml) blackcurrant vodka
1 oz. (30 ml) lemon vodka
4 oz. (120 ml) apple juice

Shake all the ingredients. Strain into a highball glass with ice.

La Dolce Vita

1 oz. (30 ml) vodka
5 seedless grapes
1 tsp. honey
Prosecco dry sparkling wine to fill

Muddle the grapes in a shaker. Add vodka and honey. Shake. Strain into a
champagne glass. Fill with Prosecco.

Limey

1 oz. (30 ml) lemon vodka
1 oz. (30 ml) orange liqueur
1 oz. (30 ml) freshly squeezed lime juice

Shake all the ingredients. Strain into a cocktail glass.

Love for Sale

1 oz. (30 ml) Absolut Mandarin vodka
½ oz. (15 ml) passion fruit liqueur
½ oz. (15 ml) pineapple juice
½ oz. (15 ml) orange juice
maraschino cherry as garnish

Shake all the ingredients with ice and strain into a chilled cocktail glass.
Garnish with a maraschino cherry.

Lucy's

1 oz. (30 ml) vodka
1 oz. (30 ml) brown crème de cacao
1 oz. (30 ml) crème de menthe

Mix all the ingredients together in a shaker, then strain into an old-fashioned
glass and serve.

Lychee Martini

1 oz. (30 ml) vodka
⅓ oz. (10 ml) lychee liqueur
⅓ oz. (10 ml) crème de banane
1 oz. (30 ml) pineapple juice

Shake all the ingredients. Strain into a cocktail glass.

Madras

1½ oz. (45 ml) vodka
4 oz. (120 ml) cranberry juice
1 oz. (30 ml) orange juice
lime wedge as garnish

Pour the liquid ingredients into a highball glass over ice. Add the lime wedge and serve.

Madroska

2 oz. (60 ml) vodka
3 oz. (90 ml) apple juice
2 oz. (60 ml) cranberry juice
1 oz. (30 ml) freshly squeezed orange juice

Pour ingredients into a highball glass filled with ice.

Mandarin Blossom

3 oz. (90 ml) Absolut Mandarin vodka
3 oz. (90 ml) Midori
dash of cranberry juice
dash of orange juice
maraschino cherry as garnish
lemon slice as garnish

Pour ingredients into a shaker with ice. Shake well and strain into a highball glass filled with ice. Garnish with a cherry and a lemon slice.

Mandarin Punch

2 oz. (60 ml) Absolut Mandarin vodka
dash of orange juice
dash of cranberry juice
dash of grapefruit juice
dash of cherry juice
dash of lemon-lime soda
maraschino cherry as garnish

Shake all ingredients, except the lemon-lime soda, with ice. Strain into a chilled cocktail glass. Add a dash of soda. Garnish with a cherry.

Mello Jell-O Shot (makes 15 3-oz. shots)

1 pint (475 ml) Stolichnaya vodka
1½ pints (710 ml) Midori melon liqueur
8 sheets baker's gelatin
1 pint (475 ml) watermelon juice
4 oz. (120 ml) gomme syrup
½ cup (120 ml) dried currants (optional)
3 oz. (90 ml) crème de cassis (optional)

Heat 8 oz. (240 ml) Midori with 3 sheets gelatin until dissolved. Cool. Add the remaining Midori. For each drink, pour 1½ oz. (45 ml) into a cordial glass. Leave for 20 minutes in the freezer. Then, blend 8 oz. (240 ml) of watermelon juice with the gomme syrup and 5 sheets gelatin. Heat until dissolved. Cool. Add the remaining watermelon juice and vodka. Pour 1½ oz. (45 ml) to fill each glass. Dried currants soaked in crème de cassis can be added before it sets.

Melon Martini

1⅔ oz. (50 ml) vodka
a quarter of a slice of watermelon
dash of freshly squeezed lemon juice

Muddle melon in a shaker. Add ice and vodka. Shake. Strain into a cocktail glass.

Metro Martini

1 oz. (30 ml) Stolichnaya Razberi vodka
dash of triple sec
dash of Rose's Lime Juice
$^1/_2$ oz. (15 ml) Chambord liqueur
juice of half a lime
lime wedge as garnish

Shake ingredients with ice. Strain into a chilled cocktail glass and garnish with a lime wedge.

Metropolis

2 oz. (60 ml) Absolut Mandarin vodka
$^1/_2$ oz. (15 ml) Mandarine Napoléon liqueur
$^1/_2$ oz. (15 ml) fresh lemon juice
dash of gomme syrup

Shake all ingredients with ice and strain into a cocktail glass.

Metropolitan 1

2 oz. (60 ml) Absolut Kurrant vodka
$^1/_2$ oz. (15 ml) Rose's Lime Cordial
$^1/_2$ oz. (15 ml) lime juice
1 oz. (30 ml) cranberry juice
lime wedge to garnish

Shake and strain into a cocktail glass and garnish with the wedge of lime.

Metropolitan 2

2 oz. (60 ml) blackcurrant vodka
$^2/_3$ oz. (20 ml) Cointreau
1 oz. (30 ml) cranberry juice
dash of freshly squeezed lime juice

Shake all the ingredients. Strain into a cocktail glass.

Milkshake

2 oz. (60 ml) vanilla vodka
1 oz. (30 ml) Frangelico
1 oz. (30 ml) Baileys Irish Cream

Shake with ice. Strain into a chilled cocktail glass.

Misty

1 oz. (30 ml) vodka
1 oz. (30 ml) Cointreau
1 oz. (30 ml) apricot brandy
dash of crème de banane

Stir all the ingredients together, then strain into a martini glass and serve.

Molotov Cocktail

3 oz. (90 ml) Finlandia vodka
¹/₂ oz. (15 ml) Black Bush Irish whiskey
¹/₂ oz. (15 ml) Irish Mist

Shake and strain into cocktail glasses.

Mother's Milk

1 oz. (30 ml) vodka
¹/₂ oz. (15 ml) gin
¹/₂ oz. (15 ml) Tia Maria
¹/₂ oz. (15 ml) orgeat syrup
4 oz. (120 ml) half-and-half or milk

Shake all the ingredients together, then pour into an old-fashioned glass and serve.

Mudslide

2 oz. (60 ml) vodka
2 oz. (60 ml) Kahlua
2 oz. (60 ml) Baileys Irish cream

Mix with cracked ice in a shaker. Strain and serve in a chilled highball glass.

New England Iced Tea

1 oz. (30 ml) vodka
1 oz. (30 ml) triple sec/Cointreau
1 oz. (30 ml) gold tequila
1 oz. (30 ml) light rum
1 oz. (30 ml) gin
1 oz. (30 ml) freshly squeezed lime juice
1 oz. (30 ml) gomme syrup
cranberry juice to fill

Pour ingredients, except cranberry juice, into a shaker. Shake. Strain into a highball glass with ice. Fill with cranberry juice.

Onion Breath

2 oz. (60 ml) vodka
$^1/_2$ oz. (15 ml) vinegar from cocktail onions
1 drop Worcestershire sauce
$^1/_2$ oz. (15 ml) lemon juice
2 cocktail onions to garnish

Shake all the ingredients together, then strain into a martini glass. Serve, garnished with the onions.

Orange Blossom

2 oz. (60 ml) vodka
2 oz. (60 ml) orange juice
dash of orange flower water

Shake all the ingredients together and strain into a cocktail glass.

Orange Caipirovska

2 oz. (60 ml) orange vodka
$^2/_3$ oz. (20 ml) freshly squeezed lemon juice
half an orange, diced
1 tsp. (5 ml) superfine sugar

Muddle the orange and sugar in an old-fashioned glass. Add remaining ingredients. Fill with crushed ice.

Orange Hush

3 oz. (90 ml) Absolut Mandarin vodka
1 oz. 30 ml) Grand Marnier
½ oz. (15 ml) fresh orange juice
½ oz. (15 ml) fresh lemon juice

Shake with ice and strain into a chilled cocktail glass with a powdered sugar rim.

Oyster Shooter (aka Heartstarter)

½ oz. (15 ml) vodka
½ oz. (15 ml) tomato juice
dash of cocktail sauce
dash of Worcestershire sauce
dash of Tabasco sauce
1 fresh oyster

Shake all the ingredients with ice and strain into a chilled cocktail glass.

Parson's Nose

2 oz. (60 ml) vodka
½ oz. (15 ml) amaretto
½ oz. (15 ml) crème de peche
dash of Angostura bitters

Stir all the ingredients together, then strain into a martini glass and serve.

Peach Molly

2 oz. (60 ml) vodka
dash of peach schnapps
lemon wedge as garnish
lime wedge as garnish

Shake with ice and strain into a chilled cocktail glass. Garnish with lemon and
lime wedges.

Pearl Harbor

1 oz. (30 ml) vodka
²/₃ oz. (20 ml) melon liqueur
1 oz. (30 ml) pineapple juice

Shake all the ingredients. Strain into a cocktail glass.

Petit Zinc

1 oz. (30 ml) vodka
¹/₂ oz. (15 ml) Cointreau
¹/₂ oz. (15 ml) sweet vermouth
¹/₂ oz. (15 ml) orange juice
orange zest or maraschino cherry as garnish

Shake all ingredients with ice and strain into a chilled cocktail glass. Garnish with orange zest or a maraschino cherry.

Pink Fetish

1 oz. (30 ml) vodka
1 oz. (30 ml) peach schnapps
2 oz. (60 ml) cranberry juice
2 oz. (60 ml) freshly squeezed orange juice
lime wedge as garnish

Shake all the ingredients. Strain over ice into an old-fashioned glass. Add a lime wedge.

Pink Lemonade

2 oz. (60 ml) lemon vodka
¹/₂ oz. (15 ml) Cointreau
1 oz. (30 ml) cranberry juice
juice of 1 lemon
lemon wheel as garnish

Shake with ice and serve in an old-fashioned glass with ice. Garnish with a lemon wheel.

Poison Arrow

1 oz. (30 ml) vodka
1 oz. (30 ml) light rum
2 dashes Midori
2 dashes blue curaçao
dash of pineapple juice

Shake all the ingredients with ice. Strain into chilled highball glass filled with crushed ice.

Polish Martini

1½ oz. (45 ml) Wyborowa vodka
½ oz. (15 ml) Krupnik vodka
dash of apple juice

Shake and strain into a cocktail glass.

Pure Bliss

3 oz. (90 ml) lemon vodka
dash of Cointreau
dash of fresh lemon juice

Coat the rim of a chilled cocktail glass with powdered sugar. Shake all the ingredients well with ice and strain into the glass.

Purple Hooter

1 oz. (30 ml) citrus vodka
½ oz. (15 ml) triple sec
½ oz. (15 ml) Chambord liqueur

Shake all the ingredients together, then strain into a shot glass.

Quiet Rage

1²/₃ oz. (50 ml) vodka
2 oz. (60 ml) guava juice
2 oz. (60 ml) pineapple juice
4 fresh lychees
1 oz. (30 ml) coconut cream
dash of grenadine

Blend ingredients with crushed ice. Pour into a highball glass.

Raspberry Martini

2 oz. (60 ml) vodka
1 oz. (30 ml) crème de framboise
10 raspberries
dash of gomme syrup

Put the gomme in a shaker and muddle the raspberries in the syrup. Add vodka and crème de framboise. Shake. Strain into a cocktail glass.

Red October

2 oz. (60 ml) Stolichnaya Razberi vodka
¹/₂ oz. (15 ml) Chambord liqueur
champagne to fill
1 fresh raspberry as garnish
lemon twist as garnish

Shake first two ingredients with ice and strain into a cocktail glass. Top up with champagne and garnish with a fresh raspberry and lemon twist.

Red Russian

1 oz. (30 ml) vodka
1 oz. (30 ml) white crème de cacao
2 dashes grenadine

Shake all the ingredients together, then strain into an ice-filled old-fashioned glass and serve.

Reggae Sundash

1 oz. (30 ml) lemon vodka
½ oz. (15 ml) coconut rum
6 oz. (170 ml) orange juice
dash of grenadine
dash of soda water

Shake all the ingredients, except soda, with ice and strain into a highball glass filled with ice. Add soda water. Serve with a straw.

Road Runner

1 oz. (30 ml) vodka
⅔ oz. (20 ml) amaretto
⅔ oz. (20 ml) coconut cream

Shake all the ingredients together, then strain into a martini glass and serve.

Royal Blush

1 oz. (30 ml) vodka
1 oz. (30 ml) crème de framboise
1 oz. (30 ml) heavy cream
2 dashes grenadine

Mix the ingredients together in a shaker, then strain into a martini glass and serve.

Russian Bear

1 oz. (30 ml) vodka
1½ oz. (45 ml) light cream
¼ oz. (8 ml) crème de cacao
1 tsp. (5 ml) superfine sugar

Shake and strain into a cocktail glass.

Russian Cocktail

1 oz. (30 ml) vodka
1 oz. (30 ml) gin
1 oz. (30 ml) white crème de cacao

Shake all the ingredients together, then strain into a martini glass and serve.

Salty Dog

2 oz. (60 ml) vodka
2 oz. (60 ml) grapefruit juice

Mix the vodka with the grapefruit juice in a shaker, then strain into a martini glass and serve.

Screwdriver

2 oz. (60 ml) vodka
5 oz. (150 ml) freshly squeezed orange juice

Pour the vodka into a highball glass with ice. Add orange juice, stir and serve with a stirrer.

Scroppino

1 oz. (30 ml) Absolut Citron vodka
6 oz. (170 ml) lemon sorbet
champagne
lemon slice (thin) as garnish

Pour all ingredients into a mixing glass and blend with a hand blender. Strain into a cocktail glass and garnish with a thin slice of lemon.

Sea Breeze

2 oz. (60 ml) vodka
3 oz. (90 ml) cranberry juice
2 oz. (60 ml) fresh grapefruit juice

Pour ingredients over ice into a highball glass. Stir and serve with a stirrer.

Sea Horse

1½ oz. (45 ml) vodka
dash of Pernod
1 oz. (30 ml) apple juice
1 oz. (30 ml) cranberry juice
¼ lime, freshly squeezed
sprig of mint as garnish

Pour ingredients into a highball glass filled with ice. Garnish with a sprig of mint.

Silver Bullet

2 oz. (60 ml) vodka
1 oz. (30 ml) kümmel

Pour the vodka and kümmel into an old-fashioned glass and serve.

Studio 54 Kiss

3 oz. (90 ml) Ketel One vodka
½ oz. (15 ml) pineapple juice
½ oz. (15 ml) peach purée
dash of peach liqueur
champagne to fill
peach wedge as garnish
2 pineapple leaves as garnish

Combine first four ingredients in a shaker with ice. Shake well and strain into a chilled cocktail glass. Top up with champagne. Garnish with a peach wedge and two neat pineapple leaves.

Sugar Cocktail

1½ oz. (45 ml) vodka
½ oz. (15 ml) peach schnapps
dash of peach nectar
dash of sour mix

Shake with ice, and strain in a sugar-rimmed martini glass.

Tablatini A fusion for 4 servings

8 oz. (240 ml) lemon-flavored vodka
1 pint (475 ml) pineapple juice
3 oz. (90 ml) fresh lemon juice
6 coarsely chopped stalks fresh lemon grass

Simmer the pineapple juice and lemon grass in a saucepan for 15 minutes.
Take off the heat and cool. Strain into a jar and place in the refrigerator. To a
pitcher filled with ice, add the pineapple juice, vodka and fresh lemon juice.
Mix well. Strain into four chilled cocktail glasses.

That Stinger

2 oz. (60 ml) vodka
1 oz. (30 ml) white crème de menthe
chocolate mint candy

In a chilled mixing glass, stir the vodka and crème de menthe. Garnsh with
the mint candy.

The Abyss

1 oz. (30 ml) vodka
$^1/_2$ oz. (15 ml) white rum
$^1/_2$ oz. (15 ml) blue curaçao
pineapple juice

Pour the blue curaçao into a chilled cocktail glass. Combine the vodka, rum
and pineapple juice in a blender with ice. Strain into the cocktail glass over
blue curaçao.

The Vacation

2 oz. (60 ml) vanilla vodka
2 oz. (60 ml) light rum
dash of pineapple juice
dash of sour mix

Shake all the ingredients with ice. Strain into a chilled cocktail glass.

Transfusion

2 oz. (60 ml) vodka
½ oz. (15 ml) pure grape juice
soda water to fill
lemon twist as garnish

Shake first two ingredients with ice, strain into an old-fashioned glass with ice.
Top up with soda and garnish with a lemon twist.

Velvet Hammer

2 oz. (60 ml) vodka
1 oz. (30 ml) white crème de cacao
1 oz. (30 ml) heavy cream

Mix the ingredients together in a shaker, then strain into a martini glass and serve.

Vesper

1 oz. (30 ml) Stolichnya Gold vodka
1 oz. (30 ml) Beefeater dry gin
dash of white Lillet
lemon twist as garnish

Vigorously shake ingredients with ice and strain into a chilled cocktail glass.
Garnish with the twist.

Vodka Martini

2 oz. (60 ml) chilled vodka
spray of dry vermouth from an atomizer
green olive or twist of lemon to serve

Pour the vodka into a chilled martini glass with a spray of dry vermouth. Add
the olive or lemon and serve.

Vodkatini

3 oz. (90 ml) vodka
2 drops dry vermouth
lemon twist as garnish

Pour the vodka into a freezing cocktail glass. Splash the vermouth on top of vodka. Add a twist of lemon.

Vulga

2 oz. (60 ml) vodka
$^1/_2$ oz. (15 ml) fresh orange juice
$^1/_2$ oz. (15 ml) fresh lime juice
2 dashes grenadine
dash of orange bitters

Shake all the ingredients together, then strain into a martini glass and serve.

What's Up, Watson

3 oz. (90 ml) Grey Goose vodka
3 oz. (90 ml) Kahlua
3 oz. (90 ml) Amaretto Di Saronno
soda water
dash of lemon-lime soda

Layer the Kahlua, then the amaretto, then vodka in an old-fashioned glass over ice. Add the lemon-lime soda and top with soda water. Serve with a straw and drink quickly.

Where the Buffalo Roam

2 oz. (60 ml) Wyborowa vodka
$^1/_2$ oz. (15 ml) Zubrowka bison grass vodka
dash of Chambery
blade of bison grass

Coat a shaker with Chambery and discard excess. Add ice and the vodka and shake. Garnish with blade of grass.

White Russian

1 oz. (30 ml) vodka
1 oz. (30 ml) Kahlua
1 oz. (30 ml) heavy cream

Mix the ingredients together in a shaker, then strain into a martini glass and serve. Alternatively, layer the ingredients in an ice-filled old-fashioned glass.

Woo Woo

1 oz. (30 ml) vodka
1 oz. (30 ml) peach schnapps
3 oz. (90 ml) cranberry juice

Shake all the ingredients together, then strain into an old-fashioned glass and serve.

Yellow Fever

2 oz. (60 ml) vodka
$^2/_3$ oz. (20 ml) Galliano
$^2/_3$ oz. (20 ml) freshly squeezed lime juice
1 oz. (30 ml) pineapple juice

Shake all the ingredients. Strain into a cocktail glass.

Gin Cocktails

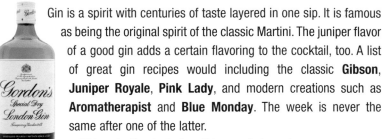

Gin is a spirit with centuries of taste layered in one sip. It is famous as being the original spirit of the classic Martini. The juniper flavor of a good gin adds a certain flavoring to the cocktail, too. A list of great gin recipes would including the classic **Gibson**, **Juniper Royale**, **Pink Lady**, and modern creations such as **Aromatherapist** and **Blue Monday**. The week is never the same after one of the latter.

This selection includes all types of gin and genever.

A1

2 oz. (60 ml) gin
1 oz. (30 ml) Grand Marnier
dash of fresh lemon juice
lemon twist as garnish

Shake the gin and Grand Marnier together, then strain into a martini glass. Add the lemon juice, stir, then garnish with the twist of lemon and serve.

Abbey

2 oz. (60 ml) gin
1 oz. (30 ml) orange juice
dash sweet vermouth
dash of Angostura bitters
maraschino cherry as garnish

Shake ingredients with ice and strain into a cocktail glass. Garnish with a maraschino cherry.

Alabama Fizz

2 oz. (60 ml) gin
1 oz. (30 ml) freshly squeezed lemon juice
dash of gomme syrup
soda water to fill
lemon wedge as garnish

Shake the gin, juice and gomme, then strain into a highball glass filled with ice. Top up with soda. Add a lemon wedge in the glass.

Alaska

2 oz. (60 ml) gin
splash yellow Chartreuse
dash of Angostura or orange bitters
lemon twist as garnish

Shake and strain into a cocktail glass. Garnish with the lemon twist.

Alexander's Big Brother

1¹/₂ oz. (45 ml) gin
³/₄ oz. (22 ml) blue curaçao
³/₄ oz. (22 ml) light cream
³/₄ oz. (22 ml) cream or half-and-half
physalis berry as garnish

Shake all the ingredients together with ice, then strain into a martini glass and serve with a physalis berry as garnish.

Alexander's Brother

1 oz. (30 ml) gin
1 oz. (30 ml) white crème de menthe
1 oz. (30 ml) heavy cream

Mix the ingredients together in a shaker, then strain into a martini glass and serve.

Alexander's Other Brother

1 oz. (30 ml) gin
1 oz. (30 ml) white crème de menthe
1 oz. (30 ml) heavy cream
grated nutmeg to serve

Mix the ingredients together in a shaker, then strain into a martini glass.
Sprinkle on the nutmeg and serve.

Alexander's Sister

1 oz. (30 ml) gin
1 oz. (30 ml) green crème de menthe
1 oz. (30 ml) heavy cream

Mix the ingredients together in a shaker, then strain into a martini glass and serve.

Alfonzo

1 oz. (30 ml) gin
2 oz. (60 ml) Grand Marnier
1 oz. (30 ml) dry vermouth
$^1/_2$ oz. (15 ml) sweet vermouth
dash of Angostura bitters

Shake the Grand Marnier, gin, and vermouths together, then strain into a
martini glass. Add the bitters, stir and serve.

Angler's Cocktail

2 oz. (60 ml) gin
dash of grenadine
2 dashes of Angostura bitters
3 dashes of orange bitters

Shake all the ingredients together with cracked ice, strain into an ice-filled old-
fashioned glass, and serve.

Angel Face

1 oz. (30 ml) gin
1 oz. (30 ml) apricot brandy
1 oz. (30 ml) calvados

Shake all the ingredients together, then strain into a martini glass and serve.

Aromatherapist

3 oz. (90 ml) gin
1 oz. (30 ml) sake
3 dashes Angostura bitters

Stir the gin, sake and bitters together, then strain into a martini glass and serve.

Aster

3 oz. (90 ml) gin
dash of fresh orange juice
dash of fresh lemon juice
orange zest as garnish

Stir all the ingredients together, then pour into an old-fashioned glass and serve
with an orange zest as garnish.

Astoria

2 oz. (60 ml) gin
1 oz. (30 ml) dry vermouth
dash of orange bitters

Shake all the ingredients together and strain into a cocktail glass.

Aussie Slinger

1¹/₂ oz. (45 ml) gin
1 oz. (30 ml) grenadine
dash of Angostura bitters
2 oz. (60 ml) lemon juice
lemonade to fill
orange slice and maraschino cherry as garnish

Half-fill a highball glass with ice and pour in ingredients. Stir, then top up with
lemonade. Stir again and serve with orange and cherry garnishes, and a stirrer.

Aviation 1

1½ oz. (45 ml) gin
½ oz. (15 ml) maraschino liqueur
½ oz. (15 ml) lemon juice
maraschino cherry or lemon twist as garnish

Shake all ingredients with cracked ice and strain into a chilled cocktail glass.
Garnish with the cherry or a lemon twist.

Baby Fingers

2 oz. (60 ml) sloe gin
1 oz. (30 ml) gin
dash of Angostura bitters

Shake both gins together with the bitters, then strain into a martini glass and serve.

Bella, Bella

1 oz. (30 ml) gin
⅔ oz. (20 ml) Aperol
½ oz. (15 ml) limoncello
½ oz. (15 ml) Mandarine liqueur
⅔ oz. (20 ml) freshly squeezed orange juice
lime spiral as garnish

Shake all the liquid ingredients together and strain into a cocktail glass. Add a
a spiral of lime.

Berlin

1 oz. (30 ml) gin
1 oz. (30 ml) orange juice
1 oz. (30 ml) Madeira
dash of Angostura bitters

Shake all ingredients together in an ice-filled shaker and strain into a cocktail glass.

Bermuda Rose

3 oz. (90 ml) gin
²/₃ oz. (20 ml) apricot brandy
²/₃ oz. (20 ml) grenadine

Shake all the ingredients together, then strain into a martini glass and serve.

Black Eye Martini

2 oz. (60 ml) chilled dry gin
spray of dry vermouth from an atomizer
black olive or lemon twist to serve

Pour the gin into a chilled martini glass with a spray of dry vermouth. Add the black olive or lemon and serve.

Blue Monday

1 oz. (30 ml) gin
1 oz. (30 ml) Cointreau
dash of blue curaçao
soda water to fill

Pour the gin and Cointreau into a highball glass filled with ice, then fill with soda water, and stir. Add a few drops of blue curaçao. Stir again and serve with a stirrer in the glass.

Bombardier

2 oz. (60 ml) Bombay gin
¹/₄ oz. (8 ml) orange juice
¹/₂ oz. (15 ml) fresh lime juice
3 oz. (90 ml) soda water
3 oz. (90 ml) tonic water
dash of grenadine
1 mint leaf to garnish

Shake all the liquid ingredients, except the tonic and soda, with ice and strain into an ice-filled highball glass. Fill up with the tonic and soda waters. Stir, then garnish with the mint leaf.

Boston Bullet

2 oz. (60 ml) chilled dry gin
spray of dry vermouth from an atomizer
green olive stuffed with an almond

Pour the gin into a chilled martini glass, then spray with the dry vermouth. Add the olive and serve.

Broadway

2 oz. (60 ml) gin
1 oz. (30 ml) sweet vermouth
dash of grenadine
dash of pineapple juice
1 egg white
grated nutmeg as garnish

Shake all the liquid ingredients together, then strain into a martini glass. Sprinkle with the nutmeg and serve.

Bronx

1 oz. (30 ml) gin
$^1/_2$ oz. (15 ml) sweet vermouth
$^1/_2$ oz. (15 ml) dry vermouth
juice of quarter of an orange
orange slice as garnish

Shake all the liquids together, then strain into a martini glass. Serve garnished with the orange slice.

Bronx View

$1^2/_3$ oz. (50 ml) gin
1 oz. (30 ml) dry vermouth
$^1/_3$ oz. (10 ml) Rose's Lime Cordial
lime spiral as garnish

Shake all the ingredients together and strain into a cocktail glass. Add a spiral of lime.

Butterfly

2 oz. (60 ml) gin
1 oz. (30 ml) dry vermouth
1 oz. (30 ml) blue curaçao
1 oz. (30 ml) Poire William

Shake all the liquid ingredients together, then strain into a martini glass and serve.

Cadillac Lady

1 oz. (30 ml) gin
1 oz. (30 ml) Grand Marnier
1 oz. (30 ml) fresh lemon juice
1 egg white

Shake all the ingredients together, then strain into a martini glass and serve.

Café de Paris

2 oz. (60 ml) gin
$^1/_2$ oz. (15 ml) light cream
$^1/_2$ oz. (15 ml) anisette
1 egg white

Mix the ingredients together in a shaker, then strain into a martini glass and serve.

Cajun Martini

2 oz. (60 ml) chilled dry gin
spray of dry vermouth from an atomizer
jalapeno chilli as garnish

Pour the gin into a chilled martini glass with a spray of dry vermouth. Add the chilli and serve.

Caruso

1 oz. (30 ml) gin
$^3/_4$ oz. (22 ml) dry vermouth
$^1/_4$ oz. (8 ml) green crème de menthe

Stir all the ingredients in a mixing glass, then strain into a cocktail glass.

Caterpillar

½ oz. (15 ml) gin
½ oz. (15 ml) yellow Chartreuse
½ oz. (15 ml) blue curaçao

Shake all ingredients with ice and strain into a cocktail glass.

Clover Club

2 oz. (60 ml) dry gin
splash grenadine
1 oz. (30 ml) lemon juice
1 egg white

Shake well for 30 seconds and strain into a cocktail glass.

Cobbler

1 tsp. (5 ml) powdered sugar
1 oz. (30 ml) soda water
2 oz. (60 ml) gin or any spirit
seasonal fruit to garnish

In an old-fashioned glass, dissolve the sugar in the soda water, then fill the glass with ice. Stir in the spirit, garnish with the fruit and serve.

Dawn

1 oz. (30 ml) gin
⅔ oz. (20 ml) Campari
1⅔ oz. (50 ml) freshly squeezed orange juice

Shake all the ingredients together and strain into an old-fashioned glass over crushed ice.

Daydream Island

1 oz. (30 ml) dry gin
½ oz. (15 ml) orange juice
½ oz. (15 ml) blue curaçao
1 oz. (30 ml) Galliano
1 egg white
maraschino cherry as garnish

Shake all the liquid ingredients well and strain into a cocktail glass. Garnish with a maraschino cherry.

Demeanor

1 oz. (30 ml) Old Tom gin
1 oz. (30 ml) sweet vermouth
½ oz. (15 ml) Parfait Amour

Stir all the ingredients together, then strain into a martini glass and serve.

Devil's Advocate

2 oz. (60 ml) gin
1 oz. (30 ml) crème de framboise
2 dashes dry vermouth

Pour the gin and vermouth into a mixing glass with ice. Strain into a cocktail glass. Add liqueur and watch it sink to the bottom of the glass.

Diamond Fizz

2 oz. (60 ml) gin
1 oz. (30 ml) fresh lemon juice
1 tsp. (5 ml) powdered sugar
chilled champagne to fill

Shake the gin, lemon juice and sugar together and pour into a sugar-rimmed highball glass. Top up with champagne and serve.

Dirty Martini

1²/₃ oz. (50 ml) gin
²/₃ oz. (20 ml) brine from cocktail olives
¹/₃ oz. (10 ml) extra dry vermouth
green olive as garnish

Pour ingredients into a mixing glass with ice and stir. Strain into a cocktail glass. Add an olive on a cocktail stick.

Dodge

2 oz. (60 ml) gin
2 oz. (60 ml) Cointreau
dash of white grape juice

Shake all the ingredients together, then strain into a martini glass and serve.

Eclipse

1 oz. (30 ml) sloe gin
1 oz. (30 ml) gin
dash of grenadine
1 olive
dash of fresh lemon juice

In a martini glass, cover the olive with the grenadine. Mix the gins with the lemon juice in a shaker, then strain into the glass taking care not to disturb the grenadine.

Eton Blazer

1 oz. (30 ml) gin
¹/₂ oz. (15 ml) lemon juice
1 oz. (30 ml) kirsch
¹/₃ oz. (10 ml) gomme syrup
soda water to fill
2 maraschino cherries as garnish

Shake all ingredients, except the soda, with ice and strain into a highball glass. Top up with soda. Garnish with two maraschino cherries.

Evergreen

1 oz. (30 ml) dry gin
$^{1}/_{2}$ oz. (15 ml) dry vermouth
$^{1}/_{2}$ oz. (15 ml) Midori
dash of blue curaçao

Shake all ingredients with ice. Strain into a chilled cocktail glass.

Fallen Angel

1 oz. (30 ml) gin
$^{1}/_{2}$ lemon, freshly squeezed
dash of crème de menthe
dash of Angostura bitters

Shake all ingredients with ice and strain into a cocktail glass.

Filby

2 oz. (60 ml) gin
1 oz. (30 ml) Campari
1 oz. (30 ml) dry vermouth
1 oz. (30 ml) amaretto

Stir all the liquids in a mixing glass, then strain into a martini glass and serve.

Fluffy Duck

1 oz. (30 ml) gin
2 oz. (60 ml) advocaat
$^{1}/_{3}$ oz. (10 ml) Galliano
lemonade to fill

Mix the advocaat and gin in a highball glass filled with ice. Top up with lemonade and stir. Float the Galliano on top.

Fluffy Duck (international)

½ oz. (15 ml) gin
1 oz. (30 ml) advocaat
½ oz. (15 ml) vodka
1 oz. (30 ml) cream
½ oz. (15 ml) Cointreau
lemonade to fill

Pour all ingredients, except the lemonde, into a highball glass over ice. Stir, then top up with lemonade.

Flying Dutchman

3 oz. (90 ml) Dutch gin
dash of triple sec

Mix the gin and triple sec together in a shaker, then strain into an ice-filled old-fashioned glass and serve.

French 75

1½ oz. (45 ml) gin
1½ oz. (45 ml) fresh lemon juice
chilled champagne to fill
lemon twist as garnish

Mix the gin and lemon juice together in a champagne flute. Top up with champagne, garnish and serve.

French 75 (alt)

¾ oz. (22 ml) gin
¼ oz. (8 ml) lemon juice
dash of gomme syrup
dash of grenadine
champagne to fill

Shake the gin, lemon juice, gomme and grenadine together, strain into a champagne flute and top with champagne.

Gene Tunney

2 oz. (60 ml) Plymouth gin
1 oz. (30 ml) dry vermouth
dash of fresh orange juice
dash of fresh lemon juice

Shake all the ingredients together, then strain into a martini glass, and serve.

Gibson

2 oz. (60 ml) chilled dry gin
spray of dry vermouth from an atomizer
1 cocktail onion to serve

Pour the gin into a chilled martini glass and spray with the dry vermouth. Add the onion and serve.

Gin Alexander

1 oz. (30 ml) gin
1 oz. (30 ml) brown crème de cacao
1 oz. (30 ml) heavy cream

Mix the ingredients together in a shaker, then strain into a martini glass and serve.

Gloom Raiser

2 oz. (60 ml) gin
1 oz. (30 ml) vermouth
2 dashes grenadine
2 dashes absinthe or Pernod

Shake the gin, vermouth and absinthe or Pernod together. Add the grenadine and strain into a cocktail glass.

Harry's Cocktail

2 oz. (60 ml) gin
1 oz. (30 ml) sweet vermouth
dash of pastis
sprig of mint as garnish

Shake all the liquids together, then strain into a martini glass and serve.
Garnish with a sprig of mint.

Hendrick's Gin Gibson

2 oz. (60 ml) Hendrick's gin
tiny dash of dry vermouth
cocktail onions

Pour the gin into a shaker filled with ice cubes. Add the vermouth, then shake.
Place several cocktail onions on a stick in a chilled cocktail glass. Pour the
cocktail over the onions to add their flavor.

Imperial

1 oz. (30 ml) gin
1 oz. (30 ml) dry vermouth
dash of maraschino liqueur
dash of Angostura bitters

Shake all the ingredients together, then strain into a martini glass and serve.

Itza Paramount

1 oz. (30 ml) gin
1 oz. (30 ml) Drambuie
1 oz. (30 ml) Cointreau
orange slice, thin, as garnish
lime twist, around orange, as garnish

Stir the liquid ingredients together, strain into a martini glass and garnish.

Jack Zeller

1 oz. (30 ml) Old Tom gin
1 oz. (30 ml) Dubonnet

Stir the gin and Dubonnet together, then strain into a martini glass and serve.

Jacuzzi

1 oz. (30 ml) gin
²/₃ oz. (20 ml) peach schnapps
1 oz. (30 ml) freshly squeezed orange juice
champagne to fill

Pour the gin, schnapps and juice into a shaker with ice. Shake, then strain into
a champagne glass. Stir gently and fill with champagne. Stir again.

Jade Lady

1 oz. (30 ml) gin
1 oz. (30 ml) blue curaçao
1 oz. (30 ml) advocaat
1½ oz. (45 ml) freshly squeezed orange juice

Shake all the ingredients together and strain into a cocktail glass.

Jasmine

1½ oz. (45 ml) gin
⅓ oz. (10 ml) Cointreau
⅓ oz. (10 ml) Campari
½ oz. (15 ml) fresh lemon juice
lemon twist as garnish

Shake all the ingredients together with ice and strain into a cocktail glass. Add a lemon twist.

Juniper Royale

1 oz. (30 ml) gin
½ oz. (15 ml) fresh orange juice
½ oz. (15 ml) cranborry juice
dash of grenadine
champagne to fill

Pour the gin, juices and grenadine into a shaker with ice and shake. Strain into a champagne glass and stir gently. Top up with champagne and stir again.

Kaiser

1 oz. (30 ml) gin
1 oz. (30 ml) kümmel
½ oz. (15 ml) dry vermouth

Stir all the ingredients together, then strain into a martini glass and serve.

Kiwi

1²/₃ oz. (50 ml) gin
²/₃ oz. (20 ml) triple sec
1 oz. (30 ml) kiwi fruit purée
dash of gomme syrup

Shake all the ingredients together and strain into an old-fashioned glass with crushed ice.

Knickerbocker

2 oz. (60 ml) gin
1 oz. (30 ml) dry vermouth
2 dashes sweet vermouth
lemon twist to serve

Stir the gin and the vermouths together, then strain into a martini glass and serve with the lemon twist.

L'amour

2 oz. (60 ml) gin
dash of cherry brandy
dash of grenadine
dash of fresh lemon juice
2 sprigs mint

Shake all the ingredients together, including the mint. Strain into a martini glass and serve.

Lady Finger

1 oz. (30 ml) gin
1 oz. (30 ml) cherry brandy
1 oz. (30 ml) kirsch
orange twist as garnish
maraschino cherry as garnish

Shake all the liquid ingredients together, then strain into a tulip glass and serve with the orange and cherry garnish.

Leap Year

2 oz. (60 ml) gin
1/2 oz. (15 ml) sweet vermouth
1/2 oz. (15 ml) Grand Marnier
dash of. fresh lemon juice
orange or lemon twist as garnish

Shake all ingredients with ice and strain into a chilled cocktail glass. Garnish with a twist of lemon or orange.

London Cocktail

2 oz. (60 ml) London dry gin
dash of maraschino liqueur
2 dashes orange bitters
dash of gomme syrup

Shake all the ingredients together, then strain into a martini glass and serve

Maiden's Prayer

1 oz. (30 ml) gin
1 oz. (30 ml) Cointreau
juice of half an orange
juice of half a lemon

Shake all the ingredients together, then strain into a martini glass and serve.

Maiden's Wish

1 oz. (30 ml) gin
1 oz. (30 ml) Kina Lillet
1 oz. (30 ml) calvados

Stir all the ingredients together, then strain into a martini glass and serve.

Main Chance

1 oz. (30 ml) gin
1 oz. (30 ml) triple sec
1 oz. (30 ml) freshly squeezed grapefruit juice
lime twist as garnish

Shake all the ingredients together, strain into a cocktail glass. Add a twist of lime.

Major Bailey

2 oz. (60 ml) gin
dash of fresh lime juice
dash of fresh lemon juice
1 tsp. (5 ml) granulated sugar
8–10 fresh mint leaves

Muddle the lime and lemon juices with the sugar and mint leaves in an old-fashioned glass. Fill the glass with ice and stir in the gin until the glass is frosted.

Mandarine Martini

1¹/₂ oz. (45 ml) gin
¹/₂ oz. (15 ml) vodka
splash Mandarine Napoléon
dash of Cointreau
mandarin twist as garnish

Pour the Mandarine Napoléon and Cointreau into an empty shaker. Coat and discard any surplus. Add ice and the gin and vodka. Shake and strain into cocktail glass. Garnish with twist.

Martini Thyme

3 oz. (90 ml) gin
³/₄ oz. (22 ml) green Chartreuse
1 sprig of thyme

Stir the gin and Chartreuse together. Strain into a cocktail glass and garnish with the thyme.

Monkey Gland 1

2 oz. (60 ml) gin
2 oz. (60 ml) fresh orange juice
dash of absinthe or Pernod
dash of grenadine
orange twist as garnish

Shake all the liquid ingredients, then strain into a chilled cocktail glass. Garnish with an orange twist.

Monkey Gland 2

2 oz. (60 ml) gin
1 oz. (30 ml) grenadine
1 oz. (30 ml) Benedictine
2 oz. (60 ml) fresh orange juice

Shake all the ingredients together. Strain into a chilled cocktail glass and serve.

Monte Carlo Highball

2 oz. (60 ml) gin
1/2 oz. (15 ml) white crème de menthe
1 oz. (30 ml) fresh lemon juice
champagne to fill
long lemon twist as garnish

Shake the gin, crème de menthe and lemon juice in a shaker, strain into a highball glass. Pour the champagne and serve with a long twist of lemon as garnish.

Moulin Rouge

1 oz. (30 ml) gin
1/2 oz. (15 ml) apricot brandy
1/2 oz. (15 ml) lemon juice
dash of grenadine
sparkling white wine (or champagne) to fill
orange slice as garnish

Shake all the ingredients, except the sparkling wine (or champagne), together, and strain into a champagne saucer. Top with sparkling wine. Garnish with an orange slice.

Mount Fuji

2 oz. (60 ml) gin
1/2 oz. (15 ml) lemon juice
1/3 oz. (10 ml) light cream
1 egg white
red cherry as garnish

Shake ingredients with ice and strain into a large cocktail glass. Garnish with a red cherry.

Naked Martini

2 oz. (60 ml) dry gin (room temperature)
1 green olive infused with vermouth

Pour the gin directly into a martini glass, add the olive. Stir and serve.

Napoleon

2 oz. (60 ml) gin
2 dashes orange curaçao
2 dashes Dubonnet

Stir all the ingredients together, then strain into a martini glass and serve.

New Orleans Gin Fizz

2 oz. (60 ml) gin
1 oz. (30 ml) Cointreau
$^1/_2$ oz. (15 ml) kirsch
1 oz. (30 ml) fresh lemon juice
2 oz. (60 ml) light cream
1 egg white
soda water to fill

Mix the ingredients together in a shaker, then strain into a highball glass. Top up with the soda water and serve.

North Pole

2 oz. (60 ml) gin
1 oz. (30 ml) maraschino liqueur
1 oz. (30 ml) fresh lemon juice
1 egg white
$^1/_2$ oz. (15 ml) heavy cream

Mix the ingredients together in a shaker, then strain into a martini glass. Float the cream on top and serve.

Nuptial

2 oz. (60 ml) gin
1 oz. (30 ml) kirsch
dash of Cointreau
dash of fresh lemon juice

Mix all the ingredients together in a shaker, then strain into a martini glass and serve.

Old Vermouth

1 oz. (30 ml) Old Tom gin
1 oz. (30 ml) dry vermouth
$^1/_2$ oz. (15 ml) sweet vermouth
2 dashes Angostura bitters
lemon slice as garnish

Pour the gin, vermouths and bitters into an old-fashioned glass. Garnish with the lemon slice and serve.

On a Wave

1 oz. (30 ml) gin
1 oz. (30 ml) light rum
$^2/_3$ oz. (20 ml) blue curaçao
3 oz. (90 ml) pineapple juice
1 oz. (30 ml) freshly squeezed lime juice
2 dashes gomme syrup
pineapple wedge as garnish

Shake all the liquid ingredients together and strain into a colada glass filled with crushed ice. Add a pineapple wedge.

Opal

1$^2/_3$ oz. (50 ml) gin
$^2/_3$ oz. (20 ml) Cointreau
1 oz. (30 ml) freshly squeezed orange juice
orange twist as garnish

Shake all the liquid ingredients together and strain into a cocktail glass. Add a twist of orange.

Orange Blossom Special

1²/₃ oz. (50 ml) gin
²/₃ oz. (20 ml) Cointreau
²/₃ oz. (20 ml) lychee liqueur
¹/₃ oz. (10 ml) freshly squeezed lemon juice

Shake all the ingredients together and strain into a cocktail glass.

Orchid

2 oz. (60 ml) gin
1 oz. (30 ml) Parfait Amour
1 egg white

Shake all the ingredients together, then strain into a martini glass and serve.

Oriental

1¹/₂ oz. (45 ml) gin
²/₃ oz. (20 ml) limoncello
1 oz. (30 ml) passion fruit purée
dash of passion fruit syrup
lemon twist as garnish

Shake all the ingredients together, then strain into a cocktail glass. Add a twist of lemon.

Original Martinez

2 oz. (60 ml) Old Tom gin
¹/₂ oz. (15 ml) sweet vermouth
2 dashes maraschino liqueur
dash of orange (or lemon) bitters

Mix all the ingredients together in a shaker, then strain into a cocktail glass and serve.

Paisley Martini

2 oz. (60 ml) dry gin (room temperature)
¹/₂ oz. (15 ml) Scotch whisky

Pour the gin directly into a martini glass, add the Scotch. Stir and serve.

Pink Gin

4 oz. (120 ml) gin
2 dashes Angostura bitters

Coat a chilled cocktail glass with the Angostura bitters. Discard the excess and top up with the gin.

Pegu

1¹/₂ oz. (45 ml) gin
¹/₂ oz. (15 ml) Cointreau
¹/₂ oz. (15 ml) fresh lime juice
2 dashes Angostura bitters
lime twist as garnish

Stir ingredients in a mixing glass with ice. Strain into a chilled cocktail glass and garnish with a lime twist.

Pink Lady

1 oz. (30 ml) gin
2 dashes grenadine
1 egg white
juice of half a lemon

Shake all the ingredients together, then strain into a martini glass and serve.

Pink Rose

2 oz. (60 ml) gin
¹/₂ oz. (15 ml) light cream
¹/₂ oz. (15 ml) fresh orange juice
2 dashes grenadine
1 egg white

Mix the ingredients together in a shaker, then strain into a martini glass and serve.

Queen Elizabeth

2 oz. (60 ml) gin
1 oz. (30 ml) dry vermouth
¹/₂ oz. (15 ml) Benedictine

Stir all the ingredients together, strain into a martini glass and serve.

Ramos Gin Fizz

1¹/₂ oz. (45 ml) gin
¹/₂ oz. (15 ml) fresh lemon juice
3–4 drops orange-flower water
¹/₃ oz. (10 ml) gomme syrup
2 oz. (60 ml) fresh cream
1 egg white
soda water to fill
small flower as garnish

Place the ingredients, except the soda, in a blender and quickly blend. Add ice and blend again quickly. Pour into a goblet and top up with soda water. Add a small flower as garnish.

Raspberry Collins

2 oz. (60 ml) gin
²/₃ oz. (20 ml) crème de framboise
1²/₃ oz. (50 ml) freshly squeezed lemon juice
¹/₃ oz. (10 ml) gomme syrup
3 oz. (90 ml) raspberry purée
soda water to fill
3 raspberries as garnish

Pour all ingredients, except the soda, into a shaker. Shake and strain into a highball glass, then top up with soda. Add three raspberries on a cocktail stick across the glass.

Red Snapper

2 oz. (60 ml) gin
4 oz. (120 ml) tomato juice
¹/₂ oz. (15 ml) lemon juice
1–2 pinches salt and pepper
2–3 dashes Worcestershire sauce
2–3 drops Tabasco sauce
lemon slice as garnish
stick of celery (optional garnish)

Shake the gin, tomato juice and lemon juice with ice and strain into a chilled highball glass filled with ice. Stir in the Worcestershire, Tabasco and salt and pepper. Add a stick of celery (if needed) and a lemon slice.

Sage Passion

1 oz. (30 ml) gin
3 fresh sage leaves
1 oz. (30 ml) fresh lime sour
$^1/_2$ oz. (15 ml) Alizé Gold Passion

Shake all ingredients, except one sage leaf, with ice and strain into a large cocktail glass. Add the sage leaf as a garnish.

Satan's Whiskers

1 oz. (30 ml) gin
1 oz. (30 ml) dry vermouth
1 oz. (30 ml) sweet vermouth
$^1/_2$ oz. (15 ml) fresh orange juice
$^1/_2$ oz. (15 ml) Grand Marnier
dash of orange bitters
orange twist as garnish

Shake ingredients with ice and strain into a cocktail glass. Garnish with an orange twist.

Scarborough Fair

2 oz. (60 ml) Plymouth gin
$^1/_4$ oz. (8 ml) Chambery
sprig of flat leaf parsley
2 fresh sage leaves
sprig of thyme as garnish
sprig of rosemary as garnish

Muddle sage, parsley and Chambery in shaker. Add gin. Shake and strain into a cocktail glass. Garnish with rosemary and thyme.

Showtime

1 oz. (30 ml) gin
$^2/_3$ oz. (20 ml) lychee liqueur
$^2/_3$ oz. (20 ml) pineapple liqueur
$^2/_3$ oz. (20 ml) fresh peach purée
peach slice as garnish

Shake all the liquid ingredients together, then strain into a cocktail glass. Add a peach slice on the edge of the glass.

Silver Bronx

2 oz. (60 ml) dry gin
1 oz. (30 ml) sweet vermouth
1 oz. (30 ml) fresh orange juice
$^1/_2$ egg white

Shake all the ingredients well and strain into a cocktail glass.

Silver Streak

2 oz. (60 ml) gin
1 oz. (30 ml) kümmel

Pour the gin and kümmel into an old-fashioned glass and serve.

Singapore Gin Sling

2 oz. (60 ml) gin
$^1/_2$ oz. (15 ml) Cointreau
$1^1/_2$ oz. (45 ml) fresh lime juice
1 tsp. (5 ml) superfine sugar
dash of gomme syrup
$^3/_4$ oz. (22 ml) Cherry Heering
soda water to fill
lime as garnish

Shake first five ingredients and strain into collins glass. Top up with soda water and float the Cherry Heering. Garnish with lime.

Smoky Martini

2 oz. (60 ml) gin
$^1/_4$ oz. (8 ml) Scotch whisky
dash of dry vermouth

Stir or shake all the ingredients together and strain into a cocktail glass.

Snakebite

1 oz. (30 ml) gin
1 oz. (30 ml) crème de menthe

Shake the ingredients and strain into a cocktail glass.

Soixante-Neuf

1 oz. (30 ml) gin
1 oz. (30 ml) fresh lemon juice
chilled champagne to fill
twist of lemon as garnish

Shake the gin and lemon juice together, then strain into a flute glass. Top up with champagne, garnish with the lemon twist and serve.

Star

1 oz. (30 ml) dry gin
1 oz. (30 ml) calvados
dash of dry vermouth
dash of grapefruit juice

Stir all the ingredients together and strain into a cocktail glass.

Straits Sling

2 oz. (60 ml) Beefeater gin
2 oz. (60 ml) fresh lime juice
½ oz. (15 ml) Benedictine
½ oz. (15 ml) Peter Heering
2 tsp. (10 ml) sugar
dash of Angostura bitters
soda water to fill

Pour the gin, lime juice and bitters onto crushed ice in a collins glass. Add the sugar and stir. Then add Benedictine and Peter Heering and top with soda.

Tail Spin Cocktail

1 oz. (30 ml) gin
1 oz. (30 ml) sweet vermouth
1 oz. (30 ml) green Chartreuse
dash of Angostura bitters

Shake all the ingredients together, then strain into a martini glass and serve.

The Swinger

2 oz. (60 ml) gin
1 tsp. (5 ml) superfine sugar
2 lemon wedges
champagne to fill
lemon twist as garnish

Fill a shaker with ice, add sugar, squeezed lemon wedges and gin. Shake and strain into a cocktail glass. Top up with champagne and garnish with a lemon twist.

Tom Fizz

2 oz. (60 ml) gin
1 oz. (30 ml) lemon juice
1 tsp. (5 ml) superfine sugar
dash of Angostura bitters (optional)
soda water to fill

Shake and strain into a tall glass, and top up with soda.

Tom Sour

2 oz. (60 ml) gin
$^3/_4$ oz. (22 ml) lemon juice
$^1/_2$ tsp. (2 ml) superfine sugar

Shake all the ingredients together and strain into a sour glass.

Top Knotch

1 oz. (30 ml) sloe gin
1 oz. (30 ml) dry vermouth
$^1/_2$ oz. (15 ml) crème de framboise
maraschino cherry to garnish

Pour the ingredients into an old-fashioned glass, garnish with the cherry and serve.

Typhoon

1 oz. (30 ml) gin
dash of anisette
¹/₂ oz. (15 ml) fresh lime juice
chilled champagne to fill

In a shaker, mix together the gin, anisette and lime juice, then strain into an ice-filled highball glass. Top up with champagne and serve.

Union Jack

2 oz. (60 ml) gin
1 oz. (30 ml) sloe gin
2 dashes grenadine

Mix the gins and grenadine together in a shaker, then strain into a martini glass and serve.

Vampire

1 oz. (30 ml) gin
1 oz. (30 ml) dry vermouth
2 dashes fresh lime

Shake all the ingredients together, then strain into a martini glass and serve.

Venus

2 oz. (60 ml) gin
1 oz. (30 ml) Cointreau
dash of gomme syrup
dash of Peychaud's bitters
9 raspberries (3 as garnish)

Shake all the ingredients together and strain into a cocktail glass. Add another three raspberries on a cocktail stick placed across the glass.

Vesper

3 oz. (90 ml) Gordon's gin
1 oz. (30 ml) Moskovskaya vodka
¹/₂ oz. (15 ml) Lillet Blanc
lemon twist as garnish

Shake the gin, vodka and Lillet Blanc together, then strain into a martini glass and serve with the lemon twist.

Ward Eight (alt)

2 oz. (60 ml) chilled dry gin
spray of dry vermouth from an atomizer
2 pieces orange peel as garnish

Pour the gin into a chilled martini glass with a spray of vermouth. Add the orange peel and serve.

White Baby

2 oz. (60 ml) gin
1 oz. (30 ml) fresh lime juice
¹/₂ oz. (15 ml) Cointreau

Shake all the ingredients together, then strain into a martini glass and serve.

White Velvet

2 oz. (60 ml) gin
1 oz. (30 ml) fresh pineapple juice
¹/₂ oz. (15 ml) Cointreau

Shake all the ingredients together, then strain into a martini glass and serve.

Why Not?

1 oz. (30 ml) gin
1 oz. (30 ml) apricot brandy
¹/₂ oz. (15 ml) dry vermouth
dash of fresh lemon juice

Shake all the ingredients together, then strain into a martini glass and serve.

Woodstock

1 oz. (30 ml) gin
1 oz. (30 ml) lemon juice
1 tsp. (5 ml) maple syrup
dash of Angostura bitters

Shake all the ingredients together, then strain into a martini glass and serve.

Yellow Rattler

1 oz. (30 ml) gin
$^1\!/_2$ oz. (15 ml) sweet vermouth
$^1\!/_2$ oz. (15 ml) dry vermouth
$^1\!/_2$ oz. (15 ml) orange juice
3 cocktail onions as garnish

Shake all ingredients (except cocktail onions) together with ice, and strain into a cocktail glass. Add the cocktail onions and serve.

Za-Za

2 oz. (60 ml) gin
2 oz. (60 ml) Dubonnet
lemon twist as garnish

Stir all the ingredients together, then strain into a martini glass. Garnish with the lemon twist and serve.

Brandy Cocktails

Smooth and dark, with the occasional fiery edge, brandy is a terrific base for cocktails. It is full of flavor, and is especially beautiful as an after-dinner cocktail. However, some of the newer recipes coming from producers have it mixing with ginger ale, tonic and even cola.

Here is a bounty of brandy cocktail recipes designed to thrill the palate, including the classic **Brandy Alexander**, **Brandy Eggnog** for cold days and **Tulip**.

This selection includes calvados and fruit brandies.

ABC

5 ice cubes
³/₄ oz. (22 ml) armagnac
³/₄ oz. (22 ml) Benedictine
dash of Angostura bitters
champagne or sparkling white wine to fill
lemon slice as garnish
orange segment as garnish
maraschino cherry as garnish

Crack two ice cubes and place in a shaker with the armagnac, Benedictine and Angostura. Shake the ingredients together. Crush the remaining ice cubes and place in a goblet, then strain contents of the shaker over the ice. Top up with champagne and add the fruit.

Adam and Eve

1 oz. (30 ml) cognac
1 oz. (30 ml) gin
1 oz. (30 ml) forbidden fruit liqueur

Shake all the liquids together, then strain into a martini glass and serve.

Ambrosia

1 oz. (30 ml) calvados
1 oz. (30 ml) cognac
dash of curaçao
chilled champagne to fill

Shake the calvados, cognac and curaçao together, then strain into a
champagne saucer. Top with champagne and serve.

American Beauty

$^1/_2$ oz. (15 ml) brandy
$^1/_4$ oz. (8 ml) dry vermouth
$^1/_4$ oz. (8 ml) sweet vermouth
$^3/_4$ oz. (22 ml) orange
dash of grenadine
dash of port

Shake and strain all the ingredients, except the port, into a cocktail glass. Float
the port on top.

Angel Face

1 oz. (30 ml) apricot brandy
1 oz. (30 ml) calvados
1 oz. (30 ml) gin

Shake all the ingredients together, then strain into a martini glass and serve.

Angel's Kiss No. 3

1 oz. (30 ml) crème de cacao
1 oz. (30 ml) gin
1 oz. (30 ml) cream
1 oz. (30 ml) brandy

Layer each ingredient in order in a cocktail glass.

Ante

1 oz. (30 ml) calvados
1 oz. (30 ml) Cointreau
1 oz. (30 ml) Pernod or Dubonnet

Shake all the ingredients together, then strain into a martini glass and serve.

Apple Special

1 oz. (30 ml) brandy
¹/₂ oz. (15 ml) Cointreau
dry apple cider to fill
apple slice as garnish

Shake all the ingredients, except for the cider, and strain into a highball glass.
Top up with the cider, garnish with the apple slice, and serve with a straw.

April Shower

1 oz. (30 ml) brandy
2 oz. (60 ml) orange juice
1 oz. (30 ml) Benedictine
soda water to fill

Pour the brandy, orange juice and Benedictine into a highball glass with ice.
Stir and top up with soda.

Aunt Jermina (Jemima)

1 oz. (30 ml) cognac
1 oz. (30 ml) Benedictine
1 oz. (30 ml) white crème de cacao

Pour all the ingredients into a brandy glass, stir and serve.

B & B

1 oz. (30 ml) brandy
1 oz. (30 ml) Benedictine

Pour the brandy and Benedictine into a brandy glass and serve.

Baked Apple

2 oz. (60 ml) calvados
1 oz. (30 ml) dark rum
4 oz. (120 ml) apple juice
dash of crème de cassis
cinnamon stick as garnish

Pour all the ingredients into a tumbler and stir. Add the cinammon stick and serve.

Banana Bliss

1 oz. (30 ml) cognac
1 oz. (30 ml) banana liqueur

Pour the ingredients into an old-fashioned glass filled with ice. Stir well and serve.

Between the Sheets

1 oz. (30 ml) brandy
1 oz. (30 ml) white rum
1 oz. (30 ml) Cointreau
1 oz. (30 ml) fresh lemon juice
$^1/_2$ oz. (15 ml) gomme syrup

Shake all the ingredients together, then strain into a martini glass and serve.

Billy Hamilton

1 oz. (30 ml) cognac
1 oz. (30 ml) crème de cacao
1 oz. (30 ml) orange curaçao
1 egg white

Shake all the ingredients together, then strain into a martini glass, and serve.

Bosom Caresser

1$^1/_2$ oz. (45 ml) brandy
1 egg yolk
$^1/_2$ oz. (15 ml) blue curaçao
dash of grenadine

Shake all the ingredients together with ice and strain into a chilled cocktail glass.

Brandy Alexander

1 oz. (30 ml) cognac
1 oz. (30 ml) brown crème de cacao
1 oz. (30 ml) heavy cream

Mix all the ingredients together in a shaker, then strain into a martini glass and serve.

Brandy Alexander (alt)

1 oz. (30 ml) cognac
1 oz. (30 ml) brown crème de cacao
1 oz. (30 ml) heavy cream
whipped cream
nutmeg as garnish

Put the cognac, crème de cacao and cream in a shaker. Shake, then strain into a cocktail glass. Add the whipped cream and sprinkle nutmeg to garnish.

Brandy Cocktail

2 oz. (60 ml) cognac
1 oz. (30 ml) sweet vermouth
2 dashes Angostura bitters

Stir the cognac, vermouth and bitters together, then strain into a martini glass and serve.

Brandy Daisy

1 oz. (30 ml) brandy
6 dashes grenadine
1 oz. (30 ml) lemon juice
soda water to fill
sprig of mint as garnish

Shake the brandy, lemon juice and grenadine, and strain into a goblet over ice. Top up with soda and garnish with a sprig of mint.

Brandy Eggnog

2 oz. (60 ml) cognac
1 oz. (30 ml) dark rum
1 oz. (30 ml) gomme syrup
1 egg
4 oz. (120 ml) half-and-half or milk
grated nutmeg as garnish

Stir the cognac, rum, gomme and egg together, then strain into a medium goblet. Stir in the milk and sprinkle the grated nutmeg over the top.

Brandy Kiss

1 oz. (30 ml) brandy
1 oz. (30 ml) lemon juice
1 oz. (30 ml) Grand Marnier

Shake all the ingredients together with ice and strain into a cocktail glass.

Brandy Smash

2 oz. (60 ml) cognac
1 tsp. (5 ml) granulated sugar
6–8 fresh mint leaves

Dissolve the sugar with a dash of the cognac in the bottom of an old-fashioned glass. Add the mint and combine. Fill with ice and stir in the remaining cognac until the glass has become frosted. Serve with a short straw.

Brighton Punch

3 oz. (90 ml) brandy
1 oz. (30 ml) bourbon
2 oz. (60 ml) orange juice
1/4 oz. (8 ml) Benedictine
3/4 oz. (22 ml) lemon juice
dash of gomme syrup

Shake all the ingredients together and strain into an ice-filled collins glass.

—〜〜—

Butterfly Flip

1 oz. (30 ml) brandy
1 egg yolk
1 oz. (30 ml) crème de cacao
¹/₂ tsp. (2 ml) superfine sugar
dash of light cream
grated nutmeg as garnish

Shake all ingredients with ice and strain into a cocktail glass. Sprinkle with grated nutmeg and serve.

Cha-Cha-Cha

2 oz. (60 ml) calvados
1 oz. (30 ml) crème de framboise

Shake all the ingredients together, then strain into a martini glass and serve.

Charlie Chaplin

1 oz. (30 ml) apricot brandy
1 oz. (30 ml) sloe gin
1 oz. (30 ml) fresh lemon juice

Shake all the ingredients together, then strain into a martini glass and serve.

Cherry Alexander

2 oz. (60 ml) cherry brandy
1 oz. (30 ml) white crème de cacao
1 oz. (30 ml) heavy cream

Mix the ingredients together in a shaker, then strain into a martini glass and serve.

Cherry Picker

1 oz. (30 ml) cherry brandy
1 oz. (30 ml) gold tequila
freshly squeezed juice of half a lime
1 oz. (30 ml) apple juice
lime twist as garnish

Put all the ingredients in a shaker. Shake, then strain into a cocktail glass and add a twist of lime to serve.

Chicago

2 oz. (60 ml) brandy
$^{1}/_{2}$ oz. (15 ml) triple sec
dash of Angostura bitters

Shake all the ingredients together, then pour into a sugar-rimmed old-fashioned glass and serve.

Combustible Edison   care needed

2 oz. (60 ml) brandy
1 oz. (30 ml) Campari
1 oz. (30 ml) fresh lemon juice

Shake the Campari and lemon juice with cracked ice. Strain into a chilled cocktail glass. Heat the brandy, ignite and pour in a flaming stream into the cocktail glass. Be careful with the flames!

Contessa

$^{1}/_{2}$ oz. (15 ml) brandy
$^{1}/_{2}$ oz. (15 ml) orange juice
$^{1}/_{2}$ oz. (15 ml) Cointreau
$^{1}/_{2}$ oz. (15 ml) fresh cream
$^{1}/_{2}$ oz. (15 ml) Galliano
maraschino cherry as garnish

Shake all the ingredients together with ice and strain into a champagne flute. Sit the cherry on the rim.

Corpse Reviver

$^{3}/_{4}$ oz. (22 ml) brandy
$^{3}/_{4}$ oz. (22 ml) calvados
$^{3}/_{4}$ oz. (22 ml) sweet vermouth

Shake all the ingredients together and strain into a cocktail glass.

Deauville

1 oz. (30 ml) brandy
³/₄ oz. (22 ml) calvados
¹/₂ oz. (15 ml) triple sec
³/₄ oz. (22 ml) lemon juice

Shake all the ingredients together and strain into a cocktail glass.

Depth Bomb

1 oz. (30 ml) calvados
1 oz. (30 ml) cognac
2 dashes fresh lemon juice
dash of grenadine

Shake all the ingredients together, pour into an old-fashioned glass and serve.

Dizzy Dame

1 oz. (30 ml) brandy
1 oz. (30 ml) cream
¹/₂ oz. (15 ml) Kahlua
¹/₂ oz. (15 ml) cherry brandy

Shake all the ingredients together with ice and strain into a cocktail glass.

Doctor Dangerous

1 oz. (30 ml) brandy
¹/₂ oz. (15 ml) milk
1 oz. (30 ml) Baileys Irish Cream

Shake all the ingredients together with ice and strain into an ice-filled old-fashioned glass.

Dream Cocktail

3 oz. (90 ml) brandy
1¹/₂ oz. (45 ml) triple sec
dash of anisette
chilled champagne to fill

Mix all the ingredients together in an ice-filled shaker, strain into a cocktail glass and serve.

East India

2 oz. (60 ml) cognac
$^1/_2$ oz. (15 ml) dark rum
dash of triple sec
dash of pineapple juice
dash of Angostura bitters

Shake all the liquids together, then strain into a martini glass and serve.

Eggnog

2 oz. (60 ml) cognac
1 egg
$^1/_2$ oz. (15 ml) gomme syrup
dash of dark rum
5 oz. (150 ml) half-and-half or light cream
grated nutmeg as garnish

Mix the ingredients together in a shaker, then pour into a highball glass.
Sprinkle on the grated nutmeg and serve.

Fjord

2 oz. (60 ml) aquavit
$^1/_2$ oz. (15 ml) cognac
1 oz. (30 ml) freshly squeezed orange juice
1 oz. (30 ml) freshly squeezed lime juice
$^1/_2$ oz. (15 ml) grenadine

Mix the ingredients together in an ice-filled shaker. Strain into an ice-filled old-fashioned glass and serve.

Frenchie

2 oz. (60 ml) cognac
2 oz. (60 ml) Grand Marnier

Pour the ingredients into a cocktail glass and stir.

French Whore

1 oz. (30 ml) cognac
1 oz. (30 ml) Tia Maria

Pour the cognac and Tia Maria into an old-fashioned glass, stir and serve.

Frozen Apple

2 oz. (60 ml) calvados
1 oz. (30 ml) fresh lime juice
dash of gomme syrup
1 egg white

Blend all the ingredients together with ice until frozen, then pour into a large goblet.

Good Fellow

1 oz. (30 ml) cognac
1 oz. (30 ml) Benedictine
2 dashes Angostura bitters
$^1/_2$ oz. (15 ml) gomme syrup

Shake all the ingredients together, then strain into a martini glass and serve.

Harmony

2 oz. (60 ml) cognac
$^1/_2$ oz. (15 ml) crème de fraises
2 dashes orange bitters
dash of maraschino liqueur

Pour the cognac, crème de fraises, bitters and liqueur into an old-fashioned glass and serve.

Headcrack

2 oz. (60 ml) Hennessy cognac
$1^1/_2$ oz. (45 ml) Kahlua
6 oz. (180 ml) cream or milk

Pour all the ingredients into an ice-filled mixing glass and stir well. Strain into a collins glass and serve.

IBF

¹/₂ oz. (15 ml) cognac
¹/₂ oz. (15 ml) orange curaçao
¹/₂ oz. (15 ml) Madeira
chilled champagne to fill

Pour the cognac, curaçao and Madeira into a champagne flute. Top up with champagne and serve.

Incredible Hulk

1 oz. (30 ml) Hennessy cognac
1 oz. (30 ml) Hpnotiq
3 maraschino cherries with stems on

Fill an old-fashioned glass with ice and pour the cognac, then float the Hpnotiq over this. Add the three cherries on a cocktail stick and serve with a straw.

Jack Rabbit

2 oz. (60 ml) applejack or calvados
dash of fresh lemon juice
dash of fresh orange juice
dash of gomme syrup

Shake all the ingredients together, then strain into a martini glass and serve.

Jack Rose

2 oz. (60 ml) applejack
1 oz. (30 ml) fresh lime juice
¹/₂ oz. (15 ml) grenadine
lime slice as garnish

Shake ingredients with ice and strain into a cocktail glass. Garnish with a slice of lime.

Lieutenant

$^1/_2$ oz. (15 ml) apricot brandy
1 tsp. (5 ml) superfine sugar
1 oz. (30 ml) bourbon
$^1/_2$ oz. (15 ml) grapefruit juice
maraschino cherry as garnish

Shake all the ingredients together with ice and strain into a cocktail glass.
Garnish with a cherry and serve.

Luxury

3 oz. (90 ml) cognac
3 dashes Angostura bitters
chilled champagne

Pour the cognac, champagne and bitters into a champagne flute, then serve.

Mikado

1 oz. (30 ml) cognac
$^1/_2$ oz. (15 ml) Cointreau
$^1/_2$ oz. (15 ml) crème de noyaux
dash of grenadine

Stir all the ingredients together, then strain into an ice-filled old-fashioned
glass and serve.

Mint Julep (alt)

1 oz. (30 ml) peach brandy
1 oz. (30 ml) brandy
12 sprigs of fresh mint
1 tsp. (5 ml) granulated sugar
chunk of pineapple

Put the mint in an old-fashioned glass, then add the sugar and brandies. Fill
the glass with crushed ice and rub the pineapple over the rim of the glass,
then serve.

Nicky Finn

1 oz. (30 ml) brandy
1 oz. (30 ml) Cointreau
1 oz. (30 ml) fresh lemon juice
dash of Pernod
lemon twist or maraschino cherry as garnish

Shake with ice and strain into a chilled cocktail glass. Garnish with a lemon
twist or a maraschino cherry.

Pierre Collins

2 oz. (60 ml) cognac
1 oz. (30 ml) lemon juice
1 tsp. (5 ml) superfine sugar
dash of Angostura bitters (optional)
soda water to fill

Place the cognac, juice, sugar and, if wanted, bitters in a tall glass half-filled
with ice, and stir to mix. Top up with soda water and stir gently.

Pierre Fizz

2 oz. (00 ml) cognac
1 oz. (30 ml) lemon juice
1 tsp. (5 ml) superfine sugar
dash of Angostura bitters (optional)
soda water to fill

Shake and strain into a tall glass, and top up with soda.

Pierre Sour

2 oz. (60ml) cognac
³/₄ oz. (22 ml) lemon juice
¹/₂ tsp. (2 ml) superfine sugar

Shake all the ingredients together and strain into a sour glass.

Prince of Wales

³/₄ oz. (22 ml) brandy
¹/₄ oz. (8 ml) Benedictine
champagne
dash of Angostura bitters
1 sugar cube
orange slice as garnish
maraschino cherry as garnish

Place the sugar cube in a highball glass and soak it with the Angostura. Add ice and brandy, then stir. Add the champagne, then the Benedictine, and serve with the slice of orange and maraschino cherry garnish.

Raja

1 oz. (30 ml) cognac
1 oz. (30 ml) champagne

Stir the cognac and champagne together, then strain into a martini glass and serve.

Sidecar (alt)

1¹/₂ oz. (45 ml) cognac
³/₄ oz. (22 ml) Cointreau
³/₄ oz. (22 ml) lemon juice
lemon twist as garnish

Sugar the rim of a cocktail glass. Shake the cognac, Cointreau and juice together. Strain, then pour into the glass and garnish with the twist of lemon.

Stinger

2 oz. (60 ml) brandy
1 oz. (30 ml) white crème de menthe

Pour the brandy and crème de menthe into a brandy glass and serve. Alternatively, mix the ingredients together in a shaker, then strain into a martini glass or an old-fashioned glass.

Thunder and Lightning

2 oz. (60 ml) cognac
1 oz. (30 ml) Cointreau
1 egg yolk
4 drops Tabasco sauce

Shake all the ingredients together, then strain into a martini glass and serve.

Tiger's Milk

1 oz. (30 ml) cognac
1 oz. (30 ml) sloe gin
lemon slice as garnish

Shake the cognac and gin together, then strain into a martini glass. Garnish with the lemon and serve.

Tulip

1 oz. (30 ml) calvados
1 oz. (30 ml) sweet vermouth
¹/₂ oz. (15 ml) apricot brandy
2 dashes fresh lemon juice
¹/₂ oz. (15 ml) gomme syrup

Shake all the ingredients together, then strain into a martini glass and serve.

Wally

1 oz. (30 ml) cognac
1 oz. (30 ml) Benedictine
2 dashes fresh lemon juice
chilled champagne to fill

Pour the cognac, Benedictine and lemon juice into a champagne flute. Top up with champagne and serve.

Xanthia Cocktail

1 oz. (30 ml) cherry brandy
1 oz. (30 ml) yellow Chartreuse
1 oz. (30 ml) gin

Stir all the ingredients together, then strain into a martini glass and serve.

Rum Cocktails

Rum comes with a sense of rhythm in every sip. This superb spirit from the Caribbean is behind many of the sensational summer cocktails we know and love. Here's a selection of remarkable rum recipes including **Hurricane**, **La Floridita**, **Mai Tai**, **Piña Colada** and **Zombie**. And, of course, there is the **Rum Punch** which comes with a rich naval history; and just one of countless recipes, the **Fish House Rum Punch** is included here. Whether you are a dark rum drinker or prefer the taste of light rum you'll discover a cocktail for your palate.

This selection includes all types of rum and cachaça.

Acid Trip

2 oz. (60 ml) Malibu rum
1 oz. (30 ml) Bacardi Spiced rum
$\frac{1}{2}$ oz. (15 ml) Jägermeister
1 oz. (30 ml) pineapple juice
dash of lemon-lime soda
lime wedge as garnish

Shake all the ingredients, except the soda, and strain into a highball glass filled with ice. Add the soda and garnish with a lime wedge.

Afternoon Delight

1 oz. (30 ml) dark rum
1 oz. (30 ml) freshly squeezed orange juice
1 oz. (30 ml) coconut cream
$\frac{1}{2}$ oz. (15 ml) crème de fraise
$\frac{1}{2}$ oz. (15 ml) heavy cream
7 strawberries

Place all the ingredients, except one strawberry, into a blender. Add crushed ice and blend. Pour into a goblet. Garnish with a strawberry and serve with a straw.

Alexander Baby

1 oz. (30 ml) navy rum
1 oz. (30 ml) brown crème de cacao
1 oz. (30 ml) heavy cream

Mix the ingredients together in a shaker, then strain into a martini glass and serve.

American Fizz

1 oz. (30 ml) dark rum
1 oz. (30 ml) banana purée
1 oz. (30 ml) pineapple juice
champagne to fill

Pour the ingredients, except champagne, into a shaker with ice. Shake and strain into a champagne glass. Fill with champagne and stir gently.

Anita's Attitude Adjuster

³/₄ oz. (22 ml) light rum
³/₄ oz. (22 ml) vodka
³/₄ oz. (22 ml) gin
³/₄ oz. (22 ml) tequila
¹/₄ oz. (8 ml) triple sec
¹/₂ lime, freshly squeezed
³/₄ oz. (22 ml) orange juice
sparkling white wine to fill

Squeeze the lime into a collins glass, add ice cubes, triple sec, orange juice and the spirits. Stir and top up with sparkling white wine.

Apollo 13

1 oz. (30 ml) white rum
dash of grenadine
¹/₂ oz. (15 ml) Galliano
1 oz. (30 ml) fresh cream
¹/₂ oz. (15 ml) Grand Marnier
maraschino cherry as garnish

Shake all the ingredients together with ice and strain into a champagne saucer. Garnish with a maraschino cherry.

Apple Colada

1 oz. (30 ml) white rum
$^2/_3$ oz. (20 ml) apple schnapps
1 oz. (30 ml) coconut cream
2 oz. (60 ml) apple juice
$^1/_2$ tsp. (2 ml) superfine sugar
$^1/_2$ apple, peeled

Place all the ingredients in a blender. Add crushed ice and blend until smooth, then pour into a colada glass. Serve with a straw.

Apple Daiquiri

2 oz. (60 ml) white rum
$^2/_3$ oz. (20 ml) apple schnapps
$^1/_2$ oz. (15 ml) cinnamon schnapps
$^1/_2$ oz. (15 ml) freshly squeezed lime juice
dash of gomme syrup

Shake all the ingredients together and strain into a cocktail glass.

Astronaut

1 oz. (30 ml) Coruba rum
1 oz. (30 ml) Smirnoff vodka
$^1/_3$ oz. (10 ml) fresh lemon juice
6 drops passion fruit pulp as garnish

Shake the first three ingredients together with ice and strain into a cocktail glass. Garnish with 6 drops of passion fruit pulp.

Aussie Crawl

$^1/_2$ oz. (15 ml) Bundaberg rum
$^1/_2$ oz. (15 ml) Scotch whisky
$^1/_2$ oz. (15 ml) gin
$^1/_2$ oz. (15 ml) vodka
cola to fill
orange slice as garnish

Pour each ingredient into a highball glass filled with ice and stir. Top up with cola and stir again. Garnish with a slice of orange and serve with a stirrer.

Australian Gold

1 oz. (30 ml) Bundaberg rum
1 oz. (30 ml) Galliano
1 oz. (30 ml) mango liqueur
pineapple wedge as garnish

Pour each ingredient into a highball glass filled with ice. Garnish with a pineapple wedge.

Bacardi Cocktail

2 oz. (60 ml) Bacardi rum
1 oz. (30 ml) fresh lime juice
dash of grenadine

Shake all the liquids together, then strain into a martini glass and serve.

Bahia

2 oz. (60 ml) white rum
1 oz. (30 ml) coconut cream
2 oz. (60 ml) pineapple juice
1 oz. (30 ml) grapefruit juice
1 oz. (30 ml) heavy cream

Blend all the ingredients together and pour into a large goblet

Banana Daiquiri

1 oz. (30 ml) white rum
1 oz. (30 ml) crème de banane
1 oz. (30 ml) fresh lime juice
$\frac{1}{2}$ oz. (15 ml) gomme syrup
$\frac{1}{2}$ banana

Blend all the ingredients together and pour into a large glass.

Banja Pantie

2 oz. (60 ml) Bacardi rum
1/2 oz. (15 ml) cream of coconut
dash of pineapple juice
dash of orange juice
dash of guava juice

Blend all the ingredients together with ice and pour into a cocktail glass.

Barracuda

1 oz. (30 ml) white rum
1 oz. (30 ml) Galliano
1 oz. (30 ml) pineapple juice
1/2 oz. (15 ml) fresh lime juice
1/2 oz. (15 ml) grenadine
chilled champagne to fill

Pour each of the ingredients into a highball glass, top up with champagne and serve.

Batida

2 oz. (60 ml) cachaça
1/2 oz. (15 ml) gomme syrup
fresh fruit

Blend all the ingredients together with ice until frozen, then pour into a large goblet. You can use any fresh fruit of your choice or even cashew nuts.

Bee's Kiss

2 oz. (60 ml) white rum
1/2 oz. (15 ml) cold black coffee
1/2 oz. (15 ml) heavy cream

Shake all the ingredients well and strain into a cocktail glass.

Beja Flor

2 oz. (60 ml) cachaça
1 oz. (30 ml) triple sec or Cointreau
1 oz. (30 ml) crème de banane

Shake all the ingredients together and strain into a cocktail glass.

Bella Donna

1 oz. (30 ml) dark rum
1 oz. (30 ml) amaretto
1 oz. (30 ml) sour mix
lime wedge

Rub the rim of a cocktail glass with a wedge of lime and then dip the glass into a saucer of sugar to coat the rim. Shake all ingredients with ice and strain into the glass.

Berry Sweet (makes two)

2 oz. (60 ml) cachaça
2 small limes, diced
few raspberries
few blueberries
6 strawberries diced, and hulled
1 Tbsp. (15 ml) brown sugar

Place the sugar and pieces of lime in a small mixing bowl. Muddle the lime, releasing the juices, then add berries. Muddle again until the juices are released. Place a scoop of this mixture into a small tumbler. Add the cachaça and some cracked ice. Stir and serve with a stirrer and a straw.

Black Widow

2 oz. (60 ml) dark rum
1 oz. (30 ml) Southern Comfort
1 oz. (30 ml) fresh lime juice

Shake all the ingredients together, then strain into a martini glass and serve.

Blow Up

1 oz. (30 ml) Bacardi rum
5 drops green crème de menthe
1 oz. (30 ml) Chartreuse
5 drops grenadine
$^1/_2$ oz. (15 ml) parfait amour
cracked ice

Pour the rum, Chartreuse and parfait amour into a mixing glass with ice and stir. Strain into a cocktail glass, then add the grenadine and crème de menthe.

Blue Boy

3 oz. (90 ml) dark rum
1 oz. (30 ml) sweet vermouth
dash of fresh orange juice
dash of orange bitters

Shake all the ingredients together, then pour into an old-fashioned glass and serve.

Blue Hawaiian

1 oz. (30 ml) white rum
1 oz. (30 ml) blue curaçao
3 oz. (90 ml) pineapple juice
1 oz. (30 ml) coconut cream

Blend all the ingredients together and pour into a large goblet.

Bondi Blue

1$^1/_2$ oz. (45 ml) Bacardi rum
1 oz. (30 ml) blue curaçao
1 oz. (30 ml) banana liqueur
1 egg white
lemonade to fill

Shake all the ingredients together with ice and strain into a highball glass filled with ice. Top up with lemonade.

Buster

3 oz. (90 ml) dark Puerto Rican rum
1 oz. (30 ml) Pernod
pineapple chunks to garnish

Shake all the ingredients together, then pour into an old-fashioned glass and serve, garnished with the pineapple.

Casablanca

2 oz. (60 ml) white rum
1 oz. (30 ml) Cointreau
1 oz. (30 ml) fresh lime juice
dash of orange bitters

Shake all the ingredients together, then strain into a martini glass and serve.

Castro

1½ oz. (45 ml) gold rum
¾ oz. (22 ml) calvados
1½ oz. (45 ml) orange juice
¾ oz. (22 ml) lime juice
¼ oz. (22 ml) Rose's Lime Cordial
dash of gomme syrup
lime wedge as garnish

Shake all the liquid ingredients together and strain into an ice-filled highball glass. Decorate with the wedge of lime.

Centenario

1½ oz. (45 ml) gold rum
1 oz. (30 ml) overproof white rum
¼ oz. (8 ml) Kahlua
¼ oz. (8 ml) Cointreau
dash of grenadine
juice of 1 lime
sprig of mint

Stir all the ingredients together, then pour over ice into a highball glass and garnish with a sprig of mint.

Citrus Rum Cooler

1$^1/_3$ oz. (40 ml) white rum

$^2/_3$ oz. (20 ml) triple sec

1$^2/_3$ oz. (50 ml) freshly squeezed orange juice

$^1/_2$ oz. (15 ml) freshly squeezed lime juice

few dashes of gomme syrup

lemon-lime soda to fill

Shake first five ingredients and strain into a highball glass with ice. Top up with soda and serve with a straw.

Cocoloco

1 oz. (30 ml) white rum

1 oz. (30 ml) vodka

1 oz. (30 ml) tequila

1 oz. (30 ml) fresh lemon juice

1 oz. (30 ml) sweetened coconut cream

Blend all the ingredients together until smooth, then pour into a large goblet.

Coconilla Delight

1 oz. (30 ml) gold rum

1 banana, peeled

1 oz. (30 ml) coconut cream

3 oz. (90 ml) pineapple juice

3 oz. (90 ml) fresh orange juice

2 scoops vanilla ice cream

Place ingredients into a blender with crushed ice. Blend and pour into a highball glass. Serve with a straw.

Constellation

1$^1/_2$ oz. (45 ml) dark rum

1$^1/_2$ oz. (45 ml) dry vermouth

dash of lime juice

1$^1/_2$ oz. (45 ml) green ginger wine

dash of Angostura bitters

Shake all the ingredients together with ice and strain into a cocktail glass.

Continental

2 oz. (60 ml) white rum
$^1/_2$ oz. (15 ml) crème de menthe
dash of fresh lime juice
lemon twist as garnish

Pour the rum, crème de menthe and lime juice into an old-fashioned glass. Garnish with the lemon twist and serve.

Cuba Libre

$1^2/_3$ oz. (50 ml) white rum
freshly squeezed juice of 1 lime
cola to fill
lime wedge as garnish

Pour the juice, then the rum into a highball glass filled with ice. Top up with cola, add a wedge of lime, then serve with a stirrer.

Cuban

2 oz. (60 ml) white rum
dash of apricot brandy
$^1/_2$ lime, freshly squeezed
dash of gomme syrup

Stir the rum, brandy, lime juice and gomme together. Strain into a martini glass and serve.

Cuban Cutie

2 oz. (60 ml) white rum
$^2/_3$ oz. (20 ml) passion fruit juice
3 oz. (90 ml) grenadine
3 oz. (90 ml) fresh orange juice
lime wedge as garnish

Shake all the liquid ingredients together and strain into a highball glass with ice. Add a lime wedge.

Cuban Island

¾ oz. (22 ml) white rum
¾ oz. (22 ml) vodka
¾ oz. (22 ml) Cointreau
¾ oz. (22 ml) lemon juice

Shake all the ingredients together and strain into a cocktail glass.

Dizzy Gillespie

½ oz. (15 ml) Appleton Special rum
½ oz. (15 ml) Captain Morgan Original Spiced rum
½ oz. (15 ml) Malibu rum
½ oz. (15 ml) cranberry juice
½ oz. (15 ml) orange juice
½ oz. (15 ml) pineapple juice
½ oz. (15 ml) fresh lime juice
dash of Bacardi Special Reserve rum

Shake all the ingredients, except the Bacardi, with ice and strain into a highball glass with ice. Float the Bacardi Special Reserve.

Dorothy Lamour

1 oz. (30 ml) Bacardi rum
1 oz. (30 ml) banana liqueur
½ oz. (15 ml) lemon juice
3 slices mango

Blend all the ingredients together and pour into a champagne flute.

Dry Presidente

2 oz. (60 ml) white rum
1 oz. (30 ml) dry vermouth
dash of Angostura bitters
olive as garnish

Shake all the liquid ingredients together, then strain into a martini glass. Garnish with the olive and serve.

El Burro

¹/₂ oz. (15 ml) Kahlua
1 oz. (30 ml) light cream
¹/₂ oz. (15 ml) rum
¹/₂ fresh banana, sliced
1 oz. (30 ml) coconut cream

Blend all the ingredients together until smooth. Pour into a chilled cocktail glass.

El Presidente

2 oz. (60 ml) white rum
1 oz. (30 ml) fresh lime juice
dash of grenadine
dash of pineapple juice

Pour the grenadine into a cocktail glass. In an ice-filled shaker, mix the rum, and the lime and pineapple juices, then strain into the glass and serve.

Esme's Peril

6 oz. (180 ml) Bacardi rum
2 oz. (60 ml) lemon juice
1¹/₂ oz. (45 ml) light cream
1 oz. (30 ml) dark rum
1 oz. (30 ml) banana liqueur
1 oz. (30 ml) orange juice
¹/₂ fresh banana
2 tsp. (10 ml) superfine sugar
4 strawberries

Blend all the ingredients together until smooth. Pour into a beer tankard and serve.

Fish House Rum Punch (makes 30 servings)

36 oz. (1 L bottle) dark rum
25 oz. (750 ml bottle) fresh lemon juice
25 oz. (750 ml bottle) cognac
4 oz. (120 ml) peach brandy
12 oz. (355 g) superfine sugar
40 oz. (1.1 L) spring water

Dissolve the sugar in some water, heating if necessary and then chilling. Add the lemon juice and the remaining water; stir until blended. Two to three hours before serving, add the spirits and refrigerate. For serving, portion part of punch into large bowl, add large blocks of ice to the punch and serve in chilled glasses, if possible.

Florida

1 oz. (30 ml) white rum
¹/₂ oz. (15 ml) crème de menthe
¹/₂ oz. (15 ml) lime juice
¹/₂ oz. (15 ml) pineapple juice
soda water to fill
sprig of mint as garnish

Shake all the ingredients, except soda, with ice and strain into a highball glass filled with ice. Top up with soda and garnish with a sprig of mint.

Floridita

1¹/₂ oz. (45 ml) white rum
¹/₂ oz. (15 ml) sweet vermouth
dash of white crème de cacao
dash of grenadine
juice of ¹/₂ lime

Shake all the ingredients over ice cubes and strain into a cocktail glass.

Frozen Daiquiri

2 oz. (60 ml) white rum
1 lime, freshly squeezed
1 tsp. (5 ml) superfine sugar
fruit (optional)

Blend all the ingredients together with ice until frozen, then pour into a large goblet. Add any fruit to turn this drink into a fruit daiquiri, adding 1 oz. (30 ml) of an appropriate liqueur.

Grapefruit Daiquiri

2 oz. (60 ml) white rum
1 oz. (30 ml) fresh grapefruit juice
dash of gomme syrup

Shake all the ingredients together and strain into a cocktail glass.

Hazy Cuban

1 oz. (30 ml) Bacardi rum
1 oz. (30 ml) coconut cream
1 oz. (30 ml) cream or milk
2 oz. (60 ml) pineapple juice
pineapple slice as garnish

Blend all the liquid ingredients together. Pour into an ice-filled old-fashioned glass and serve. Garnish with a slice of pineapple.

Hurricane

1 oz. (30 ml) white rum
1 oz. (30 ml) dark rum
²/₃ oz. (20 ml) triple sec
1 lime, freshly squeezed
²/₃ oz. (20 ml) gomme syrup
¹/₃ oz. (10 ml) grenadine
3 oz. (90 ml) freshly squeezed orange juice
3 oz. (90 ml) pineapple juice
pineapple wedge as garnish

Shake all the ingredients together and strain into a highball glass filled with ice. Add a pineapple wedge to decorate.

Hurricane (alt)

1 oz. (30 ml) dark rum
1 oz. (30 ml) white rum
¹/₂ oz. (15 ml) grenadine
2 dashes fresh lime juice

Mix both rums with the grenadine and lime juice in a shaker, then strain into a martini glass and serve.

Jerry's Juice

1 oz. (30 ml) dark rum
¹/₂ oz. (15 ml) Cointreau
³/₄ oz. (22 ml) cranberry juice
¹/₂ oz. (15 ml) passion fruit juice
dash of grenadine

Shake all the ingredients together and strain into a cocktail glass.

Jungle Juice

1¹/₂ oz. (45 ml) white rum
1 oz. (30 ml) pineapple juice
1¹/₂ oz. (45 ml) Drambuie
1 oz. (30 ml) cream
1¹/₂ oz. (45 ml) coconut cream
¹/₂ fresh banana

Blend all the ingredients together until smooth, then pour into a champagne glass.

Keep on Going

1 oz. (30 ml) white rum
¹/₂ oz. (15 ml) Pernod
¹/₂ oz. (15 ml) grapefruit juice
¹/₂ oz. (15 ml) fresh lime juice
1 oz. (30 ml) cola
lemonade or lemon-lime soda to fill
lemon slice as garnish

Shake the rum, Pernod, grapefruit juice and lime juice, and strain into a highball glass half-filled with ice. Add the cola and lemonade/lemon-lime soda to the top. Add a slice of lemon as a garnish and serve with a straw.

King's Daiquiri

1¹/₂ oz. (45 ml) Bacardi rum
¹/₂ oz. (15 ml) lemon juice
¹/₂ oz. (15 ml) parfait amour
1 tsp. (5 ml) superfine sugar
dash of egg white

Blend all the ingredients together until smooth, then pour into a cocktail glass.

Kiwi Fruit Daiquiri

1 oz. (30 ml) Bacardi light rum
1 oz. (30 ml) lemon juice
1 oz. (30 ml) Cointreau
¹/₂ oz. (15 ml) gomme syrup
1 oz. (30 ml) Midori
1 kiwi fruit, diced

Blend all the ingredients together until smooth, then pour into a cocktail glass.

Knickerbocker Knockerl

2 oz. (60 ml) white rum
¹/₂ oz. (15 ml) crème de framboise
¹/₂ oz. (15 ml) orange curaçao
¹/₃ oz. (10 ml) freshly squeezed lemon juice
pineapple wedge as garnish

Shake all the ingredients together and strain into a cocktail glass. Add a wedge of pineapple.

Knickerbocker Special

2 oz. (60 ml) white rum
¹/₂ oz. (15 ml) triple sec
dash of fresh orange juice
dash of fresh lemon juice
dash of raspberry syrup

Shake all the ingredients together, then strain into a martini glass and serve.

La Floridita

2 oz. (60 ml) Havana white rum
dash of maraschino liqueur
1 lime, freshly squeezed
dash of gomme syrup
lime wedge as garnish

Pour the liquid ingredients into a shaker filled with crushed ice. Shake, then strain into a cocktail glass over dry crushed ice. Add a wedge of lime and serve with a straw.

Latin Manhattan

3 oz. (90 ml) Bacardi Limon rum
1 oz. (30 ml) fresh lime juice
1 oz. (30 ml) sugar cane juice or gomme syrup
lime wedge as garnish

Blend all the ingredients together and pour in a martini glass. Garnish with a lime wedge.

Long Island Iced Tea

$^3/_4$ oz. (22 ml) light rum
$^3/_4$ oz. (22 ml) vodka
$^3/_4$ oz. (22 ml) gin
$^3/_4$ oz. (22 ml) tequila
$^1/_4$ oz. (8 ml) triple sec
$^1/_2$ lime, freshly squeezed
$^3/_4$ oz. (22 ml) orange juice
cola to fill

Squeeze lime into a collins glass, add ice cubes, spirits, triple sec and orange juice. Stir and top up with cola.

Madagascar Sour

2 oz. (60 ml) Appleton Special gold rum
$^1/_2$ oz. (15 ml) fresh lime juice
1 tsp. (5 ml) vanilla sugar
dash of vanilla liqueur

Shake all ingredients together with ice and strain into a chilled cocktail glass.

Madonna

1¹/₂ oz. (45 ml) Captain Morgan Original Spiced rum
2 oz. (60 ml) pineapple juice
2 oz. (60 ml) orange juice
1 oz. (30 ml) sour mix
dash of Bacardi 151 rum
dash of grenadine
2 maraschino cherries as garnish

Shake the Captain Morgan, pineapple juice, orange juice and sour mix with
ice and strain into an ice-filled highball glass. Float the Bacardi over the top,
then the grenadine, and garnish with two maraschino cherries.

Mai Tai No. 1

1 oz. (30 ml) white rum
¹/₂ oz. (15 ml) Cointreau
¹/₄ oz. (8 ml) Rose's Lime Cordial
1¹/₂ oz. (45 ml) orange juice
1¹/₂ oz. (45 ml) unsweetened pineapple juice
splash of grenadine
¹/₂ oz. (15 ml) gold rum
pineapple wedge as garnish

Shake and strain the white rum, Cointreau, lime cordial and the juices into a
collins glass half-filled with ice. Add the grenadine and gold rum and garnish
with a pineapple wedge.

Mai Tai No. 2

2 oz. (60 ml) gold rum
1 oz. (30 ml) curaçao
1¹/₂ oz. (45 ml) Rose's Lime Cordial
¹/₂ oz. (15 ml) orgeat syrup
1 tsp. (5 ml) gomme syrup
splash of grenadine
¹/₂ oz. (15 ml) overproof rum
pineapple wedge as garnish
lime wedge as garnish

Shake and strain the gold rum, curaçao, lime cordial and the syrups into a
collins glass half-filled with ice. Add the grenadine and the overproof rum and
garnish with the pineapple and lime wedges.

Mango Delicious

1 oz. (30 ml) Bacardi rum
3 oz. (90 ml) pineapple juice
1 oz. (30 ml) mango liqueur
$^1/_2$ mango, skinned and pitted
1 oz. (30 ml) coconut cream
1 small scoop crushed ice
1 oz. (30 ml) light cream

Blend all the ingredients together with ice, then pour into large tumbler, and serve.

Mary Pickford

$1^1/_2$ oz. (45 ml) white rum
dash of maraschino liqueur
$1^1/_2$ oz. (45 ml) unsweetened pineapple juice
dash of grenadine
lemon twist as garnish

Shake all the liquid ingredients and strain into a cocktail glass. Add twist.

Mickey

1 oz. (30 ml) dark rum
$^1/_2$ oz. (15 ml) Cointreau
$^1/_2$ oz. (15 ml) bourbon
dash of grenadine

Shake all the ingredients together, then strain into a martini glass and serve.

Mint Daiquiri

2 oz. (60 ml) white rum
$^1/_2$ oz. (15 ml) Cointreau
handful of mint leaves
juice of $^1/_2$ lime, freshly squeezed
1 tsp. (5 ml) superfine sugar

Blend all the ingredients together with crushed ice and strain into a cocktail glass.

Mofuco

2 oz. (60 ml) white rum
dash of Angostura bitters
$^1/_2$ oz. (15 ml) gomme syrup
1 egg
lemon peel as garnsish

Shake all the ingredients together, then strain into a martini glass and serve with lemon peel.

Mojito

2 oz. (60 ml) white rum
dash of gomme syrup
$^1/_2$ lime, freshly squeezed
fresh mint leaves
soda water to fill
sprig of mint as garnish

In a large highball glass, muddle the mint leaves and gomme. Squeeze lime juice into the glass and add lime half. Then add the rum and some ice. Stir, then add the soda, stir again, briefly, and garnish with the sprig of mint.

Naked Lady

1 oz. (30 ml) white rum
1 oz. (30 ml) apricot brandy
1 oz. (30 ml) fresh lemon juice
dash of grenadine
1 egg white

Shake all the ingredients together, then strain into a martini glass and serve.

Naked Lady (alt)

$1^1/_2$ oz. (45 ml) white rum
$1^1/_2$ oz. (45 ml) sweet vermouth
4 dashes apricot brandy
2 dashes grenadine
4 dashes lemon-lime soda

Shake all the ingredients, except the lemon-lime soda, and pour into a cocktail glass. Add the dashes of soda, stir and serve.Δ

Nevada

2 oz. (60 ml) white rum
1 oz. (30 ml) grapefruit juice
juice of 1 lime, freshly squeezed

Shake all the ingredients together, then strain into a martini glass and serve.

Olympia

2 oz. (60 ml) white rum
$^1/_2$ oz. (15 ml) Cherry Heering
juice of 1 lime, freshly squeezed

Shake all the ingredients together, then strain into a martini glass and serve.

Painkiller

2 oz. (60 ml) white rum
4 oz. (115 ml) pineapple juice
1 oz. (30 ml) freshly squeezed orange juice
1 oz. (30 ml) coconut cream

Shake all the ingredients together and strain into a highball glass filled with ice.

Passion Batida

$1^2/_3$ oz. (50 ml) cachaça
1 oz. (30 ml) passion fruit purée
$^1/_3$ oz. (10 ml) gomme syrup
lime wedge as garnish

Pour all ingredients into an ice-filled old-fashioned glass and stir. Garnish with a lime wedge.

Pear Daiquiri

1 oz. (30 ml) white rum
$^1/_3$ oz. (10 ml) pear schnapps
1 oz. (30 ml) fresh pear purée
1 oz. (30 ml) fresh lime juice
dash of gomme syrup

Put all the ingredients into a blender with crushed ice. Blend and pour into a large cocktail glass.

Piña Colada

2 oz. (60 ml) white rum
1 oz. (30 ml) sweetened coconut cream
2 oz. (60 ml) pineapple juice
4 chunks fresh pineapple
pinch of salt

Blend all the ingredients together until smooth, then pour into a large goblet.

Planters

2 oz. (60 ml) dark rum
1 lime, freshly squeezed
$^1/_2$ oz. (15 ml) gomme syrup

Shake all the ingredients together, then strain into a martini glass and serve.

President

2 oz. (60 ml) dark rum
dash of grenadine
$^1/_2$ ruby (blood) orange, freshly squeezed
dash of lemon juice

Shake all the ingredients together, then strain into a martini glass and serve.

Presidente

2 oz. (60 ml) white rum
$^1/_4$ oz. (8 ml) Cointreau
$^3/_4$ oz. (22 ml) dry vermouth
$^1/_4$ oz. (8 ml) sweet vermouth
dash of grenadine
dash of lime juice, freshly squeezed

Shake all the ingredients together and strain into a cocktail glass.

Pussy Foot

2 oz. (60 ml) white rum
1 oz. (30 ml) fresh lime juice
1 oz. (30 ml) fresh orange juice
1 oz. (30 ml) pineapple juice
2 dashes grenadine
1 oz. (30 ml) heavy cream

Mix all the ingredients together in a shaker, then pour
into a highball glass and serve.

Raspberry Mint Daiquiri

1²/₃ oz. (50 ml) white rum
handful fresh raspberries
6 leaves fresh mint
dash of gomme syrup
1 mint leaf as garnish

Place all the ingredients in a shaker. Shake and strain into a large cocktail glass,
and garnish with mint.

Ronaldo

1 oz. (30 ml) cachaça
1 oz. (30 ml) gold rum
¹/₂ oz. (15 ml) crème de banane
¹/₂ oz. (15 ml) unsweetened pineapple juice
1 lime, freshly squeezed
lime wedge as garnish

Shake and strain the liquid ingredients into a highball glass half-filled with ice.
Garnish with lime.

Rum Shrub

2 oz. (60 ml) dark rum
1 oz. (30 ml) shrub (fruit and herb syrup)
1 oz. (30 ml) soda water

Fill a wine goblet two-thirds with ice. Add the rum, shrub and soda, then stir lightly.

September Morn

2 oz. (60 ml) white rum
splash of grenadine
1 oz. (30 ml) lemon juice
1 egg white

Shake all the ingredients together for about 30 seconds, then strain into a cocktail glass.

Spice Whirl

1 oz. (30 ml) spiced rum
$^2/_3$ oz. (20 ml) triple sec
1 oz. (30 ml) fresh orange juice
1 oz. (30 ml) papaya juice
$^2/_3$ oz. (20 ml) fresh lime juice

Place all the ingredients in a shaker. Shake, then strain into a highball glass with ice and serve with a straw.

Superior

2 oz. (60 ml) white rum
1 oz. (30 ml) sweet vermouth
1 oz. (30 ml) fresh lemon juice
2 fresh apricots
orange slice as garnish

Blend all the ingredients together until frozen, then pour into a large goblet. Garnish with the orange slice and serve.

Sydney Sling

2 oz. (60 ml) white rum
$^2/_3$ oz. (20 ml) freshly squeezed lemon juice
$^2/_3$ oz. (20 ml) cherry brandy
2 oz. (60 ml) guava juice
2 oz. (60 ml) pineapple juice
few dashes peach schnapps
$^1/_2$ ripe banana

Place all the ingredients in a blender and blend. Add two scoops of crushed ice and blend again. Pour into a tumbler and serve with a straw.

Tabu

2 oz. (60 ml) rum
1 oz. (30 ml) gomme syrup
1 oz. (30 ml) cranberry juice
$^1/_2$ oz. (15 ml) fresh lemon juice
3 oz. (90 ml) pineapple juice

Blend all the ingredients together until smooth, then pour into a large goblet.

Tropical

2 oz. (60 ml) Jamaican rum
1 slice pineapple
1 tsp. (5 ml) granulated sugar
1 lime, freshly squeezed
dash of grenadine

Sprinkle a slice of pineapple with the sugar. Mix in the base of a shaker, then add the rum, lime juice and grenadine as well as some crushed ice. Shake long and vigorously, then strain into martini glass and serve.

Tropical Storm

2 oz. (60 ml) golden rum
1 oz. (30 ml) vodka
1 oz. (30 ml) fresh orange juice
$^1/_2$ oz. (15 ml) fresh lime juice
$^1/_2$ oz. (15 ml) pineapple juice
dash of grenadine
dash of Angostura bitters

Blend all the ingredients together until smooth, then pour into a highball glass.

Virgin's Answer

1 oz. (30 ml) white rum
1 oz. (30 ml) brown crème de cacao
1 oz. (30 ml) crème de banane
1 oz. (30 ml) fresh lemon juice
1 oz. (30 ml) fresh orange juice
$^1/_2$ fresh banana

Blend all the ingredients together until smooth, then pour into a large goblet.

Yellow Bird

2 oz. (60 ml) white rum
1 oz. (30 ml) Cointreau
1 oz. (30 ml) Galliano
2 oz. (60 ml) fresh orange juice

Shake all the ingredients together, then strain into a martini glass and serve.

Yellow Bird (alt)

1¹/₂ oz. (45 ml) gold rum
¹/₂ oz. (15 ml) overproof rum
³/₄ oz. (22 ml) crème de banane
dash of Galliano
¹/₄ oz. (8 ml) apricot brandy
3 oz. (90 ml) unsweetened pineapple juice
¹/₄ oz. (8 ml) freshly squeezed orange juice

Shake all the ingredients together and strain into a highball glass half-filled with ice.

Zombie

³/₄ oz. (22 ml) gold rum
2 oz. (60 ml) dark rum
³/₄ oz. (22 ml) overproof rum
³/₄ oz. (22 ml) Cherry Heering
1¹/₄ oz. (38 ml) lime juice
dash of grenadine
³/₄ oz. (22 ml) orange juice

Shake all the ingredients together and strain into a large highball glass half-filled with ice.

Whiskey Cocktails

Talk of whiskey always starts a discussion between blended and pure malts. The best cocktails are made with blended whiskey. Always use the best quality brand to retain the flavor for cocktails such as the **Godfather**, **Old-Fashioned**, **Rob Roy** and **Whisky Mac**. Whiskey is a strong spirit and needs strong-tasting mixers. These recipes are not for faint-flavor fans. However, they are all worth tasting once in a lifetime.

This selection includes bourbon, rye, Scotch, Irish and Canadian whiskies.

Admiral Cannon

1½ oz. (45 ml) bourbon
½ oz. (15 ml) lemon juice
1 oz. (30 ml) white rum
1 tsp. (5 ml) maple syrup

Shake all ingredients with ice. Strain into a cocktail glass.

Affinity

2 oz. (60 ml) Scotch whisky
1½ oz. (45 ml) sweet vermouth
1½ oz. (45 ml) dry vermouth
2 dashes Angostura bitters
lemon twist as garnish

Stir the Scotch and vermouths together, then strain into a martini glass and serve with the lemon twist.

Alcazar

2 oz. (60 ml) Canadian Club whisky
1 oz. (30 ml) Benedictine
dash of orange bitters

Shake all the liquids together, then strain into a martini glass and serve.

Algonquin

2 oz. (60 ml) rye
1 oz. (30 ml) dry vermouth
1 oz. (30 ml) pineapple juice
dash of Peychaud's bitters

Shake all the ingredients together and strain into a cocktail glass.

Alice

1 oz. (30 ml) Scotch whisky
1 oz. (30 ml) kümmel
1 oz. (30 ml) sweet vermouth

Shake all ingredients with ice and strain into a champagne flute.

Angelic

3 oz. (90 ml) bourbon
1 oz. (30 ml) crème de cacao
1 oz. (30 ml) grenadine
1 oz. (30 ml) heavy cream
grated nutmeg as garnish

Mix the ingredients together in a shaker, then strain into a cocktail glass.
Sprinkle on the nutmeg and serve.

Ballantine's

2 oz. (60 ml) Ballantine's Scotch whisky
1 oz. (30 ml) sweet vermouth
dash of crème de cassis
dash of Angostura bitters

Pour all the ingredients into a shaker and shake. Strain into a martini glass
and serve.

Berlin Binge

1 oz. (30 ml) bourbon
1 oz. (30 ml) vodka
1 oz. (30 ml) gin
1 oz. (30 ml) cognac
green cocktail olive as garnish

Mix ingredients with ice in a mixing glass, then strain into a cocktail glass.
Garnish with a green cocktail olive.

Blood and Sand

1 oz. (30 ml) Scotch whisky
1 oz. (30 ml) orange juice
1 oz. (30 ml) cherry brandy
1 oz. (30 ml) sweet vermouth
orange twist as garnish

Mix ingredients with ice in a mixing glass, then strain into a champagne
saucer. Garnish with an orange twist.

Bourbon Banana

1 oz. (30 ml) bourbon
1 oz. (30 ml) orange juice
1 oz. (30 ml) Kahlua
1 oz. (30 ml) light cream
1 banana

Blend ingredients with ice and pour into a tumbler.

Brighton Punch

1 oz. (30 ml) bourbon
2 oz. (60 ml) orange juice
3 oz. (90 ml) brandy
$^1/_4$ oz. (8 ml) Benedictine
$^3/_4$ oz. (22 ml) lemon juice
dash of gomme syrup

Shake all the ingredients together and strain into an ice-filled collins glass.

Brooklyn

1 oz. (30 ml) rye
³/₄ oz. (22 ml) vermouth rosso
dash of maraschino liqueur

Stir all the ingredients together, then strain into a cocktail glass.

Canadian Sherbet

1 oz. (30 ml) Canadian Club whisky
1 oz. (30 ml) lemon juice
¹/₂ oz. (15 ml) Tia Maria
1 oz. (30 ml) gomme syrup

Blend ingredients with ice and pour into a margarita glass.

Chapel Hill

3 oz. (90 ml) bourbon
1 oz. (30 ml) triple sec
dash of fresh lemon juice
orange twist as garnish

Shake all the liquids together, then strain into a martini glass and serve with the orange twist.

Colonel Collins

2 oz. (60 ml) bourbon
1 oz. (30 ml) lemon juice
1 tsp. (5 ml) superfine sugar
dash of Angostura bitters (optional)
soda water to fill

Place the first three ingredients in a tall glass half-filled with ice, and stir to mix. Top up with soda, stirring gently. Add a dash of bitters, if wanted. Stir again and serve.

Colonel Fizz

2 oz. (60 ml) bourbon
1 oz. (30 ml) lemon juice
1 tsp. (5 ml) superfine sugar
dash of Angostura bitters (optional)
soda water to fill

Shake and strain into a tall glass. Top up with soda.

Colonel Sour

2 oz. (60 ml) bourbon
³/₄ oz. (22 ml) lemon juice
¹/₂ tsp. (2 ml) superfine sugar

Shake all the ingredients together and strain into a sour glass.

Cyclone Tracy

1 oz. (30 ml) Tia Maria
1 oz. (30 ml) Scotch whisky
1 oz. (30 ml) Kahlua
1 oz. (30 ml) Baileys Irish Cream
cream or milk to fill

Shake all the ingredients, except the cream, with ice. Strain into an ice-filled highball glass, top up with cream and serve with a straw.

Evans

2 oz. (60 ml) bourbon
1 oz. (30 ml) Cointreau
1 oz. (30 ml) apricot brandy

Stir the bourbon, Cointreau and brandy together, then strain into an ice-filled old-fashioned glass and serve.

Frisco

2 oz. (60 ml) rye
1/4 oz. (8 ml) Benedictine
3/4 oz. (22 ml) fresh lemon juice
lemon slice as garnish

Shake all ingredients with ice and strain into a cocktail glass. Garnish with a slice of lemon.

Ginger Jest

1 oz. (30 ml) bourbon
1 oz. (30 ml) pineapple juice
2–3 slices fresh gingerroot
champagne to fill

Muddle fresh ginger in a shaker. Add the bourbon, pineapple juice and ice cubes, then shake. Strain into a champagne glass and top up with champagne.

Godfather

2 oz. (60 ml) Scotch whisky
1 oz. (30 ml) amaretto

Pour the Scotch and amaretto into an old-fashioned glass and serve.

Gumdrop

2 oz. (60 ml) Scotch whisky
1 oz. (30 ml) Galliano

Pour the Scotch and Galliano into an old-fashioned glass and serve.

H. G. Wells

2 oz. (60 ml) bourbon
1 oz. (30 ml) dry vermouth
1/2 oz. (15 ml) Pernod
2 dashes Angostura bitters

Stir all the ingredients together. Strain into an ice-filled old-fashioned glass and serve.

Hair of the Dog

2 oz. (60 ml) Scotch whisky
1 oz. (30 ml) honey
1 oz. (30 ml) heavy cream

Mix the ingredients together in a shaker, then strain into a martini glass and serve.

Harper Cranberry

2 oz. (60 ml) I.W. Harper bourbon
3 oz. (90 ml) cranberry juice

Stir into an ice-filled highball glass.

Horse's Neck

2 oz. (60 ml) bourbon
2 dashes Angostura bitters
ginger ale
lemon twist

Coat a highball glass with bitters. Add ice and the bourbon. Stir, then add the ginger ale and the twist of lemon. Stir again, briefly.

Independence

1 oz. (30 ml) bourbon
¹/₂ oz. (15 ml) lemon juice
¹/₂ oz. (15 ml) brandy
2 oz. (60 ml) orange juice
sprig of mint as garnish

Shake ingredients with ice and strain into a cocktail glass. Garnish with sprig of mint.

Ink Street

1 oz. (30 ml) Scotch whisky
1 oz. (30 ml) lemon juice
1 oz. (30 ml) orange juice
orange twist as garnish

Shake ingredients with ice and strain into a champagne glass. Garnish with a twist of orange.

Irish Nut

1 oz. (30 ml) Irish whiskey

1 oz. (30 ml) Baileys Irish Cream

1 oz. (30 ml) Frangelico

Pour the whiskey, Baileys and Frangelico into an old-fashioned glass and serve.

Jocose Julep

2¹/₂ oz. (75 ml) bourbon

¹/₂ oz. (15 ml) green crème de menthe

1 oz. (30 ml) gomme syrup

1 oz. (30 ml) fresh lime juice

8–10 fresh mint leaves

sprig of mint to garnish

Blend all the ingredients together until frozen, then pour into a large goblet. Garnish with the mint and serve.

Kentucky Sunset

2 oz. (60 ml) bourbon

¹/₂ oz. (15 ml) Strega

¹/₂ oz. (15 ml) anisette

lemon twist as garnish

Stir the bourbon, Strega and anisette together, then strain into a martini glass. Serve, garnished with the lemon twist.

Last Emperor

1 oz. (30 ml) Canadian whisky

1 oz. (30 ml) Blanco vermouth

¹/₂ oz. (15 ml) Grand Marnier

1 oz. (30 ml) orange juice

dash of Angostura bitters

strip of orange peel as garnish

Place ingredients in mixing glass with ice and stir well. Strain into a cocktail glass and stir again. Add a strip of orange peel.

Liberty Bell

2 oz. (60 ml) bourbon
1 oz. (30 ml) peach schnapps
dash of apricot brandy
dash of Campari

Stir all the ingredients together, then strain into a martini glass and serve.

Magnolia Blossom

1 oz. (30 ml) bourbon
$^1/_3$ oz. (10 ml) lemon juice
2 dashes grenadine
$^1/_3$ oz. (10 ml) light cream

Shake all the ingredients with ice and strain into a cocktail glass.

Manhattan (perfect)

$1^1/_2$ oz. (45 ml) whiskey
2 oz. (60 ml) sweet vermouth
1 oz. (30 ml) dry vermouth
dash of Angostura bitters
maraschino cherry to garnish

Fill a mixing glass halfway with ice cubes and pour in all the liquid ingredients.
Stir together, then strain into a martini glass. Garnish with the cherry and serve.

Manhattan (sweet)

2 oz. (60 ml) bourbon or rye
1 oz. (30 ml) sweet vermouth
dash of Angostura bitters
maraschino cherry to garnish

Fill a mixing glass halfway with ice cubes and pour in all the liquid ingredients.
Stir together, then strain into a martini glass. Garnish with the cherry, dropped
in the glass, and serve.

Milk Punch

3 oz. (90 ml) bourbon
3 oz. (90 ml) cream or milk
2 oz. (60 ml) light cream
¹/₂ oz. (15 ml) gomme syrup
grated nutmeg as garnish

Shake all the liquid ingredients with ice and strain into a ice-filled tumbler.
Shake grated nutmeg over the drink.

Old-Fashioned

3 oz. (90 ml) bourbon
3 dashes Angostura bitters
1 sugar cube
orange slice as garnish
maraschino cherry as garnish

Put the bitters, sugar cube and a dash of the bourbon into an old-fashioned
glass and muddle together. Add 2 ice cubes and 1 oz. (30 ml) of the
bourbon and stir. Squeeze some of the juice from the orange slice into the
glass, then add two more ice cubes and 1 oz. (30 ml) bourbon and stir again.
Finally add two more ice cubes, the remaining bourbon, the orange slice and
cherry, then serve.

Pan-Am

1 oz. (30 ml) bourbon
1 oz. (30 ml) mescal
dash of Angostura bitters
dash of gomme syrup

Pour the bourbon, mescal, bitters and gomme into an old-fashioned glass
and serve.

Rob Roy

2 oz. (60 ml) Scotch whisky
1 oz. (30 ml) sweet vermouth
dash of Angostura bitters

Stir all the ingredients together, then strain into a martini glass and serve.

Rob Roy Perfect

2 oz. (60 ml) Scotch whisky
$^1/_2$ oz. (15 ml) sweet vermouth
$^1/_2$ oz. (15 ml) dry vermouth
dash of Angostura bitters

Stir all the ingredients together, then strain into a martini glass and serve.

Rusty Nail

2 oz. (60 ml) Scotch whisky
1 oz. (30 ml) Drambuie

Pour the Scotch and Drambuie into an old-fashioned glass and serve.

Sazerac

$2^1/_2$ oz. (75 ml) bourbon
$^1/_3$ oz. (10 ml) absinthe or Pernod
dash of gomme syrup
3 dashes Peychaud's bitters
lemon twist as garnish

Pour the absinthe or Pernod into a highball glass, coat and discard the excess. Shake the other ingredients and pour over ice into the glass. Serve with the lemon twist.

Scofflaw

$1^1/_2$ oz. (45 ml) Canadian Club whisky
$1^1/_2$ oz. (45 ml) dry vermouth
$1^1/_2$ oz. (15 ml) fresh lemon juice
dash of grenadine
dash of orange bitters
lemon slice as garnish

Stir all ingredients in a mixing glass with ice. Strain into a chilled cocktail glass. Garnish with a lemon slice.

Seelbach Cocktail

1 oz. (30 ml) Old Forester bourbon
$^{1}/_{2}$ oz. (15 ml) Cointreau
7 dashes Angostura bitters
7 dashes Peychaud's bitters
5 oz. (150 ml) champagne
orange twist as garnish

Pour the bourbon, Cointreau and both bitters into a champagne flute and stir. Add the champagne and garnish with the twist of orange.

Shamrock

2 oz. (60 ml) Irish whiskey
2 oz. (60 ml) dry vermouth
3 dashes green crème de menthe
3 dashes green Chartreuse

Mix all the ingredients together in a shaker, strain and serve in a cocktail glass.

Sidney

2 oz. (60 ml) ryc or bourbon
$^{1}/_{2}$ oz. (15 ml) dry vermouth
1 splash yellow Chartreuse
dash of orange bitters
lemon twist as garnish

Stir all the liquid ingredients and strain into a cocktail glass. Add the lemon twist to decorate.

Tipperary

1 oz. (60 ml) Irish whiskey
$^{3}/_{4}$ oz. (22 ml) dry vermouth
$^{1}/_{4}$ oz. (8 ml) green Chartreuse

Shake and strain into a cocktail glass.

TNT

1¹/₂ oz. (45 ml) Canadian Club whisky
1¹/₂ oz. (45 ml) absinthe

Put both the ingredients into a shaker with ice. Shake very well, strain and serve in a cocktail glass.

Turkey Cocktail

3 oz. (90 ml) Wild Turkey
¹/₂ oz. (15 ml) Wild Turkey liqueur

Shake ingredients with ice and strain into a cocktail glass.

VIP

1 oz. (30 ml) bourbon
1 oz. (30 ml) Cointreau
1 oz. (30 ml) dry vermouth
orange slice as garnish

Pour the ingredients into an old-fashioned glass, garnish with the orange slice and serve.

Ward Eight

2 oz. (60 ml) bourbon
¹/₂ oz. (15 ml) fresh lemon juice
¹/₂ oz. (15 ml) fresh orange juice
dash of grenadine
lemon slice as garnish

Shake all ingredients with ice and strain into a chilled cocktail glass. Garnish with a lemon slice.

Whiskey Sour

2 oz. (60 ml) whiskey
1 oz. (30 ml) fresh lemon juice
¹/₂ oz. (15 ml) gomme syrup
1 egg white

Mix the whiskey, lemon juice and gomme in a shaker, then pour into an old-fashioned glass and serve.

Whisky Mac

1 oz. (30 ml) Scotch whisky
1 oz. (30 ml) Stone's ginger wine

Pour the Scotch and ginger wine into an old-fashioned glass, stir and serve.

Whizz Doodle

1 oz. (30 ml) Scotch whisky
1 oz. (30 ml) brown crème de cacao
1 oz. (30 ml) dry gin
1 oz. (30 ml) heavy cream

Mix all the ingredients together in a shaker with ice, strain and pour into a cocktail glass.

Zazarac

1 oz. (30 ml) whiskey
½ oz. (15 ml) white rum
½ oz. (15 ml) anisette
½ oz. (15 ml) gomme syrup
3 dashes absinthe
dash of Angostura bitters
dash of orange bitters
lemon twist as garnish

Mix all the ingredients together in a shaker, strain and pour into a cocktail glass. Garnish with a twist of lemon.

Tequila Cocktails

Tequila is a charismatic, dashing spirit that is sometimes drunk in high spirits, downed in a gulp and followed by a suck on a wedge of lemon. This is the famed way to drink a shot of tequila. However, there are less energetic, and more interesting, ways to drink this Mexican contribution to the spirit world. Here's a choice of tantalizing tequila cocktails, including the famous **Clam Digger**, **Silk Stocking** and **Tequila Sunrise**.

This selection includes all types of tequila and mescal.

Acapulco

1 oz. (30 ml) gold tequila
1 oz. (30 ml) gold rum
2 oz. (60 ml) grapefruit juice
3 oz. (90 ml) pineapple juice
pineapple wedge as garnish

Shake all the liquid ingredients and strain into a highball filled with ice. Garnish with a pineapple wedge.

Acapulco (alt)

1 oz. (30 ml) tequila
1 oz. (30 ml) dark rum
1 oz. (30 ml) Tia Maria
5 oz. (150 ml) coconut cream

Shake all ingredients with ice. Strain into a chilled double cocktail glass.

All Night

1 oz. (30 ml) tequila
dash of grenadine
1/2 oz. (15 ml) lime juice
1 egg white
maraschino cherry as garnish

Shake all ingredients with ice and strain into a chilled cocktail glass. Garnish with a maraschino cherry.

Astro Lime Ricky

3 oz. (90 ml) Cabo Wabo Reposado tequila
1 oz. (30 ml) agave nectar
muddled mint
star fruit as garnish

Blend ingredients with ice, and pour into a highball glass. Garnish with a star fruit.

Banana Margarita

1 oz. (30 ml) tequila
1 oz. (30 ml) lemon juice
1/2 oz. (15 ml) Cointreau
1/2 small banana
1/2 oz. (15 ml) banana liqueur

Shake the ingredients with ice. Strain into a cocktail glass.

Blackberry Margarita

1 2/3 oz. (50 ml) silver tequila
1/2 oz. (15 ml) blackberry liqueur
1/2 lime, freshly squeezed
10 blackberries

Pour ingredients into a blender filled with crushed ice. Blend, then pour into a margarita glass. Add the blackberries on a cocktail stick set across the glass. Serve with a straw.

Bloody Maria

2 oz. (60 ml) tequila
5 oz. (150 ml) tomato juice
$^1/_2$ lemon, freshly squeezed
pinch celery salt
pinch black pepper
4 dashes Tabasco sauce
4 dashes Worcestershire sauce
celery stick as garnish
lime wedge as garnish

Shake ingredients and strain into a highball glass filled with ice. Garnish with a celery stick and a lime wedge.

Brave Bull

1$^1/_3$ oz. (40 ml) tequila
$^2/_3$ oz. (20 ml) coffee liqueur

Pour the tequila and coffee liqueur into an old-fashioned glass filled with ice and stir.

Cactus Pear Margarita

2 oz. (60 ml) tequila
$^2/_3$ oz. (20 ml) Cointreau
$^1/_3$ oz. (10 ml) freshly squeezed lime juice
1 cactus pear, peeled and diced
lime wedge as garnish

Muddle the pear in the bottom of a shaker. Add a scoop of ice and other ingredients, then shake. Strain into a cocktail glass with a salted rim. Add a lime wedge.

Chapala

1$^1/_2$ oz. (45 ml) tequila
dash of triple sec
$^3/_4$ oz. (22 ml) lemon juice
2 oz. (60 ml) orange juice
dash of grenadine

Stir all the ingredients together over ice in a highball glass.

Cherry Picker

1 oz. (30 ml) gold tequila
1 oz. (30 ml) cherry brandy
$^1/_2$ lime, freshly squeezed
1 oz. (30 ml) apple juice
lime twist as garnish

Shake all the liquid ingredients together, then strain into a cocktail glass. Add a twist of lime.

Citrus Margarita

2 oz. (60 ml) tequila
2 oz. (60 ml) fresh orange or grapefruit juice
1 oz. (30 ml) triple sec
$^1/_2$ lime, freshly squeezed
$^1/_2$ lemon, freshly squeezed
lime wedge as garnish

Place all the ingredients in a shaker filled with ice. Shake, then pour into a chilled cocktail glass. Garnish with a lime wedge.

Clam Digger

$1^2/_3$ oz. (50 ml) silver tequila
3 oz. (90 ml) tomato juice
3 oz. (90 ml) clam juice
2 tsp. (10 ml) horseradish sauce
dash of Tabasco sauce
dash of Worcestershire sauce
1 lime, freshly squeezed
lime wedge as garnish

Shake all the liquid ingredients together and strain into a highball glass with ice. Garnish with a lime wedge.

Cool Gold

1 oz. (30 ml) gold tequila
1 oz. (30 ml) melon liqueur
1 oz. (30 ml) cranberry juice

Shake all the ingredients together and strain into a cocktail glass.

El Diablo

2 oz. (60 ml) silver tequila
1 oz. (30 ml) crème de cassis
1 lime, freshly squeezed
ginger ale to fill
lime wedge as garnish

Pour lime juice into a highball with crushed ice. Add tequila and crème de cassis. Fill with ginger ale. Stir. Drop in a lime wedge. Serve with a straw.

Eldorado

2 oz. (60 ml) gold tequila
1 oz. (30 ml) fresh lemon juice
1 tsp. (5 ml) honey

Shake all the ingredients together, then strain into a martini glass and serve.

Frostbite

1 oz. (30 ml) silver tequila
1 oz. (30 ml) white crème de menthe
1 oz. (30 ml) heavy cream

Mix the ingredients together in a shaker, then strain into a martini glass and serve.

Frozen Margarita

2 oz. (60 ml) tequila
$\frac{1}{2}$ lime, freshly squeezed
$\frac{1}{2}$ lemon, freshly squeezed

Blend all the ingredients together with ice until frozen, then pour into a coupette. You can add any fruit of your choice to turn this drink into a frozen fruit margarita.

Golden Margarita

2 oz. (60 ml) gold tequila
1 oz. (30 ml) Grand Marnier
1 lime, freshly squeezed
lime wedge as garnish

Shake the ingredients together and strain into a cocktail glass with a salted rim. Add a lime wedge.

Hot Pants

2 oz. (60 ml) tequila
1 oz. (30 ml) peppermint schnapps
¹/₂ oz. (15 ml) grapefruit juice

Shake all the ingredients together, then pour into a salt-rimmed old-fashioned glass and serve.

Jumping Jelly Bean

1 oz. (30 ml) tequila
1 oz. (30 ml) Grand Marnier
1 oz. (30 ml) fresh lemon juice
chilled champagne to fill

In a shaker mix the tequila with the Grand Marnier and lemon juice, then strain into a martini glass. Top up with champagne and serve.

La Bomba

1 oz. (30 ml) gold tequila
²/₃ oz. (20 ml) Cointreau
²/₃ oz. (20 ml) pineapple juice
²/₃ oz. (20 ml) freshly squeezed orange juice
2 dashes grenadine

Shake the tequila, Cointreau, pineapple and oranges juices, then strain into a cocktail glass with a salted rim. Add the grenadine.

La Conga

2 oz. (60 ml) silver tequila
¹/₃ oz. (10 ml) pineapple juice
3 dashes Angostura bitters
soda water to fill
lemon slice as garnish

Pour the tequila, pineapple juice and bitters into an old-fashioned glass filled with ice. Stir, then fill with soda. Stir again, then add a slice of lemon.

Laser Beam

1 oz. (30 ml) tequila
1 oz. (30 ml) Jack Daniel's
1 oz. (30 ml) amaretto
¹/₂ oz. (15 ml) triple sec

Shake all the ingredients together, pour into an old-fashioned glass and serve.

Matador

2 oz. (60 ml) gold tequila
²/₃ oz. (20 ml) triple sec
1 lime, freshly squeezed
5 oz. (150 ml) pineapple juice
lime wedge as garnish

Shake all the liquid ingredients, then strain into a highball glass with ice. Add a lime wedge.

Matador (alt)

2 oz. (60 ml) tequila
¹/₄ oz. (8 ml) Cointreau
¹/₂ oz. (15 ml) lime juice
dash of gomme syrup
1 chunk pineapple

Shake over crushed ice and strain into a highball glass with a sugared rim. Garnish with a chunk of pineapple.

Melon Margarita

1 oz. (30 ml) tequila
¹/₃ oz. (10 ml) Cointreau
¹/₃ oz. (10 ml) melon liqueur
¹/₂ lime, freshly squeezed
few slices yellow melon, diced

Blend all the ingredients together and add crushed ice. Blend again, then pour into a margarita glass. Add a straw.

Mexican Flag

1 oz. (30 ml) grenadine
1 oz. (30 ml) green crème de menthe
1 oz. (30 ml) tequila

In the exact order above, layer each of the ingredients in a shot glass and serve.

Mexican Hat

1 oz. (30 ml) tequila
1 oz. (30 ml) crème de cassis
1 oz. (30 ml) champagne

Fill a highball glass three-quarters full with crushed ice, then pour on the tequila, crème de cassis and champagne.

Mexican Madras

1 oz. (30 ml) gold tequila
3 oz. (90 ml) cranberry juice
²/₃ oz. (20 ml) freshly squeezed orange juice
dash of freshly squeezed lime juice
orange slice as garnish

Shake all the liquid ingredients together and strain into an old-fashioned glass with ice. Add a slice of orange.

Mexican Mule

2 oz. (60 ml) gold tequila
freshly squeezed juice of one lime
dash of gomme syrup
ginger ale to fill

Shake the tequila, lime juice and gomme syrup, and strain into a highball with ice. Top up with ginger ale.

Mexican Runner

1 oz. (30 ml) gold tequila
1 oz. (30 ml) rum
²/₃ oz. (20 ml) banana syrup
²/₃ oz. (20 ml) blackberry syrup
1 lime, freshly squeezed
6 strawberries

Put all the ingredients to a blender with crushed ice and blend. Pour into a tumbler.

Mexicana

1¹/₂ oz. (45 ml) tequila
1¹/₂ oz. (45 ml) unsweetened pineapple juice
¹/₄ oz. (8 ml) lime juice
dash of grenadine

Shake all the ingredients together and strain into a highball glass filled with ice.

Multiple Orgasm

1 oz. (30 ml) gold tequila
²/₃ oz. (20 ml) amaretto
²/₃ oz. (20 ml) coffee liqueur
²/₃ oz. (20 ml) Irish cream liqueur
1 oz. (30 ml) heavy cream
2 oz. (60 ml) half-and-half or milk

Pour all the ingredients, except the tequila, into a shaker and shake. Strain into a highball glass filled with ice. Float the tequila on top.

Peach Margarita

1 oz. (30 ml) silver tequila
¹/₂ oz. (15 ml) Cointreau
¹/₂ oz. (15 ml) peach schnapps
¹/₂ lime, freshly squeezed
1 peach, peeled and diced

Blend the peach pieces in a blender. Add the other ingredients and blend again. Pour into a margarita glass.

Pink Caddie-O

1 oz. (30 ml) gold tequila
²/₃ oz. (20 ml) Grand Marnier
1 oz. (30 ml) cranberry juice
1 lime, freshly squeezed

Shake all the ingredients together and strain into a cocktail glass.

Prado

1 oz. (30 ml) tequila
¹/₃ oz. (10 ml) maraschino liqueur
1 lime, freshly squeezed
¹/₃ oz. (10 ml) grenadine
1 tsp. (5 ml) egg white powder
maraschino cherry as garnish
lime slice, thin, as garnish

Shake the ingredients together and strain into an old-fashioned glass over ice.
Add a maraschino cherry and a thin slice of lime.

Red Desert

2 oz. (60 ml) Herradura Silver tequila
1 oz. (30 ml) Cointreau
1 oz. (30 ml) fresh lime juice
¹/₂ oz. (15 ml) sour cherry syrup
lime wedge as garnish

Shake all the ingredients and strain into a salt-rimmed highball glass. Garnish
with a lime wedge.

Rosalita

³/₄ oz. (22 ml) tequila
¹/₄ oz. (8 ml) dry vermouth
¹/₄ oz. (8 ml) sweet vermouth
¹/₄ oz. (8 ml) Campari

Shake all the ingredients together and strain into a cocktail glass.

Rude Cosmopolitan

2 oz. (60 ml) gold tequila
²/₃ oz. (20 ml) triple sec
1 oz. (30 ml) cranberry juice
¹/₂ lime, freshly squeezed
orange twist as garnish

Shake all the liquid ingredients together and strain into a cocktail glass. Add a twist of orange.

Short Fuse

2 oz. (60 ml) gold tequila
²/₃ oz. (20 ml) apricot brandy
¹/₃ oz. (10 ml) maraschino cherry juice
1 lime, freshly squeezed
3 oz. (90 ml) fresh grapefruit juice
lime wedge as garnish

Shake all the liquid ingredients together and strain into an ice-filled highball glass. Add a lime wedge.

Silk Stocking

1 oz. (30 ml) tequila
1 oz. (30 ml) white crème de cacao
1 oz. (30 ml) heavy cream
dash of grenadine

Mix the ingredients together in a shaker, then strain into a martini glass and serve.

Slowly Does It

1 oz. (30 ml) tequila
²/₃ oz. (20 ml) dark rum
2 dashes Tia Maria
1 oz. (30 ml) coconut cream
¹/₂ banana
2 oz. (60 ml) pineapple juice

Blend all the ingredients, except the dark rum, with crushed ice and pour into a tumbler. Float the dark rum on top and serve with a straw.

South of the Border

1 oz. (30 ml) tequila
³/₄ oz. (22 ml) Kahlua
¹/₂ lime, freshly squeezed

Squeeze the lime over ice in a highball glass and stir before adding the spirits.
Stir again to mix.

Strawberry Basil Margarita

2 oz. (60 ml) Sauza Hornitos tequila
2 oz. (60 ml) sliced fresh strawberries
6 fresh basil leaves
1 oz. (30 ml) fresh lime juice
dash of gomme syrup
sprig of basil to garnish

Shake the tequila, strawberries, basil, lime juice and gomme in an ice-filled
shaker. Pour into an old-fashioned glass and garnish with the sprig of basil.

Tapika

3¹/₂ oz. (105 ml) Chinaco Plata tequila
¹/₂ oz. (15 ml) Cointreau
¹/₂ oz. (15 ml) prickly pear cactus syrup
1 oz. (30 ml) lime juice
lime slice as garnish

Coat a cocktail glass with Cointreau and discard any after ensuring the rim is
moistened. Sprinkle the rim with salt. Then shake the tequila, prickly pear
syrup and lime juice together, strain into the glass and garnish with lime.

Tequila Canyon

2 oz. (60 ml) tequila
dash of triple sec
4 oz. (120 ml) cranberry juice
¹/₃ oz. (10 ml) pineapple juice
¹/₃ oz. (10 ml) freshly squeezed orange juice

Pour the tequila, triple sec and cranberry juice into a highball glass filled with
ice and stir. Add the pineapple and orange juices. Serve with a stirrer.

Tequila Manhattan

2 oz. (60 ml) tequila
1 oz. (30 ml) sweet vermouth
dash of freshly squeezed lime juice
maraschino cherry as garnish
orange slice as garnish

Shake all the ingredients together and strain into an old-fashioned glass filled
with ice. Add a maraschino cherry and a slice of orange as a garnish.

Tequila Mockingbird

2 oz. (60 ml) tequila
1 oz. (30 ml) green crème de menthe
1 oz. (30 ml) fresh lime juice

Mix all the ingredients together in a shaker, then strain into a martini glass
and serve.

Tequila Mockingbird (alt)

1 oz. (30 ml) tequila
$^1/_3$ oz. (10 ml) crème de menthe
dash of freshly squeezed lime juice
lime wedge as garnish

Pour all the ingredients into an old-fashioned glass with crushed ice and stir.
Garnish with a wedge of lime and serve with a straw.

Tequila Sunrise

2 oz. (60 ml) tequila
4 oz. (120 ml) freshly squeezed orange juice
2 dashes grenadine
orange spiral as garnish

Pour the tequila and orange juice into a highball glass filled with ice. Stir, then
slowly add the grenadine. Add an orange spiral as garnish and serve with a
straw and a stirrer.

Tequila Sunrise (alt)

2 oz. (60 ml) tequila
3½ oz. (105 ml) orange juice
dash of grenadine
1 lime, freshly squeezed

Squeeze the juice of the lime over ice into a large highball glass and drop the lime into the glass. Add the tequila and orange juice, then slowly pour in the grenadine.

Tequila Sunset

2 oz. (60 ml) tequila
1 oz. (30 ml) freshly squeezed lemon juice
1 tsp. (5 ml) honey
lemon spiral as garnish

Shake the tequila, lemon juice and honey together and strain into a cocktail glass. Garnish with a spiral of lemon.

Tequini

³/₄ oz. (22 ml) tequila
³/₄ oz. (22 ml) vodka
³/₄ oz. (22 ml) dry vermouth
dash of Angostura bitters
lemon twist as garnish

Shake all the ingredients together and strain into a cocktail glass.

Tijuana Taxi

1 oz. (30 ml) gold tequila
½ oz. (15 ml) blue curaçao
½ oz. (15 ml) tropical fruit schnapps
soda water to fill

Pour the tequila, curaçao and schnapps into a highball glass filled with ice. Top up with soda.

Tomahawk

1 oz. (30 ml) tequila
1 oz. (30 ml) triple sec or Cointreau
2 oz. (60 ml) cranberry juice
2 oz. (60 ml) pineapple juice

Shake all the ingredients together and strain into a highball glass filled with ice.

Triple Sunrise

1 oz. (30 ml) tequila
$^2/_3$ oz. (20 ml) triple sec
$^2/_3$ oz. (20 ml) freshly squeezed lime juice
half a fresh mango, diced
dash of grenadine

Pour all the ingredients into a blender and blend them. Add some crushed ice and blend them again. Pour into a tumbler.

Vampiro

2 oz. (60 ml) tequila
3 oz. (90 ml) tomato juice
1 oz. (30 ml) freshly squeezed orange juice
1 tsp. (5 ml) honey
$^1/_3$ oz. (10 ml) freshly squeezed lime juice
$^1/_2$ onion slice, finely chopped
few thin slices fresh red chilli
few drops Worcestershire sauce
pinch of salt
lime wedge as garnish

Shake all the ingredients, except the lime wedge, and strain into an ice-filled highball glass. Garnish with a lime wedge.

Viva La Donna!

2 oz. (60 ml) tequila
2 oz. (60 ml) passion fruit juice
2 oz. (60 ml) freshly squeezed orange juice
$^2/_3$ oz. (20 ml) freshly squeezed lime juice

Shake all the ingredients together and strain into a highball glass filled with ice.

Watermelon Smash

1²/₃ oz. (50 ml) tequila
²/₃ oz. (20 ml) limoncello
dash of basil syrup
¹/₄ slice watermelon
ginger beer to fill

Pour all the ingredients, except the ginger beer, into a shaker and shake.
Strain into a highball glass filled with ice. Top up with ginger beer.

White Bull

1 oz. (30 ml) tequila
1 oz. (30 ml) coffee liqueur
²/₃ oz. (20 ml) heavy cream
²/₃ oz. (20 ml) half-and-half or milk

Shake all the ingredients together and strain into a cocktail glass.

Champagne Cocktails

The bubbles fizzing up a champagne flute have intrigued man and seduced woman ever since Dom Perignon worked out a way to capitalize on such golden effervescence. A light cocktail base, champagne mixes with panache with almost anything. The sweet peach-flavored **Bellini** is among the following recipes, as are the classic **French 75**, **James Bond**, **Kir Royale** and an extraordinary combination called **Windowlene**, which also includes blue curaçao. There's no accounting for taste.

This selection includes sparkling wine.

Alfonso

1 oz. (30 ml) Dubonnet
1 sugar cube
2 dashes Angostura bitters
champagne to fill
lemon twist as garnish

Place the sugar cube in a champagne glass and soak it with Angostura bitters. Add the Dubonnet and top up with champagne. Stir gently then garnish with a twist of lemon.

Apple Blow Fizz

$^1/_3$ oz. (10 ml) apple schnapps
$^1/_3$ oz. (10 ml) cranberry juice
champagne to fill

Pour the schnapps and juice into a champagne glass, then stir and top up with champagne. Stir again, gently.

B & B Royale

$^1/_2$ oz. (15 ml) cognac
$^1/_2$ oz. (15 ml) Benedictine
champagne to fill

Pour the cognac and Benedictine into a champagne saucer, top up with champagne and serve.

Bastile

1 oz. (30 ml) white rum
4 blackberries
$^1/_3$ oz. (10 ml) crème de mure
$^1/_2$ slice of orange
dash of gomme syrup
champagne to fill

Muddle the blackberries with the gomme and crème de mure in a shaker. Add the rum and squeeze a half-slice of orange over the mixture. Add ice cubes, shake and strain into a highball glass with crushed ice, then top up with champagne and stir gently.

Bellini 1

6 oz. (180 ml) white peach purée (or peach nectar)
dash of fresh lemon juice
dash of grenadine
champagne to fill

Mix the peach purée, grenadine and lemon juice together in a champagne flute, then top up with champagne and serve.

Bellini 2

6 oz. (180 ml) fresh white peaches, puréed to juice
dash of fresh lemon juice
dash of peach brandy
sparkling wine to fill

Stir the peach juice and peach brandy together in a champagne flute, then top up with sparkling wine and serve.

Black Velvet

2 oz. (60 ml) chilled stout (or Guinness)
2 oz. (60 ml) champagne

Pour the stout then the champagne into a champagne flute and serve.

Blimey

dash of fresh lime
1 oz. (30 ml) crème de peche
champagne to fill

Squeeze a little lime juice into a champagne flute, pour on the crème de peche and top up with the champagne.

Bombay Bellini

6 oz. (180 ml) fresh white peaches, puréed to juice
2 oz. (60 ml) mangoes, puréed to juice
dash of fresh lemon juice
dash of peach brandy
sparkling wine to fill

Stir the peach juice and peach brandy in a champagne flute. Add the mango juice, then the lemon and top up with sparkling wine.

Buck's Fizz

2 oz. (60 ml) fresh orange juice
champagne to fill

Pour the orange juice into a champagne flute and top up with champagne.

Caribbean Royale

¹/₂ oz. (15 ml) white rum
¹/₂ oz. (15 ml) crème de banane
champagne to fill

Pour the rum and the crème de banane into a champagne flute. Top up with champagne and serve.

Casanova

1 oz. (30 ml) apple juice
1 oz. (30 ml) raspberry purée
champagne to fill
2 small raspberries as garnish

Pour the raspberry purée into a champagne flute. Add the apple juice and stir, then top up with champagne and stir gently. Drop two small raspberries into the glass and serve.

Champagne Cobbler

4 dashes Cointreau
champagne to fill
sliced fruit in season as garnish
sprig of mint as garnish

Fill a large goblet with crushed ice, then pour the champagne until it is three-quarters full. Stir in the Cointreau and garnish with the fruit and mint.

Champagne Cocktail

1 white sugar cube
dash of Angostura bitters
champagne to fill
lemon twist as garnish
orange twist as garnish

Place the sugar cube in a champagne flute and soak with the Angostura bitters. Top up with champagne, then add the lemon and orange twists.

Champagne Cocktail (classic)

1 oz. (30 ml) cognac
1 white sugar cube
4 dashes Angostura bitters
champagne to fill
maraschino cherry as garnish

Place the sugar cube in a champagne flute and soak with the Angostura bitters. Pour on the cognac and top up with champagne. Garnish with the maraschino cherry and serve.

Champagne Cooler

1 oz. (30 ml) Grand Marnier
$^{1}/_{2}$ oz. (15 ml) cognac
2 dashes Angostura bitters
champagne to fill
orange slice as garnish

Pour the Grand Marnier, cognac and bitters into a napoli grande glass. Top up with champagne and garnish with the orange slice.

Champagne Cup

1 bottle champagne
3 oz. (90 ml) Grand Marnier
3 oz. (90 ml) cognac
3 oz. (90 ml) maraschino liqueur
sliced fruits in season
fresh mint leaves

Mix all the liquid ingredients together in a large jug containing 10–15 ice cubes. Stir in the fruit and mint, then serve in champagne flutes.

Champagne Julep

6 fresh mint leaves
1 tsp. (5 ml) superfine sugar
dash of cognac
champagne to fill

Muddle the mint and sugar together with the cognac in a deep champagne saucer. Top up with champagne and serve.

Champers

1 oz. (30 ml) brandy
$^{2}/_{3}$ oz. (20 ml) fresh orange juice
$^{2}/_{3}$ oz. (20 ml) fresh lemon juice
champagne to fill

Pour first three ingredients into a shaker. Shake, then strain into a champagne glass and stir. Top up with champagne.

Cool Cucumber

1 oz. (30 ml) Benedictine
½ oz. (15 ml) lemon juice
champagne to fill
cucumber strip, long and thin with rind, as garnish

Pour the Benedictine and lemon juice into a chilled champagne flute and top up with champagne. Add the strip of cucumber as a garnish.

Crafty Champagne Cocktail

1 tsp. (5 ml) fresh pear, diced
pear liqueur, to marinate
champagne to fill

Place the pear segments in a plastic container and add enough pear liqueur to cover. Leave for about two hours, taking care not to saturate the pears. When ready to make the drink, place pear pieces in a champagne flute and top up with champagne.

Death in the Afternoon

½ oz. (15 ml) Pernod
1 sugar cube
champagne to fill

Place the sugar cube in a champagne flute and add the Pernod, then top up with champagne.

Dream Juice

1 oz. (30 ml) Dubonnet
½ oz. (15 ml) triple sec
½ oz. (15 ml) fresh grapefruit juice
champagne to fill

Pour the Dubonnet, triple sec and grapefruit juice into a mixing glass with ice. Stir, then strain into a champagne glass and top up with champagne.

Duke

1 egg
dash of triple sec
dash of maraschino liqueur
dash of fresh lemon juice
dash of fresh orange juice
champagne to fill

Shake all the ingredients, except the champagne, and strain into a flute. Top up with champagne and serve.

Epernay

1 oz. (30 ml) crème de framboise
dash of Midori
champagne to fill

Pour the crème de framboise and Midori into a champagne flute. Top up with champagne and serve.

Fizzing Americano

1 oz. (30 ml) Campari
$^1/_2$ oz. (15 ml) sweet vermouth
champagne or Prosecco (Italian sparkling wine) to fill
orange wheel as garnish

Shake and pour over rocks in a highball glass. Top up with Prosecco or champagne and garnish with orange.

Fraises Royale

2 strawberries
1 oz. (30 ml) crème de fraise
champagne to fill

Blend the strawberries with the liqueur and pour into a champagne flute. Top with the champagne and serve.

French 125

1 oz. (30 ml) cognac
1/2 oz. (15 ml) fresh lime juice
champagne to fill
lime twist as garnish

Mix the cognac and lime juice together in a champagne flute. Top up with champagne, garnish and serve.

French 75

1¹/₂ oz. (45 ml) gin
1¹/₂ oz. (45 ml) fresh lemon juice
champagne to fill
lemon twist as garnish

Mix the gin and lemon juice together in a champagne flute. Top up with champagne, garnish and serve.

French 75 (alt)

³/₄ oz. (22 ml) gin
¹/₄ oz. (8 ml) lemon juice
dash of gomme syrup
dash of grenadine
champagne to fill

Shake the gin, lemon juice, gomme and grenadine together, then strain into a champagne flute and top with champagne.

French 76

³/₄ oz. (22 ml) vodka
¹/₄ oz. (8 ml) lemon juice
dash of gomme syrup
dash of grenadine
champagne to fill

Shake the vodka, lemon juice, gomme and grenadine together, then strain into a champagne flute and top with champagne.

French Kiss 2

²/₃ oz. (20 ml) raspberry purée
1 oz. (30 ml) ginger beer
dash of apricot brandy
champagne to fill
1 raspberry

Pour raspberry purée, apricot brandy and ginger beer into a champagne glass.
Stir, then top up with champagne, drop a raspberry into the glass and serve.

French Sherbet

1 oz. (30 ml) cognac
¹/₂ oz. (15 ml) kirsch
lemon sherbet
champagne to fill

Stir the first three items in a deep champagne saucer, and fill with champagne.

Grand Mimosa

2 oz. (60ml) Grand Marnier
1 oz. (30 ml) fresh orange juice
champagne to fill

Pour Grand Marnier and juice into a champagne flute and fill with champagne.

Happy Youth

2 oz. (60 ml) cherry brandy
1 oz. (30 ml) fresh orange juice
1 sugar cube
chilled champagne to fill
cherry as garnish

In a champagne flute pour the cherrry brandy and orange juice over the sugar
cube. Top up with champagne, then garnish with the cherry and serve.

Hemingway

1 oz. (30 ml) Pernod
champagne to fill

Pour the Pernod into a champagne flute, then top up with champagne and serve.

Honeymoon Paradise

1 oz. (30 ml) blue curaçao
1 oz. (30 ml) Cointreau
1 oz. (30 ml) fresh lemon juice
champagne to fill

Pour the blue curaçao and Cointreau into a highball glass, then top up with champagne and serve.

IBF

$^1/_2$ oz. (15 ml) cognac
$^1/_2$ oz. (15 ml) orange curaçao
$^1/_2$ oz. (15 ml) Madeira
champagne to fill

Pour the cognac, curaçao and Madeira into a champagne flute, then top up with champagne and serve.

James Bond

1 oz. (30 ml) vodka
1 sugar cube
3 dashes Angostura bitters
champagne to fill

In a champagne flute soak the sugar cube in the bitters, then pour on the vodka. Top up with champagne and serve.

Kir Royale

$^1/_2$ oz. (15 ml) crème de cassis
champagne

Put the crème de cassis in a champagne flute, then pour on the champagne and serve.

La Dolce Vita

1 oz. (30 ml) vodka
5 seedless grapes
1 tsp. (5 ml) honey
Prosecco (dry sparkling wine) to fill

Muddle the grapes in a shaker, then add the vodka and honey. Shake and strain into a champagne glass, then top up with Prosecco.

London Special

2 dashes Angostura bitters
1 twist of orange
champagne to fill

Put the Angostura bitters and orange twist in a champagne flute. Top up with champagne and serve.

Mimosa

2 oz. (60 ml) freshly squeezed orange juice
2 dashes Grand Marnier
champagne to fill

Fill a champagne glass one-quarter full with orange juice. Add the Grand Marnier, then top up with champagne.

Pimm's Royale

1 oz. (30 ml) Pimm's
5 oz. (150 ml) champagne

Pour the Pimm's into a champagne flute, top up with champagne then serve.

Poinsettia

1 oz. (30 ml) Cointreau
champagne to fill
orange twist as garnish

Pour the Cointreau into a champagne flute and top up with champagne. Add an orange twist and serve.

Prince of Wales

³/₄ oz. (22 ml) brandy
¹/₄ oz. (8 ml) Benedictine
4 oz. (120 ml) champagne
dash of of Angostura bitters
1 sugar cube
1 orange slice
1 cherry

Place the sugar cube in a highball glass and soak it with the Angostura. Add ice, brandy and fruit. Stir, then add the champagne. Finally add the Benedictine.

Raspberry Sip

1 oz. (30 ml) fresh raspberry juice
¹/₂ oz. (15 ml) Cointreau
¹/₂ oz. (15 ml) crème de banane
champagne to fill

Pour ingredients, except champagne, into a shaker with ice. Strain into a champagne flute, and top up with champagne.

Ritz Fizz

dash of amaretto
dash of blue curaçao
dash of fresh lemon juice
champagne to fill

Pour the amaretto, curaçao and lemon juice into a champagne flute, top up with champagne and serve.

Seelbach Cocktail

1 oz. (30 ml) Old Forester bourbon
¹/₂ oz. (15 ml) Cointreau
7 dashes Angostura bitters
7 dashes Peychaud's bitters
5 oz. (150 ml) champagne
orange twist as garnish

Pour the bourbon, Cointreau and both bitters into a champagne flute and stir. Add the champagne and garnish with the twist of orange.

Slow Seducer

$^1/_2$ oz. (15 ml) crème de framboise
$^1/_2$ oz. (15 ml) Cointreau
1 oz. (30 ml) pink grapefruit juice
champagne to fill

Pour the crème de framboise, Cointreau and grapefruit juice into a shaker with ice. Shake, then strain into a champagne glass, and top up with champagne.

Soixante-Neuf

1 oz. (30 ml) gin
1 oz. (30 ml) fresh lemon juice
champagne to fill
lemon twist as garnish

Shake the gin and lemon juice together, then strain into a champagne flute. Top up with champagne, garnish with the lemon twist and serve.

Sweet Surrender

1 oz. (30 ml) orange juice
½ oz. (15 ml) peach brandy
champagne to fill
orange slice

Rub the orange slice around the rim of a champage flute, then coat the rim in sugar. Mix the orange juice and peach brandy together in an ice-filled shaker, strain, and pour into the glass. Top up with champagne.

Typhoon

1 oz. (30 ml) gin
dash of anisette
$^1/_2$ oz. (15 ml) fresh lime juice
champagne to fill

In a shaker mix together the gin, anisette and lime juice, then strain into an ice-filled highball glass. Top up with champagne and serve.

Valencia Royale

1 oz. (30 ml) apricot brandy
$^1/_2$ oz. (15 ml) fresh orange juice
champagne

Pour the brandy and orange juice into a champagne flute. Top up with champagne and serve.

Windowlene

1 oz. (30 ml) blue curaçao
$^1/_2$ oz. (15 ml) white rum
$^1/_2$ oz. (15 ml) gin
$^1/_2$ oz. (15 ml) vodka
4 oz. (120 ml) champagne
lemon spiral as garnish

Pour all the ingredients into a highball glass, then garnish and serve.

Hot Cocktails

Most hot cocktails originate from regions where the chill factor sets in for many months. These are traditional cocktails, sipped while you warm your hands around the tankard or glass. Cocktails such as **Irish Coffee**, **Mulled Wine** and any of the grogs included here were created to warm the heart and the body. They're also quite strong, and with warmed alcohol surging through your veins, after one or two you don't feel the cold as much.

Almond Chocolate Coffee

1½ oz. (45 ml) amaretto
1 oz. (30 ml) brown crème de cacao
6 oz. (180 ml) hot black coffee
whipped cream
chocolate shavings as garnish

Pour the amaretto, then the crème de cacao and finally the hot black coffee into a liqueur coffee glass. Top with the whipped cream and garnish with the chocolate shavings.

Amaretto Tea

6 oz. (180 ml) hot tea
2 oz. (60 ml) amaretto
whipped cream for topping

Place a spoon in a parfait glass, then pour in the hot tea. (The spoon prevents the glass from cracking.) Add the amaretto, without stirring, and top up with the whipped cream.

American Coffee

1 oz. (30 ml) bourbon
6 oz. (180 ml) hot black coffee
2 tsp. (10 ml) raw (demerara) sugar
heavy cream

Pour the bourbon and black coffee into a liqueur coffee glass, then add the
sugar. Float the cream on top and serve.

American Grog

2 oz. (60 ml) dark rum
½ oz. (15 ml) fresh lemon juice
1 sugar cube
hot water to fill

Put all the ingredients into a medium goblet. Top up with hot water, stir and serve.

Apple Toddy

1 lemon wheel
6 cloves
1 oz. (30 ml) calvados
1 oz. (30 ml) fresh lemon juice
1 tsp. (5 ml) brown sugar
dash of orgeat syrup
1 cinnamon stick
boiling water
¼ baked apple as garnish

Stud the lemon wheel with the cloves and put in a heatproof goblet. Add the
rest of the ingredients, then top up with boiling water. Stir with the cinnamon
stick and serve, spearing the baked apple on the rim of the goblet.

Belgian Coffee

1 oz. (30 ml) elixir d'anvers
6 oz. (180 ml) hot black coffee
2 tsp. (10 ml) raw (demerara) sugar
heavy cream

Pour the elixir d'anvers and black coffee into a liqueur coffee glass, then add
the sugar. Float the cream on top and serve.

Black Gold

$^1/_2$ oz. (15 ml) triple sec

$^1/_2$ oz. (15 ml) amaretto

$^1/_2$ oz. (15 ml) Baileys Irish Cream

$^1/_2$ oz. (15 ml) hazelnut liqueur

6 oz. (180 ml) hot coffee

dash of cinnamon schnapps

whipped cream for topping

shaved chocolate as garnish

1 cinnamon stick

Pour all ingredients, except the coffee and cinnamon schnapps, into an Irish coffee glass, then stir in the coffee and cinnamon schnapps. Top up with the whipped cream and sprinkle on the chocolate. Serve with a cinnamon stick as a stirrer.

Blue Blazer care needed

1 wine glass Scotch whisky

1 wine glass boiling water

1 tsp. (5 ml) sugar (to taste)

lemon twist as garnish

Using two silver-plated mugs with handles, pour the Scotch into one mug and the boiling water into the other. Carefully ignite the whisky with a match and pour the blazing ingredients back and forth between the two mugs several times. The aim is to create a long stream of liquid fire. Pour into an old-fashioned glass and sweeten with the sugar. Serve with the lemon twist.

Café Normandie

1 oz. (30 ml) calvados

6 oz. (180 ml) hot black coffee

2 tsp. (10 ml) raw (demerara) sugar

heavy cream

Pour the calvados and black coffee into a liqueur coffee glass, then add the sugar. Float the cream on top and serve.

Café Royale

1 oz. (30 ml) cognac
6 oz. (180 ml) hot black coffee
2 tsp. (10 ml) raw (demerara) sugar
heavy cream

Pour the cognac and black coffee into a liqueur coffee glass, then add the sugar. Float the cream on top and serve.

Calypso Coffee

1 oz. (30 ml) Tia Maria
6 oz. (180 ml) hot black coffee
2 tsp. (10 ml) raw (demerara) sugar
heavy cream

Pour the Tia Maria and black coffee into a liqueur coffee glass, then add the sugar. Float the cream on top and serve.

Canadian Coffee

1 oz. (30 ml) Canadian Club whisky
6 oz. (180 ml) hot black coffee
2 tsp. (10 ml) raw (demerara) sugar
heavy cream

Pour the Canadian Club and black coffee into a liqueur coffee glass, then add the sugar. Float the cream on top and serve.

Caribbean Coffee

1 oz. (30 ml) white rum
6 oz. (180 ml) hot black coffee
2 tsp. (10 ml) raw (demerara) sugar
heavy cream

Pour the rum and black coffee into a liqueur coffee glass, then add the sugar. Float the cream on top and serve.

Dutch Coffee

1 oz. (30 ml) genever

6 oz. (180 ml) hot black coffee

2 tsp. (10 ml) raw (demerara) sugar

heavy cream

Pour the genever and black coffee into a liqueur coffee glass, then add the sugar. Float the cream on top and serve.

Gaelic Coffee

1 oz. (30 ml) Scotch whisky

6 oz. (180 ml) hot black coffee

2 tsp. (10 ml) raw (demerara) sugar

heavy cream

Pour the Scotch and black coffee into a liqueur coffee glass, then add the sugar. Float the cream on top and serve.

German Coffee

1 oz. (30 ml) kirsch

6 oz. (180 ml) hot black coffee

2 tsp. (10 ml) raw (demerara) sugar

heavy cream

Pour the kirsch and black coffee into a liqueur coffee glass, then add the sugar. Float the cream on top and serve.

Grog

1 lemon wheel

6 cloves

2 oz. (60 ml) dark rum

1 oz. (30 ml) gomme syrup

$^{1}/_{2}$ oz. (15 ml) fresh lemon juice

1 cinnamon stick

boiling water

Stud the lemon wheel with the cloves, then place in a heatproof glass or tankard. Pour on the rum, gomme and lemon juice. Top up with boiling water, stir and serve.

Hot Brandy Alexander

1 oz. (30 ml) brandy
1 oz. (30 ml) brown crème de cacao
4 oz. (120 ml) steamed cream or milk
whipped cream
chocolate shavings as garnish

Pour the brandy, crème de cacao and steamed cream into a heated mug. Top with the whipped cream and chocolate shavings as garnish, then serve.

Hot Brandy Flip

2 oz. (60 ml) cognac
$^1/_2$ oz. (15 ml) gomme syrup
1 egg yolk
4 oz. (120 ml) hot cream or milk
grated nutmeg as garnish

Mix the cognac, gomme and egg yolk together in a highball glass. Stir in the hot cream and sprinkle with the nutmeg.

Hot Eggnog

1 oz. (30 ml) dark rum
1 oz. (30 ml) cognac
1 oz. (30 ml) gomme syrup
1 egg
6 oz. (180 ml) hot cream or milk
grated nutmeg to decorate

Mix the rum, cognac, gomme and egg together in a shaker, then strain into a highball glass. Stir in the hot cream and sprinkle with the nutmeg.

Hot Toddy

1 lemon wheel
6 cloves
1 oz. (30 ml) Scotch whisky
1 oz. (30 ml) fresh lemon juice
1 tsp. (5 ml) brown sugar
dash of orgeat syrup
1 cinnamon stick
boiling water

Stud the lemon wheel with the cloves and put in a heatproof goblet. Add the rest of the ingredients, then top up with boiling water. Stir with the cinnamon stick and serve.

Indian Summer

2 oz. (60 ml) apple schnapps
6 oz. (180 ml) hot apple cider
1 tsp. (5 ml) ground cinnamon to decorate

Pour the schnapps and cider into an old-fashioned glass rimmed with ground cinnamon, then serve.

Irish Coffee

1 oz. (30 ml) Irish whiskey
6 oz. (180 ml) hot black coffee
2 tsp. (10 ml) raw (demerara) sugar
heavy cream

Pour the whiskey and black coffee into a liqueur coffee glass, then add the sugar. Float the cream on top and serve.

Italian Coffee

1 oz. (30 ml) strega
6 oz. (175ml) hot black coffee
2 tsp. (10 ml) raw (demerara) sugar
heavy cream

Pour the strega and black coffee into a liqueur coffee glass, then add the sugar. Float the cream on top and serve.

Jen's Creamy Sighs

1 oz. (30 ml) amaretto
1 oz. (30 ml) Baileys Irish Cream
dash of Grand Marnier
7 oz. (210 ml) hot coffee
whipped cream

Combine the amaretto and the Baileys in a liqueur coffee glass. Add the hot black coffee, then layer with a mound of whipped cream. Finally, float the Grand Marnier over the whipped cream.

Joyful Bull

1 oz. (30 ml) tequila
1 oz. (30 ml) Kahlua
½ oz. (15 ml) Tia Maria
6 oz. (180 ml) hot coffee
heavy cream
maraschino cherry or sprig of mint as garnish

Pour the hot black coffee into a liqueur coffee glass. Add the tequila, Kahlua and Tia Maria, then float the cream on top. Garnish with a maraschino cherry or sprig of mint.

Mexican Coffee

1 oz. (30 ml) Kahlua
6 oz. (180 ml) hot black coffee
2 tsp. (10 ml) raw (demerara) sugar
heavy cream

Pour the Kahlua and black coffee into a liqueur coffee glass, then add the sugar. Float the cream on top and serve.

Midnight Snowstorm

1 oz. (30 ml) white crème de menthe
7 oz. (210 ml) hot chocolate
1 oz. (30 ml) heavy cream

Pour the crème de menthe and hot chocolate into a highball glass. Float the cream on top and serve.

183

Monte Cristo

1 oz. (30 ml) Kahlua
1 oz. (30 ml) Grand Marnier
6 oz. (180 ml) hot black coffee
1 oz. (30 ml) heavy cream

Pour the Kahlua, Grand Marnier and coffee into a heatproof mug. Float the cream on top and serve.

Mulled Wine (serves 10)

1 bottle claret
4 oz. (120 ml) port
rind of 1 lemon
rind of 1 orange
4 Tbsp. (60 ml) sugar
10 cloves
2 whole cinnamon sticks
4 oz. (120 ml) boiling water

Heat the wine and port with all the other ingredients in a saucepan for a minimum of 15 minutes and serve hot in heatproof glasses.

Russian Coffee

1 oz. (30 ml) vodka
6 oz. (180 ml) hot black coffee
2 tsp. (10 ml) raw (demerara) sugar
heavy cream

Pour the vodka and black coffee into a liqueur coffee glass, then add the sugar. Float the cream on top and serve.

Scandinavian Coffee

1 oz. (30 ml) aqvavit
6 oz. (180 ml) hot black coffee
2 tsp. (10 ml) raw (demerara) sugar
heavy cream

Pour the aqvavit and black coffee into a liqueur coffee glass, then add the sugar. Float the cream on top and serve.

Snow Bunny

1 oz. (30 ml) triple sec
6 oz. (180 ml) hot chocolate
cinnamon stick as garnish

Pour the triple sec into a mug and fill with the hot chocolate. Garnish with the cinnamon stick and serve.

Sorrento Café

1 oz. (30 ml) limoncello
1 oz. (30 ml) Grand Marnier
6 oz. (180 ml) hot coffee
2 tsp. (10 ml) raw (demerara) sugar
heavy cream

Pour the limoncello, Grand Marnier and black coffee into a liqueur coffee glass, then add the sugar. Float the cream on top and serve.

Tom and Jerry

1 egg
1 oz. (30 ml) cognac
1 tsp. (5 ml) superfine sugar
2 oz. (60 ml) dark rum
4 oz. (120 ml) hot cream or milk

Separate the egg yolk from the white and thoroughly beat both independently. Stir the beaten egg yolk and white together, then add the sugar and $1/2$ oz. of the rum to preserve the mixture. Put $1/2$ oz. of the mixture in a heatproof mug, then add the rest of the rum and stir in the hot cream to almost fill the mug. Pour in the cognac and serve.

Liqueur Cocktails

Some of you will already know the difference between a cream and a crème. The former is a mixture of cream and a spirit, for example, Baileys Irish Cream; the latter is a liqueur with a flavor. Liqueurs add the oomph to an after-dinner experience. Traditionally, they're sipped, especially if they're taken after a long dinner. Try some of the following sweet-tasting cocktails, including the **Fuzzy Navel**, **Pineapple Upside-down Cake** and **Toasted Almond**.

This selection includes cream and crème liqueurs, as well as bitters and vermouths.

Adonis

1 oz. (30 ml) sweet sherry
²/₃ oz. (20 ml) sweet vermouth
1 dash of Angostura bitters
3 ice cubes

Stir all the ingredients together, then strain into a cocktail glass and serve.

After Eight

1 oz. (30 ml) Kahlua
1 oz. (30 ml) crème de menthe
1 oz. (30 ml) brown crème de cacao
1 dash of cognac

Shake all the ingredients together, then strain into a martini glass and serve.

Alabama Slammer

1 oz. (30 ml) amaretto
1 oz. (30 ml) Southern Comfort
1 oz. (30 ml) sloe gin
dash of fresh lemon juice

Stir the amaretto, Southern Comfort and gin together, then strain into a shot glass. Add the lemon juice and serve.

Alfonzo

2 oz. (60 ml) Grand Marnier
1 oz. (30 ml) gin
1 oz. (30 ml) dry vermouth
$^1/_2$ oz. (15 ml) sweet vermouth
dash of Angostura bitters

Shake all the ingredients together, then strain into a martini glass and serve.

Allies

1 oz. (30 ml) dry vermouth
1 oz. (30 ml) kümmel
1 oz. (30 ml) gin

Stir all the ingredients together, then strain into a martini glass and serve.

Amaretto Comfort

2 oz. (60 ml) amaretto
2 oz. (60 ml) Southern Comfort
1 oz. (30 ml) heavy cream

Stir the amaretto and Southern Comfort together and strain into a martini glass. Float the cream on top, then serve.

Americano

1 oz. (30 ml) Campari
¹/₂ oz. (15 ml) sweet vermouth
soda water to fill
orange slice as garnish

Put the Campari and sweet vermouth into a highball filled with ice. Top up with soda and stir. Garnish with an orange slice.

Angel's Kiss No. 1

¹/₄ oz. (8 ml) white crème de cacao
¹/₄ oz. (8 ml) sloe gin
¹/₄ oz. (8 ml) brandy
¹/₄ oz. (8 ml) light cream

In the exact order above, layer each of the ingredients in a shot glass and serve.

Angel's Kiss No. 2

¹/₃ oz. (10 ml) crème de cacao
¹/₃ oz. (10 ml) prunelle
¹/₃ oz. (10 ml) crème de violette
¹/₃ oz. (10 ml) light cream

In the exact order above, layer the ingredients in a liqueur glass.

Angel Wing Shooter

¹/₂ oz. (15 ml) crème de cacao
¹/₂ oz. (15 ml) Baileys Irish Cream
¹/₂ oz. (15 ml) brandy

In the exact order above, layer the ingredients in a liqueur glass.

Angelique

1 oz. (30 ml) ouzo
1 oz. (30 ml) light cream
1 oz. (30 ml) advocaat
1 oz. (30 ml) orange juice
1 oz. (30 ml) Strega
maraschino cherry as garnish

Pour all the ingredients in an ice-filled shaker. Shake and strain into a champagne saucer. Garnish with a maraschino cherry.

Anisette

1 oz. (30 ml) anisette
1/2 oz. (15 ml) Benedictine
2 dashes Angostura bitters
spring water to fill

Shake the anisette, Benedictine and bitters together, then strain into a frosted martini glass and serve. Top up with water poured through a sieve filled with crushed ice.

Aqua Thunder

1/3 oz. (10 ml) blue curaçao
1/3 oz. (10 ml) lemon juice
1/3 oz. (10 ml) banana liqueur
1 oz. (30 ml) Midori
3 oz. (90 ml) soda water
lemon slice as garnish

Pour the ingredients into a mixing glass with ice. Stir and strain into a cocktail glass. Garnish with a slice of lemon.

Aristocrat

2 oz. (60 ml) Poire William
1 oz. (30 ml) white rum
3 oz. (90 ml) pineapple juice
dash of orgeat syrup
1/2 pear

Blend all the ingredients together and pour into a large goblet.

Avalanche

1 oz. (30 ml) Cointreau
1 oz. (30 ml) orange juice
1 oz. (30 ml) Tia Maria
1½ oz. (45 ml) light cream

Shake all ingredients together with ice and strain into a champagne flute.

B-52

⅔ oz. (20 ml) Tia Maria
⅔ oz. (20 ml) Baileys Irish Cream
⅔ oz. (20 ml) Cointreau

In the exact order above, layer the ingredients in a shot glass and serve.

Baccile Ball

1 oz. (30 ml) amaretto
2 oz. (60 ml) orange juice
1 oz. (30 ml) soda water

Pour ingredients over ice into an old-fashioned glass, stir and serve.

Bad Girl

½ oz. (15 ml) Malibu coconut liqueur
⅓ oz. (10 ml) Galliano
½ oz. (15 ml) banana liqueur
1 oz. (30 ml) heavy cream
½ oz. (15 ml) advocaat

Place all the ingredients in a blender with ice. Blend, then pour into a
cocktail glass.

Bamboo

1 oz. (30 ml) dry vermouth
1 oz. (30 ml) dry sherry
2 ice cubes
dash of orange bitters
2 dashes Angostura bitters
maraschino cherry as garnish

Mix all the ingredients together in an ice-filled mixing glass, then strain into a cocktail glass. Garnish with a maraschino cherry.

Banana Bender

1 oz. (30 ml) Cointreau
2 oz. (60 ml) heavy cream
1 oz. (30 ml) banana liqueur
¹/₂ banana

Blend ingredients with ice until smooth, then strain into a champagne glass.

Bango

1¹/₂ oz. (45 ml) mango liqueur
¹/₂ oz. (15 ml) Malibu
2 oz. (60 ml) pineapple juice
6 pineapple chunks
¹/₂ banana

Blend all ingredients together with ice, then strain into a champagne flute.

Banshee

2 oz. (60 ml) crème de banane
1 oz. (30 ml) white creme de cacao
2 oz. (60 ml) heavy cream

Mix all the ingredients together in a shaker with ice, then strain into a medium goblet and serve.

Bee Stinger

2 oz. (60 ml) white crème de menthe
1 oz. (30 ml) crème de cassis

Pour the crème de menthe and crème de cassis into a brandy glass. Stir and serve.

Berry Nice

1 oz. (30 ml) strawberry liqueur
½ oz. (15 ml) peach schnapps
½ oz. (15 ml) melon liqueur
½ oz. (15 ml) coconut cream
¼ oz. (8 ml) gomme syrup
1 oz. (30 ml) heavy cream
2 oz. (60 ml) mixed berry fruit juice
2 strawberries as garnish

Mix all the liquid ingredients together in an ice-filled shaker, strain and serve in a cocktail glass. Make a slice halfway up one strawberry and place it on the rim of the glass. Spear the other strawberry with a cocktail stick and balance it across the top of the glass.

Big Apple

1 oz. (30 ml) apple schnapps
1 oz. (30 ml) amaretto
1 oz. (30 ml) Drambuie
1 oz. (30 ml) fresh lemon juice

Shake all the ingredients together, then strain into a martini glass and serve.

Black and Tan

2 oz. (60 ml) sweet vermouth
1 oz. (30 ml) Pernod
1 oz. (30 ml) crème de cassis

Shake all the ingredients together, then strain into a martini glass and serve.

Black and White

1 oz. (30 ml) green crème de menthe
1 oz. (30 ml) Kahlua
½ oz. (15 ml) white crème de menthe
1 oz. (30 ml) heavy cream

Stir the Kahlua and green crème de menthe together in an ice-filled old-fashioned glass. Mix the white crème de menthe and cream in a mixing glass and float on the top.

Blackjack

1 oz. (30 ml) kirsch
1⅓ oz. (40 ml) iced coffee
1¾ oz. (52 ml) brandy

Stir all ingredients over ice in a mixing glass. Strain into a chilled cocktail glass.

Blackjack Shooter

1 oz. (30 ml) Kahlua
½ oz. (15 ml) ouzo

Layer ingredients in a shot glass and serve

Black Sombrero

2 oz. (60 ml) Kahlua
1 oz. (30 ml) tequila
1 oz. (30 ml) vodka

Stir all the ingredients together, then strain into a martini glass and serve.

Blanche

2 oz. (60 ml) Cointreau
1 oz. (30 ml) anisette

Mix the Cointreau and anisette together in a shaker, then strain into a martini glass and serve.

Blue French

1 oz. (30 ml) Pernod
dash of lemon juice
dash of blue curaçao
bitter lemon soda to fill

Shake the Pernod, lemon juice and curaçao together with ice, then strain into a cocktail glass. Top up with the bitter lemon soda.

Blueberry Delight

$^1/_2$ oz. (15 ml) Opal Nera
1 oz. (30 ml) light cream
$^1/_2$ oz. (15 ml) strawberry liqueur
$^1/_2$ oz. (15 ml) Malibu

Put all the ingredients in a shaker with ice. Shake and strain into a cocktail glass.

Body Heat

1 oz. (30 ml) Malibu
1 oz. (30 ml) pineapple juice
1 oz. (30 ml) banana liqueur
1 oz. (30 ml) orange juice
2 oz. (60 ml) lemon juice
dash of grenadine

Blend all the ingredients, except the grenadine, with ice until smooth. Strain into an ice-filled highball glass. Add the grenadine and serve with a straw.

Brighton Rock

2 oz. (60 ml) crème de fraise
3 oz. (90 ml) cranberry juice
1 oz. (30 ml) heavy cream

Mix all the ingredients together in a shaker with ice, then strain into a highball glass.

Bush Peak

$^{1}/_{2}$ oz. (15 ml) Cointreau
$^{1}/_{2}$ oz. (15 ml) Galliano
$^{1}/_{2}$ oz. (15 ml) Grand Marnier
$^{1}/_{2}$ oz. (15 ml) brandy
3 oz. (90 ml) orange juice
dash of grenadine

Shake all the ingredients, except grenadine, with ice. Strain into an ice-filled highball glass. Add the grenadine and serve with a straw.

Cadiz

1 oz. (30 ml) crème de mure
1 oz. (30 ml) dry sherry
$^{1}/_{2}$ oz. (15 ml) triple sec
$^{1}/_{2}$ oz. (15 ml) heavy cream

Shake all the ingredients together with ice, then strain into an ice-filled old fashioned glass.

Café Nero care needed

1 oz. (30 ml) Galliano
6 oz. (180 ml) hot black coffee
heavy cream
2 tsp. (10 ml) superfine sugar

Coat a heatproof glass with the Galliano and light it. Sprinkle the sugar inside and twirl it around so flames burn. Gently pour black coffee into the glass. Layer the cream on top and serve.

Campino

$^{1}/_{2}$ oz. (15 ml) Campari
$^{1}/_{2}$ oz. (15 ml) sweet vermouth
$^{1}/_{2}$ oz. (15 ml) dry vermouth
$^{1}/_{2}$ oz. (15 ml) gin
2 dashes crème de cassis
soda water to fill
orange spiral as garnish

Mix all the ingredients, except soda, in a mixing glass with ice, then strain into a small tumbler and top up with soda. Add a spiral of orange as garnish.

Cappuccino

2 oz. (60 ml) Tia Maria
1 oz. (30 ml) vodka
1 oz. (30 ml) Baileys Irish Cream

Shake all the ingredients together, then strain into a martini glass and serve.

Chastity Belt Shooter

$^1/_2$ oz. (15 ml) Tia Maria
$^1/_3$ oz. (10 ml) Baileys Irish Cream
$^1/_3$ oz. (10 ml) Frangelico
$^1/_3$ oz. (10 ml) light cream

In the exact order above, layer the ingredients in a shot glass and serve.

Chocolate-Chip Mint

1 oz. (30 ml) white crème de menthe
1 oz. (30 ml) brown crème de cacao
1 oz. (30 ml) Tia Maria
1 oz. (30 ml) vodka
1 oz. (30 ml) heavy cream

Mix the ingredients in a shaker with ice, then strain into an ice-filled highball glass.

Climax

2 oz. (60 ml) Southern Comfort
1 oz. (30 ml) Kahlua
$^1/_2$ oz. (15 ml) heavy cream

Mix all the ingredients together in a shaker, then strain into a martini glass and serve.

Curious Comfort

1 oz. (30 ml) blue curaçao
2 oz. (60 ml) Southern Comfort
3 oz. (90 ml) pineapple juice
pineapple slice as garnish

Pour the blue curaçao, Southern Comfort and half the pineapple juice into a shaker. Shake well, then strain into an ice-filled highball glass, top up with the remaining pineapple juice and garnish.

Dandy

2 oz. (60 ml) Dubonnet
1 oz. (30 ml) bourbon
1 oz. (30 ml) Cointreau
dash of Angostura bitters

Shake all the ingredients together, then strain into a cocktail glass and serve.

Death by Chocolate No. 1

1 oz. (30 ml) Baileys Irish Cream
1 oz. (30 ml) crème de cacao
1 oz. (30 ml) Kahlua
1 oz. (30 ml) Tia Maria
2 oz. (60 ml) heavy cream
grated chocolate as garnish

Shake all the ingredients together with ice and strain into a large champagne saucer. Garnish with grated chocolate.

Death By Chocolate No. 2

1 oz. (30 ml) Baileys Irish Cream
1 oz. (30 ml) Kahlua
1 oz. (30 ml) crème do cacao
1 oz. (30 ml) chocolate liqueur
3 oz. (90 ml) heavy cream
grated chocolate as garnish

Shake all the ingredients together with ice and strain into a champagne saucer. Garnish with grated chocolate.

Deep Throat Shooter

$^1/_2$ oz. (15 ml) Kahlua
$^1/_2$ oz. (15 ml) Grand Marnier
$^1/_2$ oz. heavy cream

In the exact order above, layer the ingredients in a shot glass and serve.

Desert Island

1 oz. (30 ml) Midori melon liqueur
1 oz. (30 ml) white rum
2 oz. (60 ml) pineapple juice
2 oz. (60 ml) heavy cream

Shake all the ingredients, except the cream, and strain into a deep champagne saucer. Float the cream on top and serve.

Dianna

3 oz. (90 ml) white crème de menthe
1 oz. (30 ml) cognac

Pour the crème de menthe over crushed ice in an old-fasioned glass. Float the cognac on top.

Due Campari

$^3/_4$ oz. (8 ml) Campari
$^3/_4$ oz. (22 ml) Cordiale Campari
$^3/_4$ oz. (22 ml) lemon juice
champagne or sparkling wine to fill

Shake the Camparis and lemon juice together, then strain into a champagne flute and top up with champagne or sparkling wine.

Dunny

1 oz. (30 ml) Drambuie
1 oz. (30 ml) Islay malt whisky
dash of fresh lime juice

Pour the Drambuie, whisky and lime juice into an old-fashioned glass and serve.

Elixir

1 oz. (30 ml) Grand Marnier
1 oz. (30 ml) sweet vermouth
dash of Punt e Mes
2 dashes Angostura bitters

Pour all the ingredients into an old-fashioned glass and serve.

Flying Grasshopper

1 oz. (30 ml) crème de menthe
1 oz. (30 ml) vodka
1 oz. (30 ml) crème de cacao

Shake all the ingredients together with ice, then strain into a cocktail glass.

Fragile Baby

1 oz. (30 ml) Frangelico
2 oz. (60 ml) Baileys Irish Cream
2 tsp. (10 ml) raw (demerara) sugar
1 oz. (30 ml) heavy cream

Pour the Frangelico, Baileys Irish Cream and sugar into a coffee liqueur glass. Float the cream on top, then serve.

Fuzzy Navel

1 1/2 oz. (45 ml) peach schnapps
orange juice to taste

Pour the peach schnapps into ice-filled highball glass. Fill with orange juice and stir to combine.

Goddess

1 oz. (30 ml) Pernod
1 oz. (30 ml) amaretto

Blend the Pernod and amaretto together in a shaker and strain into a shot glass.

Golden Cadillac

1 oz. (30 ml) crème de cacao
1 oz. (30 ml) Galliano
1 oz. (30 ml) heavy cream

Mix all the ingredients together in a shaker with ice, then strain into a cocktail glass.

Gone Troppo

1¹/₂ oz. (45 ml) peach liqueur
1 oz. (30 ml) banana liqueur
3 strawberries
1 oz. (30 ml) pineapple juice
pineapple wedge as garnish
2 pineapple leaves as garnish

Blend the strawberries, peach and banana liqueurs together until smooth. Pour into a wine glass and float the pineapple juice on top. Garnish with a pineapple wedge and the pineapple leaves.

Grasshopper

1 oz. (30 ml) crème de menthe
1 oz. (30 ml) white crème de menthe
1 oz. (30 ml) heavy cream

Mix all the ingredients together in a shaker with ice, then strain into a cocktail glass.

Half and Half

2 oz. (60 ml) dry vermouth
2 oz. (60 ml) sweet vermouth
lemon twist as garnish

Pour the vermouths into an old-fashioned glass, garnish with the lemon twist and serve.

Happy Birthday

1 oz. (30 ml) Cointreau
1 oz. (30 ml) blue curaçao
$^1/_2$ oz. (15 ml) Galliano
$^1/_2$ oz. (15 ml) white rum

Stir all the ingredients together, then strain into a martini glass and serve.

Iron Lady

1 oz. (30 ml) white crème de cacao
1 oz. (30 ml) noix de coco
1 oz. (30 ml) crème de cassis
2 oz. (60 ml) heavy cream

Mix all the ingredients together in a shaker filled with ice, then strain into an ice-filled highball glass.

Japan Cocktail

3 oz. (90 ml) dry sake
3 oz. (90 ml) plum wine
maraschino cherry as garnish

Shake the sake and plum wine together with ice, then strain and serve in a cocktail glass. Garnish with a maraschino cherry.

Kahlua Cocktail

1 oz. (30 ml) Kahlua
1 oz. (30 ml) brandy

Pour the Kahlua and brandy into an old fashioned glass and serve.

Knee-breaker

1 oz. (30 ml) Cointreau
1 oz. (30 ml) Parfait Amour
$^1/_2$ oz. (15 ml) cherry brandy
$^1/_2$ oz. (15 ml) Frangelico
dash of grenadine

Shake all the ingredients together, then strain into a martini glass and serve.

Legend

1 oz. (30 ml) Midori melon liqueur
1 oz. (30 ml) Kahlua
1 oz. (30 ml) Frangelico

Pour all the ingredients into an old-fashioned glass and serve.

Limp Dick

1 oz. (30 ml) Southern Comfort
1 oz. (30 ml) Grand Marnier
$^1/_2$ oz. (15 ml) amaretto
$^1/_2$ oz. (15 ml) white crème de menthe

Stir all the ingredients together, then strain into a martini glass and serve.

Melonball

2 oz. (60 ml) Midori melon liqueur
1 oz. (30 ml) vodka
pineapple juice or orange juice to fill

In a tall glass half-filled with ice, pour in the Midori and vodka. Top up with the juice.

Mother's Milk

1 oz. (30 ml) vodka
$^1/_2$ oz. (15 ml) gin
$^1/_2$ oz. (15 ml) Tia Maria
$^1/_2$ oz. (15 ml) orgeat syrup
4 oz. (120 ml) half-and-half or cream

Mix all the ingredients together in an ice-filled shaker, then strain into an old-fashioned glass.

Negroni

1 oz. (30 ml) Campari
1 oz. (30 ml) sweet vermouth
splash of soda water (optional)
orange slice as garnish

Pour the Campari and sweet vermouth into an ice-filled old-fashioned glass
and stir. Add the soda, if using, then garnish with the orange slice and serve.

Neopolitan

2 oz. (60 ml) Cointreau
1 oz. (30 ml) Grand Marnier
1 oz. (30 ml) white rum

Shake all the ingredients together, then strain into a martini glass and serve.

Nineteen

2 oz. (60 ml) dry vermouth
½ oz. (15 ml) kirsch
½ oz. (15 ml) gin
2 dashes Angostura bitters
½ oz. (15 ml) gomme syrup

Shake all the ingredients together, then strain into a martini glass and serve.

Nuclear Rainbow

½ oz. (15 ml) grenadine
½ oz. (15 ml) peppermint schnapps
½ oz. (15 ml) Jägermeister
½ oz. (15 ml) melon liqueur
½ oz. (15 ml) whiskey
½ oz. (15 ml) Bacardi 151-proof rum
½ oz. (15 ml) amaretto

In the exact order above, layer over a spoon each of the ingredients in a
champagne flute and serve.

Orange Cadillac

1 oz. (30 ml) white crème de cacao
1 oz. (30 ml) Galliano
¹/₂ oz. (15 ml) Cointreau
¹/₂ oz. (15 ml) fresh orange juice
1 oz. (30 ml) heavy cream

Mix the ingredients in a shaker with ice, then strain into a cocktail glass.

Pacific Gold

1 oz. (30 ml) crème de banane
1 oz. (30 ml) Cointreau
¹/₂ oz. (15 ml) Grand Marnier
2 dashes kümmel

Stir all the ingredients together in a mixing glass with ice, then strain into a cocktail glass.

Parked Car

1 oz. (30 ml) Campari
1 oz. (30 ml) tequila
¹/₂ oz. (15 ml) Cointreau
1 egg white

Mix all the ingredients together in shaker, then strain into a martini glass and serve.

Peach Bowl

2 oz. (60 ml) peach liqueur
4 oz. (115ml) freshly squeezed orange juice
orange slice as garnish

Pour the liqueur and the juice into an ice-filled highball glass, stir and serve with a slice of orange as garnish.

Peach Cocktail

2 oz. (60 ml) crème de pêche
1 oz. (30 ml) dry vermouth
dash of grenadine

Shake all the ingredients together, then strain into a martini glass and serve.

Pernod Cocktail

2 oz. (60 ml) Pernod
2 oz. (60 ml) iced water
2 dashes Angostura bitters

Pour all the ingredients into an old-fashioned glass and serve.

Picon-Limón

1¹/₂ oz. (45 ml) Amer Picon
¹/₂ oz. (15 ml) grenadine
dash of Rose's Lime Cordial
soda water to fill
lemon twist as garnish

Stir the Amer Picon, grenadine and lime cordial in an ice filled mixing glass, then strain into a chilled highball glass. Top up with soda and add a lemon twist.

Picon Punch

1¹/₂ oz. (45 ml) Amer Picon
dash of grenadine
soda water to fill
brandy to float
lemon twist as garnish

Coat the inside of a tumbler with grenadine. Add the Amer Picon and ice, top up with soda water and stir. Float the brandy over the drink and serve with a lemon twist.

Pineapple Upside-down Cake

¹/₂ oz. (15 ml) Baileys Irish Cream
¹/₂ oz. (15 ml) vodka
¹/₂ oz. (15 ml) butterscotch schnapps
¹/₂ oz. (15 ml) pineapple juice

Stir all the ingredients together in a mixing glass, then strain into a shot glass.

Pink Cadillac

1 oz. (30 ml) crème de cacao
$^1/_2$ oz. (15 ml) Galliano
$^1/_2$ oz. (15 ml) grenadine
1 oz. (30 ml) heavy cream
dash of fresh orange juice

Mix all the ingredients together in a shaker with ice, strain into a cocktail glass.

Red Death

1 oz. (30 ml) Southern Comfort
1 oz. (30 ml) amaretto
1 oz. (30 ml) sloe gin
dash of vodka
dash of triple sec
dash of orange juice
maraschino cherry as garnish

Shake all the ingredients together with ice and strain into an old-fashioned glass filled with ice. Garnish with a maraschino cherry.

Sake Sunrise (makes 10 4-oz. servings)

2 pints (1 L) sake, room temperature
8 oz. (250 ml) hot sake, just below boiling point
1 Tbsp. (15 ml) dried apricot
1 Tbsp. (15 ml) dried peach
$^1/_2$ tsp. (2 ml) ginger
$^1/_4$ stick vanilla pod

Combine the apricot, peach, ginger and vanilla pod in a basket strainer and immerse in hot sake. Steep for two hours, then add the room temperature sake and leave in a cool place. Infuse for one week, then remove the strainer, and place in a refrigerator until ready to serve. This mixture will keep for one week in the refrigerator.

Screaming Multiple Orgasm

1 oz. (30 ml) Baileys Irish Cream
1 oz. (30 ml) light cream
1 oz. (30 ml) Cointreau
$^1/_2$ oz. (15 ml) Galliano

In the exact order listed, layer in a brandy glass and serve.

Sex on the Beach

$^1/_2$ oz. (15 ml) Chambord
$^1/_2$ oz. (15 ml) Midori
$^1/_2$ oz. (15 ml) vodka
1 oz. (30 ml) pineapple juice
cranberry juice to fill

Stir all the ingredients together, then strain into a shot glass. Top up with the cranberry juice and serve.

Shooting Star

1 oz. (30 ml) Midori
1 oz. (30 ml) light cream
1 oz. (30 ml) peach liqueur
1 slice rockmelon, diced
$^1/_2$ oz. (15 ml) orange curaçao

Blend all the ingredients together until smooth, then pour into a colada glass.

Sicilian Kiss

$^2/_3$ oz. (20 ml) amaretto
$^2/_3$ oz. (20 ml) Southern Comfort

Layer over ice in an old-fashioned glass.

Slippery Nipple

$^2/_3$ oz. (20 ml) butterscotch schnapps
$^2/_3$ oz. (20 ml) Baileys Irish Cream

Pour butterscotch schnapps into a shot glass and layer the Baileys on top.

Southern Bull

1 oz. (30 ml) Kahlua
1 oz. (30 ml) Southern Comfort
1 oz. (30 ml) tequila

Shake all the ingredients together, then strain into a martini glass and serve.

Spanish Fly

2 oz. (60 ml) mescal
1 oz. (30 ml) Grand Marnier
1 tsp. (5 ml) instant coffee as garnish

Pour the mescal and Grand Marnier into an old-fashioned glass. Sprinkle with the coffee and serve.

Strawberry Cream Tea

1 oz. (30 ml) Kahlua
1 oz. (30 ml) Baileys Irish Cream
1 oz. (30 ml) crème de fraise
1 oz. (30 ml) vodka
1 oz. (30 ml) Lassi (Indian yogurt drink)

Blend all the ingredients together and pour into an ice-filled highball glass. Lassi gives this cocktail a lighter, cleaner flavor.

Swamp Water

1 oz. (30 ml) green crème de menthe
1 oz. (30 ml) Baileys Irish cream
1 oz. (30 ml) cherry brandy

Pour all the ingredients together into an ice-filled brandy glass, stir and serve.

Swan Song

1 oz. (30 ml) Midori
$1/2$ oz. (15 ml) Cointreau
$1/2$ oz. (15 ml) Frangelico
grated chocolate to serve

Mix all the ingredients together in a shaker, then strain into a martini glass. Sprinkle with the chocolate and serve.

Toasted Almond

2 oz. (60 ml) amaretto
2 oz. (60 ml) Kahlua
2 oz. (60 ml) light cream

Shake all the ingredients together, then strain into a highball glass.

Traffic Light

1 oz. (30 ml) crème de noix
1 oz. (30 ml) Galliano
1 oz. (30 ml) Midori

Layer the ingredients in the exact order above, in a shot glass, and serve.

Yellow Monkey

1 oz. (30 ml) Galliano
1 oz. (30 ml) white crème de cacao
1 oz. (30 ml) crème de banane
1 oz. (30 ml) white rum
1 oz. (30 ml) heavy cream

Mix all the ingredients together in a shaker, strain into a martini glass and serve.

Zanzibar

2 oz. (60 ml) dry vermouth
½ oz. (15 ml) gin
2 dashes fresh lemon juice
2 dashes gomme syrup
lemon twist as garnish

Shake all the ingredients together, then strain into a martini glass and serve with the twist of lemon.

Nonalcoholic Cocktails

Some nonalcoholic cocktails are divine both in looks and taste. With more and more exotic fruit juices becoming available, the advent of coconut cream and the modern addition of spices, such as fresh ginger, nonalcoholic cocktails have evolved tremendously. With the added bonus of being good for you, they will, without doubt, enhance your reputation at your cocktail parties. Try **Ginger Alert** on a summer's day, and a **Virgin Mary** whenever you feel like one.

Alice in Wonderland

3 oz. (90 ml) grapefruit juice
1 oz. (30 ml) green tea
²/₃ oz. (20 ml) lemon juice
¹/₂ oz. (15 ml) gomme syrup
soda water to fill

Place a few ice cubes to a champagne flute, then add the green tea, lemon juice, gomme syrup and grapefruit juice. Stir, then top up with soda.

Angel Punch

3 oz. (90 ml) apple juice
1 oz. (30 ml) green tea
²/₃ oz. (20 ml) lemon juice
dash of gomme syrup
soda water to fill

Pour the juices, tea and gomme syrup into an ice-filled highball glass and stir. Top up with soda.

Belly Dancer

1 oz. (30 ml) light cream
1/2 oz. (15 ml) lime juice
2 oz. (60 ml) coconut cream
1/2 oz. (15 ml) grenadine

Shake all the ingredients together with ice and strain into a chilled cocktail glass.

Coconut Groove

3 oz. (90 ml) pineapple juice
2 oz. (60 ml) coconut cream
2 oz. (60 ml) fresh pink grapefruit juice
grapefruit wedge as garnish

Place all the ingredients into a blender with crushed ice. Blend and pour into a colada glass. Add a thin grapefruit wedge on the edge of the glass.

Ginger Alert

3 oz. (90 ml) apple juice
2 oz. (60 ml) pear juice
1/2 lemon, freshly squeezed
small piece gingerroot, sliced
ginger ale to fill

Muddle the ginger in the bottom of a cocktail shaker. Add ice, then pour in all the ingredients, except the ginger ale. Shake, then strain into an ice-filled goblet and top up with ginger ale.

Lime Lifesaver (serves 2)

2 fresh limes
8 medium carrots
knob of gingerroot
2 fresh apples

Cut the limes in half and juice, then juice the carrots, peel and juice the knob of gingerroot and juice the apples. Stir and pour equally into two tumblers.

Mango Masher

$^1/_2$ ripe mango
1 orange, freshly squeezed
1 lime, freshly squeezed
handful fresh raspberries
ice cubes

Take the seeds out of the mango and scoop out the flesh. Halve the orange and the lime and juice them. Put everything in a blender with ice cubes and blend until smooth. Pour into a large tumbler.

On the Beach

$^1/_4$ ripe yellow melon, diced
8 fresh raspberries
3 oz. (90 ml) freshly squeezed orange juice
$^1/_2$ lime, freshly squeezed
dash of grenadine
lemon-lime soda to fill

Pour all the ingredients, except the soda, into a blender and blend for a few seconds, then add a scoop of ice. Blend again and pour into a tumbler with ice. Top up with soda, stir gently and serve with a straw.

Orange Flamingo

6 oz. (180 ml) orange soda
1 oz. (30 ml) grenadine
whipped cream

Put a little ice into a highball glass and pour in the orange soda. Slowly add the grenadine to the soda and float the whipped cream on top.

Pine Smoothie

quarter of a large fresh pineapple
1 orange, freshly squeezed
2 handfuls raspberries
ice cubes

Peel the pineapple, dice the flesh, then place in a blender along with the orange juice and rinsed raspberries. Add the ice cubes last, then blend.

Pink Awakening (serves 2)

2 large handfuls raspberries
1 ripe banana
1 pink grapefruit, freshly squeezed

Rinse the raspberries and place in a blender. Add peeled banana and
grapefruit juice, then blend.

Prairie Oyster

1 tsp. (5 ml) olive oil
3 dashes Worcestershire sauce
1 egg yolk
pinch of salt
pinch of black pepper
1 oz. (30ml) ketchup
dash of white wine vinegar

Rinse a wine glass with the olive oil and discard the excess. Add ketchup and
egg yolk and season with Worcestershire sauce, wine vinegar, salt and
pepper. Serve a small glass of iced water on the side.

Red Apple Highball

1 oz. (30 ml) fresh apple juice
dash of passion fruit syrup
dash of grenadine
ginger beer to fill

Pour juice, passion fruit syrup and grenadine into an ice-filled highball glass,
then stir. Top up with ginger beer, stir again gently and serve with a stirrer.

St. Clement's

5 oz. (150 ml) freshly squeezed orange juice
5 oz. (150 ml) bitter lemon soda
lemon twist as garnish
orange twist as garnish

Pourt the juice and soda into a highball glass filled with cracked ice. Stir and
serve garnished with twists of orange and lemon.

Sangrita (serves 10)

2 pints (1 L) tomato juice

1 pint (500 ml) freshly squeezed orange juice

5 tsp. (25 ml) honey

3 oz. (90 ml) freshly squeezed lime juice

pinch salt and black pepper

1 chilli, finely chopped

1/4 oz. (8 ml) white onion, finely chopped

10–20 dashes Worcestershire sauce

Pour all the ingredients into a bowl and stir well. Place the bowl in a refrigerator to chill for two hours. Take out, then strain into a large glass pitcher. Serve in wine glasses.

Sensation

3 oz. (90 ml) tomato juice

2 oz. (60 ml) passion fruit juice

2 oz. (60 ml) fresh carrot juice

1/2 lemon, freshly squeezed

1 tsp. (5 ml) honey

3–4 dashes Worcestershire sauce

Pour all ingredients together into a shaker. Shake, then strain into a goblet.

Shirley Temple

7 oz. (210 ml) ginger ale

1 oz. (30 ml) grenadine syrup

lemon slice as garnish

cherry as garnish

Build a pile of ice in a highball glass. Add ginger ale over the ice and sprinkle grenadine syrup over it. Garnish with a lemon slice and a cherry.

Tropicana

1 oz. (30 ml) coconut milk

2 oz. (60 ml) pineapple juice

2 oz. (60 ml) mango juice

1 banana

Blend all the ingredients together, add crushed ice, then blend again. Pour into a tumbler and serve with a straw.

Virgin Lea

4 oz. (120 ml) tomato juice
2 oz. (60 ml) passion fruit juice
¹/₂ yellow pepper, sliced
1 tsp. (5 ml) honey
1–2 dashes Worcestershire sauce

Place the pepper slices in a blender and add the juices. Blend at low speed,
then add the honey, Worcestershire sauce and ice cubes. Blend at high
speed. Pour through a strainer into an ice-filled highball glass.

Virgin Mary

5 oz. (150 ml) tomato juice
1 oz. (30 ml) freshly squeezed lemon juice
1–2 dashes Worcestershire sauce
1–2 dashes Tabasco sauce
dash of salt
dash of black pepper
1 stick celery

Pour the tomato juice into a highball glass and season to taste with spices.
Stir, then add celery stick as a stirrer.

Classic Cocktails

Some cocktails have been mixed for decades, or in the case of the **Martini** and **Manhattan**, more than a century. The early classics were simple cocktails, a spirit mixed with another and perhaps a vermouth, and lemon juice, but not much more.

In the 1930s and 1940s, glamor was queen and the names of recipes reflected that: **Adonis**, **Between the Sheets**, **Mimosa** and the **Gimlet**. There was a lot of gin, vermouth, whiskey and champagne, and a dash of liqueur would occasionally make an appearance. Everything changed after World War II, when vodka came out of the cold and into America. So what makes a classic? It is the ultimate combination of sweet and bitter – not too much of one or the other. A classic case of good taste.

Some of the drinks we know as classics are from the Prohibition era – knock on the door of the speakeasy and enter into a world of lethal spirits designed to make you forget the world you just left.

Exotic rum and tequila cocktails of the 1950s returned to the U.S. with travelers who'd been partying in Havana, South America and the Caribbean, making the **Daiquiri** and the **Margarita** famous. The 1960s, 1970s and 1980s added more juices and mixers to a spirited cocktail. And the **Cosmopolitan** (called the "stealth Martini" by Barnaby Conrad III) was created, reflecting the flavor of the era in the same way the **Martini** reflected the hard-drinking era into which it was born. Long live a classic!

The following are all classic cocktails, either modern inventions or handed down through the decades by bartenders blessed with a touch of genius.

Cheers: Clark Gable offers a Martini toast to Constance Bennett in the 1934 movie *After Office Hours*

Bloody Mary

Ask anyone who regularly has a hangover and they will probably say that a Bloody Mary fixes their day just right. Whether they prefer a celery stalk in their drink is a matter for heated debate. Some people love it, others find it useful to swat flies with.

It was in 1921 that Fernand "Pete" Petiot first combined tomato juice, vodka, salt, pepper and Worcestershire sauce at Harry's New York Bar in Paris. Vodka and tomato had been mixed together before in Europe (vodka was still unknown in the United States back then) but it was the addition of Worcestershire sauce that gave this drink the edge.

Hotel magnate John Astor tasted it, and asked Petiot to go to New York, to the St. Regis Hotel. Astor insisted Petiot rename this drink Red Snapper because he felt "bloody" was too much for customers to take. Petiot used gin because vodka was not available in the U.S. at that time. A customer, Prince Serge Obolensky, requested his drink be "spiced up." Petiot added the Tabasco sauce. After a time, it became known as a Bloody Mary in the U.S. too. American George Jessel was hired in the 1950s by Heublein, who had just acquired the rights to vodka, to introduce the Bloody Mary to America. He succeeded.

As with many classics, confusion reigns as to whom the cocktail is named after. Was it named after Mary I, the Tudor Queen of England who had a reputation for butchering Protestants? Or after another Mary who had caught Petiot's eye?

The use of a celery stick as a garnish originated in the 1960s at Chicago's Ambassador East Hotel. An unnamed celebrity asked for a Bloody Mary, but didn't get a swizzle stick in the glass. He grabbed a stalk of celery from the relish tray to stir his Bloody Mary and history was made.

Cocktail Recipe

Bloody Mary

1½ oz. (45 ml) vodka

5 oz. (150 ml) tomato juice

½ oz. (15 ml) fresh lemon juice

pinch celery salt

2 dashes Worcestershire sauce

2 dashes Tabasco sauce

ground black pepper

celery stick (optional)

lemon wedge as garnish

Fill a highball with ice, then pour in the tomato and lemon juices. Add the vodka. Add the spices. Add black pepper. Garnish with a lemon wedge, a stirrer and a celery stick, if requested.

Caipirinha

This crisp cocktail is making a comeback with groups of thirtysomethings, who love a bit of rhythm and are ready to rock on all night after a few of these classics. It's possibly the best loved of all Brazilian cocktails, with a flavor to sigh for. Literally translated it means "peasant's drink."

The kick comes from cachaça, a Brazilian spirit distilled from sugarcane juice. The cocktail had such an effect that in the 1920s and 1930s the king of the car lot, Henry Ford, decreed cachaça be outlawed at Fordlandia, his company town in Brazil. He wanted law and order to reign, not frivolity.

The problem was the quinine the workers were meant to take. Not liking the taste of it, the Brazlians mixed it with cachaça, not lime juice as recommended by the management.

Real bartenders make this sling-type drink with a long pestle-type muddler, strong enough to break down the lime skin and its fruit and bring out the flavor of the juice. Make sure you select medium-sized limes with thin skins and an even color – sure signs the lime is ripe enough to muddle.

It is one of the first rules of bartending that limes should always be rolled before they are diced. This assists in the release of the fruit's aromatic oils and it is an essential part of the method when you make a Caipirinha. Neglect to do so at your peril.

No fiery cachaça? Then use vodka and make a Caipirovhka, or rum and make a Caipirissima. As always, you can fiddle with the formula until it suits your palate. If you prefer it less fiery, use more lime juice. Like it sweeter? Then use more sugar (or syrup).

Should you decide you like this kind of cocktail, you might like to try other similar drinks such as the Pisco Sour, the Mojito and the Batida.

Cocktail Recipe

Caipirinha

2 oz. (60 ml) cachaça
1 medium fresh lime
1 tsp. (5 ml) superfine sugar

Cut the lime into quarters vertically and
place them in the base of a chilled
tumbler. Add the sugar
and crush the lime
pieces until the sugar
is dissolved. Add the
cachaça, then ice
cubes, and stir.

Cosmopolitan

For a drink that has made cocktail history, very little is known about its creation. Nothing printed to date gives a real clue as to the identity of the person who first mixed vodka, Cointreau, fresh lime juice and a splash of cranberry juice to make the sexiest drink in New York City.

There are several theories, one of which leads to the gay community in Provincetown, Massachusetts. The name Cheryl Cook is whispered in connection with this snazzy snifter, but no one of that name comes forward. From its success there, it went to New York (in search of fame and fortune) and became the most requested cocktail for some years.

In the past decade or so, this cocktail has become a megastar as a new-style Martini. Author Hunter S. Thompson mentioned the Cosmopolitan in an affidavit used in his legal case, *The People of the State of Colorado v. Hunter S. Thompson*. It gained notoriety, too, in *Sex and the City* as the one cocktail both good and bad girls drink.

It has become a favorite worldwide and, as such, is guaranteed a place in the history books. The best Cosmopolitans are those which succeed in balancing the sweet and sour; for instance, if not enough freshly squeezed lime juice is used it becomes too sweet. And sweet is not how a Cosmopolitan should taste. Nor should it be so tart that it makes you salivate. It should be served in a chilled cocktail glass, its sides glistening with moisture (this chill factor keeps the drink colder for longer).

Martini historian Barnaby Conrad III once described the Cosmopolitan as the "stealth Martini," and stealthy it is, having worked its way into the very fabric of our cocktail culture without too much trouble. Its critics claim it is not complex enough in flavor, but those who love it, adore it.

Cocktail Recipe

Cosmopolitan

1½ oz. (45 ml) vodka
¾ oz. (22 ml) Cointreau
splash cranberry juice
⅓ oz. (10 ml) fresh lime juice

Shake all ingredients with ice. Strain into a cocktail
glass. Garnish with a lime wedge.

Daiquiri

The Daiquiri is an ice-cold masterpiece of mixing. And President John F. Kennedy agreed, making this one of his preferred pre-dinner cocktails. This tidbit of information, once out there in the public consciousness, put this humble Cuban cocktail right up there with the Martini in importance.

The oft-repeated myth about its origins involves an American engineer named Jennings Cox, who was working near the town of Daiquiri, on the east coast of Cuba. In the long, hot summer of 1896, Jennings Cox is said to have run out of his gin supplies when expecting important guests. His local colleagues drank a mixture of rum and lime juice and it was this, with the addition of granulated sugar, that he offered his guests, naming it a Daiquiri after the town.

A ship's junior medical officer, Lucius W. Johnson, had met Jennings Cox during a tour of the area, imbibed the notorious mixture and introduced the cocktail to the Army & Navy Club back in Washington, D.C. A plaque recognizing the fact still hangs in the club's Daiquiri Lounge.

Another famous person to be associated with the Daiquiri was the German actress Marlene Dietrich, who was seen to sip one or two at the American Bar in the Savoy Hotel when she visited London.

Some cocktail historians dismiss Jennings Cox's claim and say the locals were drinking a version of the Daiquiri well before his period of duty there. And, these same historians note, gloomily, the apalling trend of premixed Daiquiris which bear no resemblence to the real thing.

King of the Frozen Daiquiri, Constantino Ribailagua, mixed his unique drink at La Floridita, Havana. He squeezed the limes gently with his fingers to avoid even the tiniest drop of bitter oil from the rind getting in the drink, and he strained it through a sieve into the glass so that no ice would slip through.

Cocktail Recipe

Daiquiri

1½ oz. (45 ml) white rum
½ oz. (15 ml) lime juice
2–3 dashes gomme syrup
lime wedge as garnish

Pour the ingredients into a shaker with cracked ice.
Strain into a chilled cocktail glass and garnish with a
lime wedge in the glass.

Manhattan

The Manhattan has a history dating back to 1874 and New York's Manhattan Club. William J. Tillden was elected New York's governor. Lady Randolph Churchill, Winston's American mother, threw a party to celebrate the occasion and the bartender invented the cocktail with its cute cherry.

The rye whiskey flavor was well received and has been ever since, because even now the Manhattan is still one of the most requested cocktails in bars worldwide, especially in fall and winter months when the body needs a shot of dark liquor.

However, another urban myth credits a Supreme Court judge, one Charles Henry Truax, with having a hand in the cocktail's birth. He was on a diet and this was the low-calorie drink created by a bartender at the Manhattan Club for him to sip. Let's go with the first Manhattan Club tale. This cocktail, too, has had its moment of cinematic fame, with the title of a movie to its credit.

Traditionally, the Manhattan is served sweet and always garnished with a red maraschino cherry. If the cocktail has been made correctly, the taste of the whiskey is complemented by the vermouth and the bitters. As always, the ideal Manhattan is a matter of balance between the ingredients, to the satisfaction of your palate.

If you are going to serve a Dry Manhattan, use French vermouth instead of Italian and garnish with a lemon twist. If someone asks for a Perfect Manhattan, don't panic. This version requires $1/4$ oz. (8 ml) each of sweet and dry vermouths. Again, add a lemon twist to finish the drink.

This is the perfect aperitif, one to have at hand when watching the stock market fall, then rise, and fall again, all in the same day's trading, and wonder what it's all about.

Cocktail Recipe

Manhattan

2 oz. (60 ml) rye whiskey
$^1/_2$ oz. (15 ml) sweet vermouth
dash of Angostura bitters
maraschino cherry as garnish

Pour all the ingredients into a mixing glass and stir.
Strain into a cocktail glass. Drop a maraschino
cherry in and watch it settle.

Margarita

Spare a thought for the Margarita and how its reputation has been ruined by the mixes and canned garbage available from supermarket shelves. It's enough to make you want to have another to forget about it. Keep your palate pure and drink only the real thing.

The original, enchanting Margarita was created after the mid-1930s. But take your pick as to whether it was Mexico, California, New Mexico or Texas where it was created.

One legend involves Margaret Sames, an American living in Texas. In 1948, she and her husband entertained friends in Acapulco. Nicky Hilton, of the hotel chain, and Shelton A. McHenry, owner of the Tail o' the Cock restaurant in Los Angeles, were among those invited to share their revelry. Mrs. Sames allegedly took Cointreau, added tequila and lime juice and rubbed salt on the rim of the glass to make it look attractive.

However, others repeat a tale of the day a starlet named Marjorie King walked into Carlos "Danny" Herrera's Rancho La Gloria restaurant, near Tijuana, Mexico. He mixed this cocktail especially for her because she was, apparently, allergic to every spirit but tequila.

Supporters of the Margarita having a Mexican birthplace point to Doña Bertha, proprietor of Bertita's Bar in Tasca, Pancho Morales of Tommy's Place in Juarez, and Daniel Negrete of the Garci Crespo Hotel in Puebla, all of whom are talked about when this cocktail's origins are questioned.

The proportions of the ingredients change from recipe to recipe, with any of the known brands of tequila serving as the base and any of the available liqueurs such as Grand Marnier, orange curaçao and triple sec substituting for Cointreau. The amount of lime or lemon juice varies too.

Cocktail Recipe

Margarita

1 1/2 oz. (45 ml) silver tequila
1/2 oz. (15 ml) fresh lime juice
3/4 oz. (22 ml) Cointreau
lime wedge
saucer of salt
lime slice to garnish

Rub a wedge of lime around the rim of a margarita
glass and dip the glass into a saucer of salt to
create a salt-crusted rim. Pour all the ingredients
into a shaker containing cracked ice and shake.
Strain into the glass. Garnish with a lime slice.

Martini

In a classic Martini there are only two ingredients: gin and dry vermouth. Purists keep the gin and the glasses in the freezer, and an hour before visitors arrive for cocktails, meaning Martinis, they take both out of the freezer. The trick with a Martini is to make it as cold as you can.

A recipe for a Martinez first appeared in an 1884 bartender's guide, although in 1862 a Gin Cocktail, much like the Martinez, had appeared in Jerry Thomas's book *Bon Vivant's Companion*. By 1887, this gin cocktail had become the Martinez, and Thomas was claiming credit.

The myth associated with Thomas involves a traveler walking into the San Francisco Occidental Hotel bar, and Thomas mixing him the Martinez. Step back in time to the small town of Martinez, California, and watch bartender Julio Richelieu mix what might have been the first Martinez (which became the Martini).

The people of Martinez claim the traveler was on his way to San Francisco. Richelieu mixed the cocktail for him so he could get change from a gold nugget and buy a bottle of whiskey. So much for his taste. However, in 1929 the town's mayor put up a brass plaque stating that Martinez was the birthplace of the Martini. And you can't argue with that!

How to make a Martini is a matter of personal opinion. The drink that symbolized so much for so many (mainly decadent) people has changed from a 2 part gin to 1 part vermouth cocktail to a 25 to 1 ratio. That's some alcohol. But spare a thought for the grand old man of the cocktail kingdom. Chocolate? Blueberry? Strawberry? Dirty? It was hard enough to get used to the flavor of vodka instead of gin, but really, these fruits and sweet things are an insult to the original dry Martini, the most famous icon of American culture.

Cocktail Recipe

Martini

3 oz. (90 ml) gin
1/2 oz. (15 ml) extra dry vermouth
thin twist of lemon or green olive as garnish

Pour the dry vermouth into a mixing glass filled with
the coldest ice you can imagine. Let it dribble down
the ice and then strain it from the mixing glass. Add
the chilled gin and stir quickly with a barspoon.
Strain into a chilled cocktail glass. Add a thin twist of
lemon or an olive before serving.

Mint Julep

The Mint Julep and Kentucky are tied together forever in the cocktail drinker's mind. For an easily made drink, it has captured the world's imagination. However, in the words of Alben Barkley, a Kentucky-born statesman: "A Mint Julep is not the product of a formula."

And he is right. Some people make the mint and sugar mix the night before, thinking it will make the mint flavor stronger, but does it just make it sweeter? Others use only the smallest, freshest mint leaves, discarding the larger leaves because they feel they don't have as much flavor. Or is it the other way around?

The word "julep" is derived from Arabic, translated as "julab," meaning "rose water." The bourbon-based cocktail may originate from Virginia, although other states lay claim to its origin, including Kentucky, Pennsylvania, Maryland and Mississippi.

A 1975 paper, by Richard B. Harwell, states: "Clearly the Mint Julep originated in the northern Virginia tidewater, spread soon to Maryland, and eventually all along the seaboard and even to Kentucky." Since Virginia once owned Bourbon County, birthplace of bourbon, its claim to be the first to sip the cocktail has the most validity.

The horse racing association dates back to the opening of the Churchill Downs racetrack in Louisville in May 1875. America's best-known race, the Kentucky Derby, was held on the track's first day of business and the Mint Julep took advantage of two important factors: the bourbon behind the bars and the mint growing around the track.

These days, however, the racetrack bars serve an imitation concoction that spurts from guns into glasses by the thousands each race day, making people drunk with despair if they've lost on a horse, or ecstatic if they've won!

Cocktail Recipe

Mint Julep

2 oz. (60 ml) bourbon
6 sprigs fresh mint
1 tsp. (5 ml) superfine sugar
$\frac{1}{2}$ oz. (15 ml) cold spring water
soda water

Place the mint in a highball glass and then add the sugar and water. Mix for about a minute. Add the bourbon. Fill the glass with crushed ice. Stir. Add a sprig of mint as a garnish. Serve with a straw and a stirrer.

Moscow Mule

When the Moscow Mule was released into the drinks market in the United States, it was as the direct result of a clever marketing strategy devised by the man had who bought the rights to Smirnoff, a Russian vodka – John G. Martin of Heublein Inc., a distributor of food and drink.

Martin's decision nearly lost him his reputation. Remember this was the 1950s, and the Soviet Union and the U.S. were hardly the best of friends. Smirnoff had been manufactured in Russia since 1820, and the Smirnoff family were masters of the art of vodka making, with a monopoloy on the supply of the spirit to the royal court of Tsar Alexander III. The family's fate was less exalted after the Revolution, and the recipe for vodka escaped with the Smirnoff family to France, and eventually to America, when Martin saw the future was white and clear.

The purchase became known as Martin's folly in the trade, and he took off on a nationwide trip to promote the spirit. In Hollywood, he met with the owner of the Cock 'n' Bull, the astute Jack Morgan. Morgan had a glut of ginger beer, and a friend who was trying to sell a whole load of copper mugs. The three of them created the Moscow Mule—vodka, ginger beer and an ounce of lime juice, to be sold in a copper mug. The mug was stamped with a kicking mule, a symbol of the cocktail's kick.

The Moscow Mule caught the imagination of the younger generation, if only because its gimmickry was appealing. The effervescence of ginger beer, a tart flavor from lime juice and the smooth nontaste of alcoholic vodka ensured its success in a country keen to adopt anything new and exciting.

You can replace ginger beer with ginger ale, but it won't taste the same. But, more important, make sure you serve it cold!

Cocktail Recipe

Moscow Mule

1½ oz. (45 ml) vodka
½ oz. (15 ml) fresh lime juice
ginger beer to fill
lime wedge as garnish

Pour the vodka and the lime juice into a
highball over ice. Fill to the top with ginger
beer. Stir. Garnish with a lime wedge and
serve with a stirrer.

Pimm's No. 1 Cup

This terribly British tall drink, made with gin and usually associated with summer, tennis and the Wimbledon championships, has an unusual garnish. It's cucumber, with or without the skin, and it helps to soften the bitter flavor of the Pimm's.

Pimm's No. 1 was created in 1840 as a digestive tonic by a James Pimm and served at his Oyster Bar in London's financial district. It's a refreshing concoction of herbs and quinine, but it was another 20 years before Mr. Pimm started to distribute the mixture more widely. By the 1920s, Pimm's No. 1 was distributed throughout England and exported to the far-flung colonies of the British Empire, and even as far as the Sudan, in Africa, where it was most welcome among expatriates. After World War II, the Pimm's company introduced Pimm's No. 2 with Scotch as a base, No. 3 with brandy, No. 4 with rum and No. 5 with rye whiskey. No. 6 was, and is still, made with a vodka base. Today, all but Nos. 1 and 6 are practically impossible to find.

Traditionally, the British drink lemonade instead of ginger ale with their Pimm's No. 1 Cup. However, ginger ale gives it more bite.

In England, it is consumed by the pitcher during long hot afternoons of cricket and other summer sports. When your team, or your favorite, loses, the Pimm's takes on another property, that of helping dull the embarrassment. During Wimbledon, bad weather can be very inconvenient and depressing but, again, the many pitchers of Pimm's help the fans through these wet moments.

Pimm's has also found favor with the younger generation because it can be bought by the pitcher for a reasonable price. As a drink, it is very refreshing, and has a pleasant, almost healthy taste. It is easy to forget the alcohol hidden beneath the gingery flavor.

Cocktail Recipe

Pimm's No.1 Cup

2 oz. (60 ml) Pimm's No. 1 Cup
ginger ale to fill
few strips cucumber peel
lemon slice as garnish

Pour the Pimm's into a pint glass filled
with ice. Top up with ginger ale. Add the
cucumber to the drink. Garnish with a slice
of lemon, and serve with a straw.

Pisco Sour

Pisco, as anyone who has traveled there will tell you, is a South American brandy, distilled from Muscat grapes and matured in clay jars. It is named after the town of Pisco in Peru. Its inhabitants have imbibed pisco since the 1500s. Its bittersweet flavor certainly has a long tradition in the region.

However, Chileans also like to claim it originated in their country. In the 1930s, the Chilean president, Mr. Riesco, trademarked the term and thus hijacked the spirit of a nation.

Pisco is an interesting liquor, perhaps with hallucinogenic qualities (well, after eight shots you might think that). It has a sweet taste, with a zesty tang that tends to hide its strength.

It is drunk in small bars and cafés throughout Peru, Argentina and South America. The origins of the powerful and delicious Pisco Sour are steeped in controversy. The Chileans proclaim the cocktail was created during the 1920s and 30s, when passengers from both American and European ships en route to San Francisco would be taken ashore at Coquimbo.

The Whiskey Sour was a popular drink at the time, and perhaps the passengers demanded a local version of that, using pisco. On the other hand, Peruvians are adamant that the port of Pisco is the real port of call where it happened. The story leaves a sour taste in both countries' mouths.

You may have to hunt for a bottle of genuine pisco but the effort is well worth the potent experience. Generally, the Pisco Sour was served by townies during the heat of a summer's day around Christmas as a refreshing yet very potent act of hospitality.

Try mixing Pisco Sours at the start of the evening to get everyone relaxed. Stand back and watch the results.

Cocktail Recipe

Pisco Sour

2 oz. (60 ml) pisco
1/2 oz. (15 ml) lime juice
1 Tbsp. (15 ml) egg white, beaten
dash of Angostura bitters
dash of gomme syrup

Pour all ingredients into a shaker with ice. Shake.
Strain into a white wine glass or a champagne bowl.

Sidecar

One thing is certain with this classic cocktail: the ratio of two measures strong, one measure sweet and one measure sour are firmly laid down in cocktail history, and one to be changed at your peril. The Sidecar is an elegant drink with a wan appearance that belies its beauty.

Because the balance of ingredients is important, the Sidecar is one of the more complicated cocktails to create, so watch how the bartender makes it. Too much Cointreau and not enough lemon juice leaves the drinker in a sticky situation. So take great care.

The origin of this fine cocktail is shrouded in mystery, although it is always associated with an army captain and his chauffeur-driven motorcycle sidecar in Paris during World War I. It's one classic guaranteed to take you back in time to the quiet backstreets of a darkened Paris at war.

What cocktail historians do know is that a recipe appeared in Harry Craddock's *The Savoy Cocktail Book*, which was first published in England in 1930, so either the cocktail caught his eye during an earlier trip to Paris, or a customer may have asked for it and given him the recipe. Harry Craddock's recipe doubled the amount of brandy in this version of the sour-like Sidecar.

During your next trip to Paris, walk along the small side street that is rue Daunou, in the second Arrondisement, and you'll easily imagine a motorcycle sidecar pulling up outside number 5, an unassuming joint, the door being pushed open and a man of military bearing stepping inside for a Sidecar to quench his desire.

Whether it was created by bartender Harry at Harry's New York Bar in Paris is uncertain. Duncan MacElhone, Harry's grandson, admits its history is confusing. Perhaps one day we will find out. Until then, try this recipe.

Cocktail Recipe

Sidecar

1 oz. (30 ml) brandy
⅔ oz. (22 ml) Cointreau
⅔ oz. (22 ml) fresh lemon juice
lemon wedge as garnish

Pour the ingredients into a shaker with cracked ice.
Shake and strain into an ice-cold cocktail glass.
Garnish with a discreet lemon wedge.

Singapore Sling

One simply cannot travel to Singapore without walking into the bar at Raffles Hotel and ordering a Singapore Sling. Along with the sublime taste of the cocktail, one has to take in the ambience of a bar where history was life, or life is history depending upon how many you have.

A sling can be traced back to 1759, its name perhaps being derived from the German word "schlingen," meaning to swallow quickly. Its origin is uncertain and there could even be a connection to the Collins.

This original recipe, adored by expatriate Brits living in the Far East, is refreshing. This version of the Singapore Gin Sling was created at Raffles Hotel in 1915 by bartender Ngiam Tong Boon. He had created a long and exotic cocktail his female customers liked to sip. That way they could enjoy watching and being watched.

By 1930, however, the cocktail known as the Singapore Sling had arrived in Europe and the United States, without its fruit juices and reduced to gin, cherry brandy, fresh lemon juice and soda.

To really enjoy a Singapore Sling you have to go back to its roots, to a region where fruit juices abound, frangipani leaves are au naturel and the pineapples are as common as sirens on a bad day in Manhattan. It's the kind of long, tall sling you drink while slinking in a hammock, your arms slung over your head in that oh-so-chic casual way, and your eyes are on the talent across the pool. The heady mix of gin, cherry brandy, Benedictine, fresh lime juice (there really is no other taste like it), the tang of fresh orange and pineapple juices need to be sipped slowly though a straw to while away the time. It's a cocktail made for Paradise.

Whichever recipe you prefer, always use fresh ingredients for that extra flavor.

Cocktail Recipe

Singapore Sling

$^1/_2$ oz. (15 ml) gin
$^1/_2$ oz. (15 ml) cherry brandy
$^1/_4$ oz. (8 ml) Cointreau
$^1/_4$ oz. (8 ml) Benedictine
$^1/_4$ oz. (8 ml) lime juice
2 oz. (60 ml) orange juice
2 oz. (60 ml) pineapple juice
slice of pineapple to garnish
maraschino cherry to garnish

Pour the ingredients into a shaker with ice. Shake
and strain into a highball with ice. Garnish with a
pineapple slice and a maraschino cherry and serve
with a straw and a stirrer.

Tom Collins

A Collins is a summer drink, similar in style to a sling. You might be confused as to which Collins is which. If you think of them as a family, you have a Tom and a John. The John Collins was the first of the two long and refreshing cocktails to be created.

The most-quoted story of its humble origins can be traced back to a John Collins, the headwaiter at a hotel and coffee-house named Limmer's, in London, around 1790. His original version used genever, a Dutch-style gin, with the addition of soda water, lemon and sugar.

It wasn't until the 1880s that the drink surfaced in America, where it was viewed as a type of gin sling. When an enterprising bartender used Old Tom gin, a London gin with a sweet flavor, the Collins became known as a Tom Collins. However, in America the gin was replaced with whiskey and thus it became a John Collins.

This story gives you an idea of just how muddled the history of some cocktails is, although by tracing the records of gin companies and ancient recipe books the truth might one day be known.

When asking for one of these delicious refreshing cocktails, check which one the bartender knows. Someone once alluded to an extended family of Collins cocktails, but to most purists there are still only the two brothers. If you wanted them to have a cousin, then perhaps the Singapore Sling might qualify.

The interesting thing about the Collins is that a glass shape was made to show off the cocktail at its best. Many recipes state "a collins glass," which holds up to 14 oz. and retains the effervescence, but in reality you can't find many in stores today. Now most people use a highball glass – which is slightly shorter, has a wider neck, but still holds the fizz well.

Cocktail Recipe

Tom Collins

2 oz. (60 ml) London dry gin
1 oz. (30 ml) fresh lemon juice
2 dashes gomme syrup
soda water
maraschino cherry as garnish
lime or orange slice as garnish

Add the gin, lemon juice and syrup to a collins
or highball glass filled with lots of ice. Top up
with soda. Add a slice of orange and a
maraschino cherry if you live on the East Coast
of America, and a cherry and a slice of lime if
you live on the West Coast. Serve with a stirrer.

White Lady

Lo! What pale and wan creature inspired this classic cocktail? Someone must have been the muse behind the name of this one, created by legendary bartender Harry MacElhone (later of Harry's New York Bar in Paris) while he was working at Ciro's Club, in London.

Imagine this: the year was 1919. The night was chilly. Snow was probably thick on the ground. The bar was busy when a woman in white walked in, a vision to behold, snow flecks glinting and melting in her hair. To Harry, this meant only one thing: crème de menthe, Cointreau and lemon juice for the white lady. Ten years later, and without any crème de menthe, Harry substituted gin for the minty liqueur.

Fast-forward to the modern day. In Molly Keane's novel, *Good Behavior*, one of the chief protagonists drinks a White Lady cocktail intermittently throughout the entire book. So this classic, too, has found five minutes of literary fame in the 21st century.

Here is a clean, fresh and citrus-flavored cocktail with a touch of sweetness. If you make it correctly, you will achieve the ideal balance of sweet and sharp flavors. However, the big question is: what is the correct recipe?

Only a few recipes call for the original white crème de menthe, and some even call for light cream! Don't do it with cream, please! When a White Lady is made with either gin or white crème de menthe the cocktail has a pale transparency, with the lemon juice making a slight frothy finish on top. Use cream and you take away that ghostly effect.

Perfect for after dinner, the White Lady is popular with women. To change it to a Pink Lady, add a dash of grenadine. Just a dash or you'll end up with a Red Lady! And a red face to match.

Cocktail Recipe

White Lady

1 oz. (30 ml) gin
1 oz. (30 ml) Cointreau
1 oz. (30 ml) fresh lemon juice

Shake all ingredients with ice. Strain into a chilled
cocktail glass.

World Bars

It's six o'clock in the evening, you're new in town and like the idea of sliding onto a barstool, leaning your elbows on the bar and ordering a cocktail to chill out. The concierge is busy, and besides, you don't think he'd know your kind of place. Where to go?

There are bars and there are bars. Watering holes with watered-down drinks. Where the bartender responds to your request for a Caipirinha with, "A Caiprinhuh?" Where the cocktails come ready mixed, neither stirred nor shaken. Where the bartender looks like a bouncer as ready to kick you out as serve you.

Bars open with loud fanfare on a regular basis, but close with a whimper not so long afterward. Drinkers are fickle beings, and unless a bar has all of the qualities that make it a great place to hang out, drink interesting cocktails and meet even more interesting people, it isn't going to make the grade.

In this section, intrepid bar researchers have selected a final list of bars from a thousand suggestions. How were they chosen? A set of criteria was established. Of prime importance was the quality of the cocktails served, then interior style and ambience, followed by the type of clientele.

Some are more nightclubs than cocktail bars, yet they still mix and shake great cocktails behind the bar. Others are specialist bars serving only one spirit. Also included are famous bars where some of the classics were created, for instance **Harry's Bar**, Venice, birthplace of the Bellini, the **Long Bar**, at Raffles Hotel, Singapore, where the Singapore Sling was first mixed, and **La Floridita**, Havana, where the Hemingway Daiquiri poured its way into our affections.

This is a personal overview and if your favorite bar is not here, we apologize.

24-hour nightlife: Visitors to Las Vegas might never see dawn, noon, dusk or anytime in between

U.S.

Atlanta

Tongue & Groove

3055 Peachtree Road N.E., Buckhead

Couldn't resist the name of this club and late-night bar. It's named after the floor boards. Here's a free-spirited and funky scene, complete with cigars for aficionados, cognac for the discriminating drinker and whiskey, too. It has chic décor and equally chic guests, many of whom are from the ranks of the famous. This is definitely a place to dress up for. Velvet curtains let you through into a vast bar area with cool velvet stools. There is a great cocktail list and the bartenders like to invent new cocktails. On certain nights, if you're really lucky you might even get a massage and a manicure to really de-stress you.

Eleven 50

1150B Peachtree Street

A bar and art gallery venture built on the site of a former theater. Brick walls set the style for the décor, with large banquettes for those who want to survey the scene. The bar is on the mezzanine level of this chic multi-story venue in the heart of Atlanta's midtown. Live music helps Eleven 50 to rock most nights.

Halo Lounge

817 W. Peachtree Street N.W.
(entrance on 6th Street)

This relatively new club on the Midtown scene has a following among Atlanta's singles crowd. A confusing place to find because the entrance is on 6th Street, not Peachtree, but the sleek club décor,

long, narrow bar and a cool-looking crowd to match make it worth the effort. There is a wide range of expertly made, striking cocktails to sip.

Martini Club

1140 Crescent Avenue N.E.

A Midtown hangout for drinkers who appreciate the classic Martini. The bar staff mixes more than 100 different martinis, including the Garden, made with asparagus in it. Cigar lovers are also catered to, with 40-plus varieties available, some of which are flavored. Don't expect a cheap night out at this award-winning bar.

Beluga Martini Bar

3115 Piedmont Road

This is another downtown bar specializing in martinis, including the expected classics and a few that will surprise you. At Beluga, you can mix Martinis and jazz, with live music on Friday and Saturday. Why not spend a little on the other half of the house name, and eat some caviar while sipping on the Martini specialties?

Lobby Lounge

Swissotel, 3391 Peachtree Road

The Lobby Lounge is situated in the lobby of the Swissotel hotel, but it is a piano bar and there's nothing like a bit of piano music when you want to drink classic cocktails on a steamy Georgian evening. There are rotating art exhibits in the lobby every day. When the hotel is two-thirds full, they open "Life in the Lobby" — a full bar serving up classic cocktails to Atlanta travelers.

Austin

Cedar Street Courtyard

208 West Fourth Street

Cedar Street, a cocktail lounge located in the Warehouse District, with a cigar bar and live jazz and swing, calls itself "King of Gin Joints." You'll have great fun just studying the names of the house specialties, from the 007 to the Koffee Kerouac, the Yellow Cab Calloway, the Silhouette and the Killer Martini, among others. Enjoy the courtyard during the long (4–8 p.m.) happy hour every weeknight, where you can get Frozen Martinis for just $3, and complimentary food, including burgers, tacos and a pasta bar, depending on the night.

Iron Cactus Southwestern Grill & Margarita Bar

Two locations: 606 Trinity Street (Sixth Street)
10,001 Stonelake Road (North)

Scoping out the urban, L.A.-type crowd and sorting through the 80 brands of tequila will keep you entertained all night. With live music, spicy tortilla soup, elaborate desserts and the house specialty, the "El Agave" Margarita, it is no wonder this was named one of the top 10 tequila bars in the country by *Spirits and Cocktails* magazine. Other Margaritas worth trying are: Top Shelf, the Cadillac and, after a long day wandering in the desert, the Cactus Juice.

Brown Bar

201 West 8th Street

The Brown Bar offers a chic array of delicious and elegant cocktails, including the Kir Royale, Mojitos, Margaritas and the house specialties, the Brown Bar Martini – with Godiva Chocolate – and the Wedding Cake Martini. The Brown Bar doubles as a waiting room for the upscale, seafood-centered Gumbo's Restaurant. This is a place to strut yourself, but remember "life is short" when you get the bill. The décor is more East Coast than Southwestern, with a long marble bar and subtle lighting.

Boston

Abbey Lounge

3 Beacon Street, Inman Square, Somerville

A dive that seems to pride itself on being one with the motto "Cheap booze ... rock 'n roll," at Abbey Lounge beers are $2.25, well drinks only 25 cents more. In a separate room for a $5 or $6 cover you can see local indie bands get their start. It's dark and comfortable, and a nice change from the trendy, fraternity-type bars that abound in Central Square. According to the regulars, of which there are many, you'll feel like you're miles away from Boston, closer, in fact, to the heartland.

Sligo's Pub

Davis Square, Somerville

At Sligo's in Somerville, the dark, scratched-up wood betrays the lively antics that go on here nightly. The clientele is great, a frolicking combination of yuppies, Tufts kids and neighborhood regulars. There is a wonderful classic rock jukebox, but if the bartender doesn't like your selections he will freely skip them. Plenty of great Irish beers, but the house specialties are Mike's Pet Parrot, made with rum, amaretto and pineapple juice, and the Sligo Punch made with Southern Comfort. Sligo's is open at 8 a.m. for those who like a Bud for breakfast. The liquor license here dates back to the Prohibition era.

***Overleaf*: My Kinda Town:** Chicago offers all kinds of entertainment to locals and visitors alike

Lucky's

355 Congress Street

Local jazz and funk bands entertain the relaxed crowd at Lucky's four times a week at this bar-diner hybrid on Congress Street, just two blocks from Fort Point Channel. There's no sign outside, but if you follow the red glow you'll find a friendly, affluent after-work crowd. A fun place to relax and meet up with friends, but if you're looking to live up to the bar's name, you might want to head deeper into the interior.

Venu

100 Warrenton Street, Theater District

Venu, the heart of the theater district, attracts Boston's most beautiful people to gorgeous surroundings, pastel wall decoration in an art deco room. Top cocktails help to make the night go by.

Chicago

The Bar at Peninsula Chicago Hotel

108 East Superior Street

Looks like this is the place to meet and greet an important associate or to make a great first impression on a new date. Rich colors and textures combined with modern prints hanging on the walls create a lush cocktail environment. A fine selection of premium cocktails is complemented by an extensive choice of port and cigars.

Matchbox

770 North Milwaukee Avenue

A busy bar, and crowded at the best of times, this is a narrow, candle-lit space with bartenders who

have won awards for their concoctions. Yippee. There are a dozen or so coveted bar stools in this 1930s room (revived in 1995) and that's it. You have to mingle with the rest of them. Try the Chocolate Martini–style cocktail.

Narcisse Champagne Salon and Caviar Bar

710 North Clark Street

Set for seduction, this bar is a magnet for loft-dwelling, cocktail-swilling patrons. The space has a metallic ceiling, and a dark mahogany bar runs the length of the room. The crowd is wannabe models in Donna Karan. As might be expected this place is not for the faint of wallet. As well as a wide range of champagne, Narcisse's bartenders mix some mean Martinis and other cocktails from on and off a diverse menu.

The Signature Lounge

John Hancock Center,
875 North Michigan Avenue

For a night of sophisticated live jazz, the Signature Lounge, perched 96 stories above the city, is the place to go! Located atop the John Hancock Center, where you can watch Chicago come to life as you enjoy the Signature Sensation Martini.

Green Mill Cocktail Lounge

4802 N. Broadway Street

The Green Mill Cocktail Lounge was one of the famous venues of the Roaring Twenties, and its notoriety dates back to Prohibition, when Chicago gangsters – including Al Capone – used the club as a headquarters. Memorabilia from that era is shown in a corner of the bar. Today it is crowded with hip young people and jazz lovers. It probably has the world's oldest jazz bar, and Sunday nights are given over to poetry readings.

Green Dolphin Street

2200 N. Ashland Avenue, Lincoln Park

Green Dolphin Street is the largest jazz venue in Chicago, covering everything from traditional to big band to swing. And if that's not enough, pick the right night and you get R&B. Keeping with the bar's theme, try its special Dizzy Gillespie cocktail, or just choose from a full menu of other drinks and food.

Nacional 27

325 W. Huron Street

Nacional 27 is a Latino club with representative selections from 27 countries. Its specialty cocktails are made with pisco. The Pisco Sour is especially recommended. Salsa music enlivens the weekends.

Ghost

440 W. Randolph Street

The bartenders at Ghost create cocktails that bring a smile to your face. They include their Ghostini, made with vodka, a dash of Midori and a festive swizzle-stick. The sleek, futuristic styling and the beautiful people can make for a surreal, if not quite ghostly, experience.

Café Ba-Ba-Reeba

2024 N. Halsted Street

The Café Ba-Ba-Reeba in Lincoln Park features two lively bars serving suitably colorful cocktails. Don't miss the patio adorned with flowers and artwork or the Mango Sangria. There is a full menu available with great tapas and paellas. The owner-chef of Chicago's first tapas bar draws on the traditions of Spain's Basque region – where his mother comes from – and his father's Galician culture to bring a taste of Spain to hungry Chicago diners.

Cleveland

Velvet Dog

1280 West 6th Street

In the heart of the Warehouse District, this multi-level lounge features a lovely rooftop patio with both an indoor and outdoor bar and a view of the Cleveland skyline. The bamboo and tiki light decorations against the electric buildings of West 6th Street create a charming, surreal ambience. DJs spin dance-remix and retro 1980s. Specialty drinks include Electric Lemonade, Flirtini Martini and Orange Cream Sickle. Also don't miss the Chandon Splits champagne.

Bottoms Up of Cleveland

1222 Prospect Avenue East

Set in Cleveland's redeveloped Gateway district, Bottoms Up serves a range of cocktails, wines and beers. The triangular building makes for a light and airy atmosphere with windows along two sides. Downstairs is the Abbasso Lounge music venue.

Liquid Fusion

1212 West 6th Street

The liquid side of the high-class tapas attraction of the West 6th Street scene, Liquid Fusion offers 126 different martinis with delightfully evocative names such as One Night Stand, Tie Me to the Bedpost and Fallen Angel. The magical looking Blue Devil is among the most popular. In what *Cleveland Plain Dealer* reporter Clint O'Connor describes as "the blue-collar, shot-and-a-beer, non-wallop-packing, beer-bottle-hurling" city of Cleveland, you'll have fun just watching the locals puzzle through the menu.

Overleaf: **Downtown:** The Lower Downtown or LoDo district is Denver's entertainment sector

Dallas

Minc Bar

813 Exposition Avenue

"Sake bomb Sundays" begin at 7 p.m. in Minc Bar, an exotic, cosmopolitan lounge in Exposition Park. For something a bit different in cocktails, try a Hot Kiss or a Causeway Spray. From the patio you can watch the stars burn bright, deep in the heart of Texas.

Martini Ranch

2816 Fairmount Street

When you're looking for good cocktails in the Wild West, don't miss the Martini Ranch, where the Martini is "more than just a cocktail." The Dean Martini is service with a Lucky Strike and a book of matches; for the Chocolate Martini you choose whatever vodka you want, served with Godiva in a chocolate-rimmed glass. They serve Martinis individually or by the pitcher – after all, this is Texas – and offer a wide variety of food, from goat cheese baguettes to pork dumplings to cheeseburgers, fried calamari and vegetable quesadillas.

Nikita

3699 McKinney Avenue, Suite A306

Nikita, a vodka and rum bar in Dallas's vibrant West Village, attracts all the local style divas. The cocktails have some far-out names, such as Citrus Bitch, Iron Kitten and Redhead in Boots, but the fantastic service from beautiful bar staff only adds to the allure. The décor is sort of "Russia opens the Iron Curtain" with heavy drapes and drab walls but ultra-modern Scandinavian furniture. Downstairs is a restaurant, where the food on offer is definitely not a reminder of Cold War days. This Nikita is a more glamorous femme fatale than Khrushchev.

Denver

Mynt Lounge

1424 Market Street

Brightly colored, delicious cocktails double as dessert in this sleek lounge on Market Street. Try the Mojitos, served with a sugar stick to stir. In the European tradition, bar staff encourages customers to while away the afternoon and evening as long as they like, enjoying the cocktails and the work of local artists, an unusual counterpoint to the simple, elegant design with low-white booths.

Red Room

320 E. Colfax Avenue

The house specials at the Red Room include the Cosmopolitans and Doggy Style. Don't miss the tapas and the chocolate fondue for dessert. Delicious brunch on Saturday and Sunday, served with your choice of Mimosas, Bloody Marys or, for the gritty, outdoorsy types, a Red Beer to go with your omelettes and fruit platters. The Red Room was opened by the same people who run the nearby Goosetown Tavern, the low-key neighborhood bar complete with Foosball, pool and chess.

Detroit

The Bosco

22,930 Woodward, Ferndale

Bosco is a swanky lounge club in downtown Ferndale with outrageous design, cocktails and general ambience. Décor is clean lines, space, low-slung couches and tables and stools. The various rooms include a narrow front section with a bar with a white-pine counter. There are about 20 stools. Beyond this is an open-air courtyard with a waterfall and locust trees lit up in the dark. Guests sip cocktails in fold-up chairs on the lawn. Top of the cocktail list are flavored Saketails – sake stirred with a mixer and served in a carafe or by the cup.

Buddha Bar

21,633 W. 8 Mile Road

A hip spot serving cocktails despite its unlikely locale. Same name as the ultra trendy Parisian bar near the Champs Élysées. The crowd is cool yet down-to-earth and less pretentious than the one in Paris. The intimate lounge interior is dark, and drinkers can sit in booths or on couches. The décor is Asian themed, while the cocktails include strong Martinis.

Goodnite Gracie Cigar & Spirit

222 S. Sherman Drive in Washington Square Plaza, Royal Oak

A gem, Goodnite Gracie Cigar & Spirit is a classic 1940s cigar bar. Enter through a velvet curtain doorway and you are in an authentic chic dive. A large selection of cigars is available plus you can have a private humidor for storage. There are more than 30 Martinis on the list. The service is good.

The Corner

100 Townsend Street, Birmingham

The Corner is part of the Townsend Hotel in Birmingham, 25 miles northwest of downtown Detroit. The décor screams opulence: a mahogany bar counter, stools with blue suede covers, and neon-blue lighting reflected in a domed ceiling. Add delicate mosaics, huge bay windows and Old French–style beveled mirrors and it becomes obvious that style is everything. Mind you, the local clientele seems equally ready for a fashion shoot. There is a choice of 100 Martinis but the Corner's top drink is a Billionaire Margarita made with Patron Silver tequila and 100-year-old Grand Marnier.

Houston

The Social

3730 Washington Street

Chase away those Sunday night blues with "Sundown at the Social" on the first Sunday of every month, when a mix of funk and house heats up the dance floor at this trendy scene for the post-college set. Known for its colorful vodka cocktails, this Washington Corridor lounge has a retro feel and a snazzy décor.

The Mercury Room

1008 Prairie Street

For 1920s speakeasy glamor, try the art deco Mercury Room, the bar *Inside Houston* magazine named the "Hottest Place to Be Seen on a Saturday Night." Live music, a VIP lounge, the selection of classic cocktails and Humphrey Bogart wannabes smoking stogies will transport you to another era. Performers have included George Strait, Avril Lavigne, Alicia Keys, Asleep at the Wheel, Faith Hill and Tim McGraw. Guest celebrities from stage, screen, sport and television have been seen at the Mercury.

The Boaka Bar

1010 Prairie Street

This "serious dance club for the serious club goer" built in Houston's original silent movie theater, the Boaka Bar is an extravagant club featuring DJs spinning house, trance and hip-hop. A custom-made European chandelier hangs from a 45-foot ceiling over the dance floor. The DJ spins from 30 feet above the floor. A huge blue and gold drapery creates a suspended tent. The decadent Russian and Egyptian inspired ambience is further enhanced by a palace-like staircase leading to the mezzanine, which surrounds the dance floor.

Lake Tahoe

Beacon Bar & Grill

1900 Jameson Beach Road, South Lake Tahoe

For an enchanted evening lakeside in the Sierra Nevadas, try the Beacon Bar & Grill, located at the Camp Richardson Resort & Marina. It is the home of the Rumrunner, voted the Best Drink in Tahoe for eight years according to a local newspaper. After dinner, take a walk along the beach and watch the moon light up the mountains and the lake. The Rumrunner is so good it may give you a run for your money, but this is worth it for the view alone.

The Tudor Pub

1041 Freemont Avenue

If the West Coast leaves you longing for the good beer and cheer of an authentic British-style tavern, head to the cozy Tudor Pub, offering a first-rate selection of British beers and ales on tap. Owner Keith Simpson, originally from Surrey, comes with a high recommendation – he catered for the Royal Family. Spend the night (after skiing) by the fireplace with a pint of Fullers London Pride, or stop by the award-winning Dory's Oar downstairs for dinner. If you're still thirsting for cocktails, however, you have to try the Elvis Liquid Love – made with Absolut Citron – or the Chocolate Tini, served in a chocolate-rimmed glass.

Las Vegas

V Bar

Venetian Hotel-Casino, 3355 S. Las Vegas Boulevard

V-Bar's stylish, low-key, comfy but elegant interior and ever-expanding cocktail selection are perfect after a night of wheeling and dealing. Located at the Venetian Hotel-Casino, V-bar is the brainchild of David Rabin and Will Regan, co-owners of Lotus in New York, and Brad Johnson, who currently owns Menemsha in L.A. They opened V-Bar to bring a sleek, minimalist New York style to the glitzy city. With that hook they've attracted tons of stars from Shaq to Dennis Quaid, Jerry Bruckheimer, Puffy and Ja Rule. George Clooney was often seen during the filming of *Ocean's 11*.

Risqué

Paris Hotel, 3655 S. Las Vegas Boulevard

Risqué is an ultra cool nightclub with daybeds for seating. It is just one of six bars and 11 restaurants at the enormous Paris Hotel.

Rain Bar / Ghostbar

Palms Hotel, 4321 W. Flamingo Road

The most happening nightspots at Palms Hotel are Rain and Ghostbar. The latter is on the 55th floor and is more exclusive. Leonardo DiCaprio held his birthday party there in 2002. Be ready to line up and pay a steep cover charge.

Light

Bellagio Hotel, 3600 S. Las Vegas Boulevard

One thousand orchestrated fountains from this multi-million dollar collection of art; you can dine beneath original Picassos and marvel at the lobby's 2,000 hand-blown glass flowers in a work by Dale Chihuly. Oh, and cocktails are served in the Light Bar somewhere amidst all this art. In fact, Light is just one of six bars in the Bellagio and each is distinctly different from the other in ambience and specialty cocktails.

Le Strip: The neon-lit Eiffel Tower means this can only be the Paris Hotel, Las Vegas

Caramel

Bellagio Hotel, 3600 S. Las Vegas Boulevard

A new bar modeled on mega-chic New York lounges. Numerous celebrities – including Bruce Willis, Jewel, Luke Wilson and Christian Slater – turned up for the opening night in March 2003. Low-slung furniture and wheat-grass planters, votive candles, Apple Martinis, all behind the velvet ropes. Clientele is slightly older sophisticated club-goers.

Fontana Lounge

Bellagio Hotel, 3600 S.. Las Vegas Boulevard

Go to Fontana in the Bellagio Hotel for the rich, sultry atmosphere – velvet curtains and fountain views – as well as the delectable cocktails such as the Metropolitan made with rock candy syrup, the Fresh Peach Bellini, the Bellagio Cocktail (made with Italian sparkling wine and fresh fruit purée) and the 430 made with guava nectar. A cabaret stage features live entertainment nightly. If you're looking for love, you might try your luck on the patio; the scene there is classic seductive Vegas, old-school style.

Los Angeles

Bar Marmont

Chateau Marmont, 8171 W. Sunset Boulevard at Havenhurst Drive

Bar Marmont is in the famous Sunset Strip hotel, Chateau Marmont, where the great and the good have been coming to stay for more than 70 years. An extravagant place to die for, it's where you will spot the stars you want to see, if they come by the bar. Fabulous luxury inspires fabulous cocktails served by fabulous waiters. It's dream heaven in the City of Angels.

Goldfingers

423 Yucca Street

Pussy Galore is in the cockpit at this amazing club, with giant chandeliers, black booths and gold lamé padded walls as the décor – 1960s interior style at its most mod. Martinis are Goldfingers' specialties, shaken – not stirred – we trust.

Sky Bar

The Mondrian Hotel, 8440 Sunset Boulevard

An Ian Shrager hotel full of hype and glamor and, as usual, a great bar. The pool terrace becomes a bar at night. This is definitely a bar for the sophisticated set. The views of the city from Sky Bar are matched only by the beauty of the waitresses, all of whom seem to be models between jobs or "resting" actresses.

Standard Bar

The Standard Hotel, 8300 W. Sunset Boulevard

Swanky cocktail sipping on sofas in the paneled Lobby bar here, right near the Sky Bar location, so if you didn't get into the Mondrian, you might make it here. Slick place and same type of people. If you fancy it, you can play ping-pong on the terrace or, if voyeurism is your thing, there are telescopes to look through. Beware: this is not a bar for those on a tight budget.

The Mint

6010 W. Pico Boulevard

The Mint serves great rum cocktails. The recommendation is that you try the Acid Trip, and even if it doesn't conjure up images of Janis and Jimi, it may transport you off to a groovier time. You can enjoy yourself in the present at The Mint with its menu of jazz, blues and dinner.

Deep

1707 N. Vine Street, cnr Hollywood Boulevard

Louche bar for louche cocktails in a basement where the glamor boys and girls go to get chilled. Erotic dancers groove in French boudoirs sited behind the bar as a tempting special effect.

Good Luck Bar

154 Hillhurst Avenue, Hollywood

Want to try Pacific-style drinking? The Good Luck Bar is a chic Hollywood after-hours Polynesian bar which fits the bill perfectly.

Lava Lounge

1533 N. La Brea Avenue

Enter Lava Lounge, a black-walled, hardcore music and cocktail lounge-lizard bar, at your own risk!

Formosa Café

7156 Santa Monica Boulevard at Formosa Avenue, South Hollywood

Legendary is a word that suits the Formosa, which is more restaurant than bar, but it does have a great top shelf. The walls are adorned with black and-white photographs of Hollywood stars, past and present, and you can sit there knowing you're sitting in the bar where the movie L.A. Confidential was shot.

The Derby Club

4500 Los Feliz Boulevard, Hollywood

Here's a very chic, 1940s swing bar that's perfect for sipping Martinis late at night. The Derby Club's house special, the Derby Punch, is definitely well worth sampling.

Sunset Trocadero Lounge

8280 W. Sunset Boulevard, West Hollywood

If you want to drink the best cocktails in L.A. and feel like a movie star for one night, then spend a night at the Sunset Trocadero Lounge! Music is pop, Latin, acid jazz, hip-hop. Try PCH Liquid Sunshine and the Doheny Martini.

The Firm

6311 Wilshire Boulevard, Hollywood

Get there late and you may have to wait, but the scene inside is worth it, with players and wannabes all sharing the couches. Take advantage of the Firm's penchant for new-style Martinis, such as the Black Martini.

Crazy Jack's Country Bar & Grill

4311 W. Magnolia Boulevard, Burbank

Crazy Jack's, in Burbank, serves up such classic cocktails as the Slippery Nipple. Whether or not that name puts you in a laughing mood, this bar and restaurant is not far from where The Tonight Show is recorded. Go to watch Jay Leno for your laughs and get your cocktails at Crazy Jack's.

The Four Seasons Hotel Gardens

690 Newport Center Drive, Newport Beach

The Four Seasons is always classy and this hotel lounge does not disappoint. Relax in this elegant resting place with pleasant views of the pool and foliage and enjoy the Martinis and the live entertainment.

Overleaf: **That's entertainment:** Top bars are just part of Hollywood and Los Angeles' attraction

Joe's Café

536 State Street, Santa Barbara

Opened in 1928, it still has its old-fashioned charm. Joe's Café is known for superb drinks, with a full bar range and a fine bartender who knows all the classics.

Miami

Rose Bar

Delano Hotel, 1685 Collins Avenue, Miami Beach

International interior designer Philippe Starck created the Rose Bar, a shrine in this exclusive hotel on the oceanfront in the heart of the Art Deco District. The hotel is a short walk from the bistros, shops, and galleries of South Beach. Delano is a favorite haunt of rock and movie stars.

Azul

Mandarin Oriental Hotel, 500 Brickell Key Drive

On the third floor of the Mandarin Oriental Hotel, Azul offers views of Biscayne Bay from inside the bar or on the outdoor terrace. The restaurant was designed by Tony Chi of New York and has a white marble-clad open kitchen and "raw" bar. The cocktail bar serves great Martinis and good wines.

Les Deux Fontaines

Golden Tulip Ocean Hotel, 1230 Ocean Drive

A bar serving more than 25 different martinis, with a correspondingly broad choice of cigars. The hotel's restaurant, of the same name, is highly regarded.

New Orleans

The Red Room

2040 Saint Charles Avenue

The most interesting part of this retro supper club is that it includes pieces of the Eiffel Tower, brought to the Big Easy in the 1970s and reassembled here. The night begins with live music – big band, a salsa band, swing or jazz – then turns into a wilder dance floor with DJs. The glass-enclosed cocktail lounge encircles the sophisticated supper club, where lush red décor abounds.

Whiskey Blue

W Hotel, 333 Poydras Street

You may be singing the blues in this bar when the check comes, but it will have been worthwhile in this glamorous hotel. Blue is the theme, but that was obvious from the luminous blue entrance. Inside the Whiskey Blue, everything is designed for comfort, from the great cocktails to the leather club chairs.

Coyote Ugly Saloon

225 N. Peters Street

Not to be outdone by New York's Coyote Ugly – featured on the big screen in the 2000 movie of the same name – the hot, wild, lightning-quick moves of the all-female bartenders here will keep customers on their toes, as long as they're still standing. The cheap beer and discarded bras define this rowdy, estrogen-empowered establishment that *The Times-Picayune* of New Orleans describes as "Hooters meets Urban Cowboy." Capturing the wacky charm of New Orleans, it is tucked away in the French Quarter, and worth a visit for the atmosphere alone.

Previous page: **Life's a Beach:** Great weather, super bars and fine architecture are Miami features
Right: **The Big Easy:** It is easy to enjoy yourself in the myriad bars in New Orleans' French Quarter

Bombay Club

Prince Conti Hotel, 830 Conti Street

Located in the heart of the French Quarter, the Bombay Club is less than a block from Bourbon Street. It features casual late dining in an elegant atmosphere, or you can select one of 115 Martini-style cocktails from an extensive cocktail list. There is also a magnificent range of expensive cognacs.

New York

Apt

419 W. 13th Street (at 9th Avenue)

For years the owners of Apt didn't even publish their address – the bar didn't have a telephone either – but they have now relented. Too cool for words, comic duo Andrew and Andrew are in charge of guest DJs who get seven minutes to mix their tracks. It's tough to get in through the large green metal doors in the Meatpacking District but, hey, when wasn't it!

Milk and Honey

134 Eldridge Street (Lower East Side)

You need the phone number before you get past the door and grab one of five tables in this corridor-shaped bar on the Lower East Side. The place is run like a Prohibition bar. Open until dawn, it serves fab cocktails. Go late when it is less busy.

Craft Bar

43 E. 19th Street

This small bar is attached to Tom Colicchio's restaurant of the same name. Great cocktails, and the food is both excellent and reasonably priced.

Bungalow 8

515 W. 27th Street

In the revived and vibrant Chelsea West neighborhood, Bungalow 8 is just a block from the waterfront and close to the popular Chelsea Piers. An interior boasting palm trees galore, Amy Sacco's bar is based on the Bungalow 8 at the Beverly Hills Hotel.

Serena

Chelsea Hotel, 222 W. 23rd Street

Under the fabled Chelsea Hotel, home to many famous writers and artists – including Dylan Thomas, William Burroughs and Sid Vicious (who died there) – Serena is a dark place with a bordello-like interior décor. It serves suitably dive-y cocktails. Serena still occasionally attracts stars from the worlds of rock, stage and screen, but this is more a place for relaxing with a long drink than for staring at the glitterati.

A60 Bar

Thompson Hotel, 60 Thompson Street

The private rooftop bar of the Thompson Hotel is still the place to be in summer. Very chic with lots of Armani and L.A. types, A60 Bar has amazing views of the Hudson River as well as downtown and uptown vistas. Purple is the key to entry. The hotel's public bar, Thom's, is on the second floor.

Barmacy

538 E. 14th Street
(between Avenues A and B)

A doctors and nurses theme bar with alcoholic potions dispensed to perk you up. Barmacy is popular so be prepared for a crowd. The cocktails are typically New York – strong, no messing.

Town

Chambers Hotel, 15 W. 56th Street

In the luxurious Chambers Hotel, Town is a central Manhattan bar with cocktails in a sleek environment. It is the hangout of bankers and publishers. The bar overlooks the high-quality Chambers Restaurant, which is known for truffles in season. In winter, head a few blocks downtown for the skating at the Rockefeller Center; in any weather, a few blocks uptown will get you to Manhattan's great Central Park.

Pastis

9 Ninth Avenue, Little W. 12th Street, West Village

Keith McNally's latest bistro bar is always full of interesting folk. An unrivaled bistro-of-the-moment, snugly hidden deep within the cobblestone streets of the Meatpacking District, is regularly visited by celebrities: Madonna has been spotted there. McNally has created a new low-attitude, friendly place that's noisy, busy and French. He even imported two painters from Paris to observe the clientele. He doesn't mind people painting, playing chess or kissing even, but he's not fond of people talking on cellphones. Switch it off and leave it off if you want to go back. The food is good, but you don't go to Pastis to eat. Stick to bistro staples like steak-frites and frisée salads. Come for the cocktails and olives or a late-night snack in the unreserved front room.

The Four Seasons Restaurant and Bar

99 E. 52nd Street

The Four Seasons Restaurant, located in Midtown Manhattan in the Seagram Building, is considered to have one of the most beautiful dining rooms in the world. Designed in 1959 by Ludwig Mies Van Der Rohe and Philip Johnson, the Four Seasons is the only Manhattan restaurant that is also an architectural landmark. Now a listed building, this 70s-style bar is really wonderful, located in one corner of a vast room and designed in a large square. The bar stools are the right height, and the bartenders are friendly and can make real classic cocktails with flair. A Cosmopolitan is compulsory, as is staring in awe at the 70s décor looking as good as new in the 21st century. The place for journalists, publishing people and retro design fans.

Hudson Bar

Hudson Hotel, 356 W. 58th Street

Arriving at Ian Shrager's Hudson Hotel at night is an experience in itself. The escalator quietly drifts you up in a glow of bright light and then the noise hits you (loud, loud music thuds in your head) as you reach the reception area located in a vast foyer. Run through here as quick as you can and head to the right and the long walk to the outdoor bar area where you can order any cocktail in town and it will taste fine. A home-away-from-home for pop stars like J-Lo and Madonna, and other music biz types, it's a great bar but not with what you might call friendly staff. The old schmoozer Bill Clinton was seen there recently leaving with a team of bodyguards, only to be hugged from the sidelines by a female friend dressed in Chanel. Boy, did he smile!

Suite 16

127 Eighth Avenue

There are 16 exclusive banquette booths – suites – in this bar with a hotel theme. Beautiful people make a real effort here, but it may all be undone in the gaps between the booths. The cocktails are in keeping with everything else at Suite 16, top-quality and definitely high-octane.

***Overleaf*. Never asleep:** Times Square in New York makes 24/7 seem almost part-time

Potion Lounge

370 Columbus Avenue

A popular European-style lounge on the Upper West Side, Potion Lounge is known for colorful and unique cocktails served in what look like chemistry set beakers by stylish staff. Water-filled walls could make you shiver but once you're inside the leather booths, under the moody, blue lighting and have had a few sips of one of their awesome special layered liqueur drinks, you'll be fine. Try the signature potion drinks: two great ones are the Love Potion – made with peach schnapps and an array of layered fruit juices – and the Ocean Potion – made with blue curaçao and Malibu rum. If you're there early enough in nice weather, feel the magical effects of whatever potion you choose with a stroll around the grand Museum of Natural History.

Verlaine

110 Rivington Street
(between Ludlow and Essex)

Recommended by New York's leading cocktail consultant, this is a great bar created by Gary Williams of 147 fame. Verlaine, named after the French poet, is a little slice of Vietnam in downtown Manhattan, not only with the food but also with cocktails, such as Sake Cosmo and Vietnamese Mary. The décor is very relaxed, with apricot-colored walls and banquettes covered in soft furry black fabric. Comfort always makes you want to linger and so will the cocktails.

Pravda

281 Lafayette Street

At Pravda, in the heart of SoHo, the bartenders make a Vespa with vodka, dry gin and Lillet with a lemon twist. Welcome to spy heaven. The passion fruit Bohemian will transport you to the politically charged climate of a bygone era.

Remedy

E. 20th Street (near Park Avenue South)

Remedy is a bar/nightclub with dining room. The cool clientele work their cellphones, while stretching lithe legs along the low seating as a crystal chandelier revolves overhead. A full-length glass wall lets you look out from inside and vice versa. The cocktail menu features custom-blended sakes infused with dried lemons, rose petals, Asian teas, ginger and vanilla, served in little ceramic cups and carafes to a background of Stevie Wonder songs.

Palm Beach

Bliss

313 Clematis Street, West Palm Beach

Bliss is velvet couches and red-leather banquettes lit in a decadent glow. The walls are draped in crimson velvet and the love seat sofas are kooky. Champagne or vodka-based cocktails will be delivered to your table in the three VIP sections.

Monkey Club

219 Clematis Street, West Palm Beach

The Monkey Club bar's décor is island inspired, with wood plantation-style shutter windows, French doors and tall palm trees obscuring gazebos. It is a haunt for trendy and tanned clubsters looking like they just came in from the beach. A vast dance floor invites you to dance along, a drink in hand.

E.R. Bradley's Saloon

104 Clematis Street, West Palm Beach

Very stiff Margaritas and Cosmopolitans are the drinks of choice at E.R. Bradley's on the seafront.

Philadelphia

Alma de Cuba

1623 Walnut Street

Stephen Starr, one of Philadelphia's top restaurateurs, teamed up with celebrity chef Douglas Rodriguez to create Alma de Cuba, an ultra-trendy, Cuba-themed restaurant-bar. It gives a romantic view of pre-Castro Cuba with touches of the present-day country – images of Habana Vieja streets and people projected onto the walls downstairs. Cuban metal sculptures are by the bar, and fruity classics – Mojitos and Daiquiris – served behind it. The opulent first-floor lounge has dark tables covered in red glass mosaic tiles. Latino background music completes the ambience.

Avenue B

260 Avenue of the Arts
(corner of Broad & Spruce Streets)

Avenue B is opposite the new Kimmel Center for the Performing Arts, but there are more than a few works of art here; the multi-roomed bar and restaurant combine glitz and glamour. For example, the piano lounge invites upmarket types to sit on ivory-upholstered banquettes listening to music from a black, refurbished 1902 Steinway grand piano. The lively bar-lounge is set around a dark, oval-shaped African wood counter, while the main dining room has ornate bronze-framed French windows.

Continental

134 Market Street

This bar-restaurant has been featured on MTV's *Sex in the 90s* series and earned awards from magazines as diverse as *Food and Wine* and *Playboy*. Continental's décor reinforces the classic cocktails image: even the lamps are designed to look like a Martini olive skewered by a toothpick. The Martinis are innovative and imaginative and include chocolate and raspberry flavors. The bar food is equally good.

Pod

3636 Sansom Street

Here, your seats are plastic pods straight out of *Brave New World*, and the giant, red-foam sculpture in the bar is actually for sitting on. Lit from below by white neon, the bar counter is made of a translucent amber resin. Pod's drinks are as chic as the modern Asian décor and food, with a selection of flavored sakes and colorful cocktails. For designated drivers or those not drinking alcohol, there are even Japanese sodas to savor.

Swann Lounge

Four Seasons Hotel,
18th Street and the Benjamin Franklin Parkway

The Swann Lounge is the best hotel bar in town, offering outstanding style, service and sophistication. The bar's selection of Scotch and cognacs is exceptional, while the staff specializes in Martinis and Cosmopolitans. The fireplace and the antique piano, plus the Swann Memorial Fountain outside, are all attractions here.

Trust

121–127 S. 13th Street

This retro-hip spot offers eclectic décor, magnificent food and fantastic – in more ways than one – drinks. Trust has a selection of "electronic cocktails," containing illuminated ice cubes that glow in the drink. There is a granite-topped circular bar for 28, a space-age lounge seating 20 and a communal washroom decorated to look like a swimming pool. The pretentiousness doesn't extend to the clientele.

Portland

The Gypsy

625 N.W. 21st Avenue

This laid-back restaurant has both upper and lower lounges. The lower lounge is especially for cigar aficionados so they can smoke to their heart's content.

Momo

725 S.W. 10th Street

This out-of-the-way haunt, which features a back patio as well as DJs spinning electronica and house, is home to the young after-work crowd as well as neighborhood prowlers. Come to Momo if you're looking for dinner to accompany your cocktails, or if you just want to let loose on the dance floor.

East Chinatown Lounge

322 N.W. Everett Street

A dark, mysterious, pan-Asian style bar on Everett, the East Chinatown Lounge features a variety of intriguing cocktails, including the Blackberry Kazi. The rugged/chic décor has a very woodsy, Northwest feel. You can get well drinks for just $2 during weekday happy hours. Don't let the unisex bathrooms take you by surprise.

San Diego

Hotel Del Coronado

Del Mar

Set on a beach in the pretty seaside village of Del Mar, just north of San Diego, the Hotel Del Coronado is a destination hotel with elegance and

romance in spades. It's probably the most famous hotel in America. Greta Garbo, Charlie Chaplin, Marilyn Monroe, Sly Stallone and Steven Spielberg have stayed here; and it is rumored that Edward VII (before he became King of England and then abdicated) romanced Mrs. Wallis Simpson here. Classic cocktails are served in the bar.

The Whaling Bar

La Valencia Hotel, Clifftop site above La Jolla

If you're looking for perfect weather and beautiful beach, head for La Jolla. While there, check out The Whaling Bar, which is a hit with tourists and locals alike for cocktails. The oak-paneled Long Bar was once frequented by author Raymond Chandler and Frank Sinatra.

The Bitter End

770 Fifth Avenue

The Bitter End is a multi-roomed, three-floored café/club-bar in the oldest building in San Diego's Gaslamp Quarter. A hangout for the local glitter crowd, it has an upstairs lounge with purple walls, ceiling frescos, sofas, overstuffed chairs, tapestries, antiques and two marble fireplaces. Cocktails include over 20 martinis mixed behind a 40-foot-long mahogany bar counter. Their signature cocktail is the Black Martini made with Absolut, Kahlua, chilled espresso and a whisk of cream and served in double cocktail glass.

On Broadway

615 Broadway

An all-in-one entertainment center close to the Gaslamp Quarter, On Broadway has three lounges, a bar called Ruby Red, live music and great food.

Retro chic: San Diego's historic Gaslamp Quarter has turned into the city's vibrant new hub

Martini Ranch and Shaker Room

528 F Street

A high-end stylish haunt for the cocktail connoisseur, the multi-award-winning Martini Ranch and Shaker Room is located in the historic Gaslamp Quarter. Clientele are mostly laid-back successful southern Californians. The split-level building has five bars, a dance floor, a patio and two plush mezzanine lounges with private booths, sofas, wingback chairs and ottomans. Bar staff can shake up more than 30 cocktails ranging from the 007 to the Tombstone.

Red Circle Café

420 E Street

Retro-chic Russian vodka bars are now big business and this vast, upscale vodka and champagne bar is an outstanding example. The interior design harks back Soviet style. Russian military uniforms adorn the walls as well as murals of pre- and post-Stalin life. Fab faux fur softens the entrance, silver curtains frame the high windows. The vodka selection is exceptional; there are more than 100, from 18 countries, to choose from.

San Francisco

Redwood Bar

Clift Hotel, 495 Geary Street

Designed by Philippe Starck, the bar is carved from redwood and sits in a vast space. Once a traditional bar, it now has trademarks of the Starck look, which include a tall, yellow-lit bar display and digital screens displaying individual portraits which might wink at you when you're watching. You may begin to wonder what was in your last cocktail and meander back to the plush tables away from that stare.

Top of the Mark

Number One Nob Hill

Perched high atop San Francisco's legendary Nob Hill, the Top of the Mark's extraordinary views and colorful history have drawn locals and visitors to this sophisticated landmark since it first opened in 1939. Located on the 19th floor of the Mark Hopkins Inter-Continental Hotel, the Mark first became famous during World War II, when Pacific-bound servicemen gathered there for a final toast before shipping out. Renovated in 1996, the Mark features an elevated mahogany dance floor surrounded by comfortable sofas, classic settees and elegantly upholstered chairs. Take the California Street cable car to the top of the hill.

Bix

56 Gold Street (between Montgomery & Sansome Streets)

Bix is consistently voted one of the best bars in America. It is part jazz bar, part supper club tucked away in a tiny alley just far enough away from the hustle and bustle. The atmosphere is 1930s retro, so Martinis are a must.

Matrix

3138 Fillmore Street

Posh red booths, felt walls and a roaring fire attract the young and the beautiful. Located in the heart of über-trendy Cow Hollow. But don't look for a big neon sign: part of the appeal of this watering hole is the simple exterior. The Matrix bar opened in 2001, but it is in a building with a famous rock history. In the late 1960s, the Doors, the Grateful Dead and Jefferson Airplane all played concerts at the Matrix, which closed in 1972.

No escape: While Alcatraz, middle background, may be closed, San Francisco is alive and kicking

Harry Denton's Starlight Room

Sir Francis Drake Hotel, 450 Powell Street

Located on the 21st floor of the Sir Francis Drake Hotel, Harry Denton's Starlight Room is an elegant old-time nightclub and bar, offering an incredible 180-degree view of the City by the Bay. The Starlight Orchestra gets crowds moving in the evenings with jazz, Motown, disco, funk and soul. The 1930s-style lounge is well known for the Cable Car Martini, made with spiced rum and Cointreau; the Tom Sweeny Martini, made with crème de cassis; and the Grand Fashion, or Millennium Cocktail, made with a rouge aperitif wine. Sean Penn, Sharon Stone and Michael Stipe are among the Starlight Room's many prestigious guests.

Julie's Supper Club

1123 Folsom Street (south of Market)

Opened in 1987 in the heart of San Francisco's SoMa district, Julie's Supper Club is famous for great cocktails and an array of free tantalizing appetizers during the 5–7:30 p.m. happy hour. The Supper Club menu is wonderfully diverse, with offerings from vegetarian lasagna with a pesto tomato sauce to grilled salmon with thyme and braised lamb shank. You'll love the campy 1950s/1960s décor too.

Amber

718 14th Street

A lounge bar with modern retro décor, Amber replaced the Zodiac in 2002. Its popularity stems from the fact that because it is an owner-staffed establishment, and smoking is permitted. In non-smoking California, this makes it a haven for ex–New Yorkers. Peach Mojitos are the house specialty. There are exhibitions featuring local artists to create an interesting counterpoint to the zebra-print rugs and trendy cocktails.

Vesuvio

255 Columbus Avenue

Vesuvio channels the spirits of Jack Kerouac and Allen Ginsberg in their old haunt in North Beach just across from the famous City Lights Bookstore. Established in 1948, Vesuvio is open every day of the year. House drinks include, of course, the Jack Kerouac, served in a bucket glass, and Bohemian Coffee made with brandy, amaretto and a twist of lemon. Rotating displays of local artwork open on the 1st and 15th of every month. The 2nd-floor view of Jack Kerouac Alley and the Columbus/Broadway intersection make for great people watching and you don't have to shout over loud music to be heard.

Specs

12 Saroyan Place

On Columbus and the tiny William Saroyan Alley, this former speakeasy and Alaska Fisherman's club is hidden across the street from Vesuvio. A chill, nautical atmosphere (complete with hanging shark jaw) attracts all kinds. Despite its central location in North Beach, finding a seat, even on a Friday night, is not a problem. In a travel guide to San Francisco, *The New York Times* wrote that this "old-fashioned watering hole" is "worth looking for." You'll be amused by the giant pieces of Monterey Jack cheese on sale.

Santa Fe

El Mason La Cocina de Espana

213 Washington Avenue

Don't miss the signature sangria served at this charming Spanish restaurant in Santa Fe. The sangria is a traditional recipe made with a splash of brandy and handed down by generations of the Heurtas family; owner David Heurtas opened El Mason at this venue in 1997. The dinner menu includes such delicacies as Mediterranean Mussels, and Rice Pudding Catalunyan Style. With his wife, Kelly, David opened an adjoining tapas bar called Chispa with a full bar and a wine list that includes a wonderful selection of sherries and liqueurs imported from Spain.

Swig

135 W. Palace Avenue

Santa Fe meets New York in this lively five-room, three-bar restaurant/lounge/bar. A bit pricey, but the lush interior and balcony seating with a spectacular view of sunset adds significant value, and the free pool tables help the dent in the wallet. When you've had enough chillies, tamales and guacamole in this high desert located in the beautiful Sangre de Cristo Mountains, Swig offers a diverse pan-Asian/global menu.

Seattle

Baltic Room

1207 Pine Street

Make a night of it by heading first to the Baltic Room on lower Capitol Hill. Close to the Cha Cha Lounge, it has a trendier after-work crowd, with its own spectacle of blues bands, torch singers, energetic DJs and a balcony from which to survey the scene. Owner Linda Derschang also owns Linda's Tavern at 707 East Pine – known for DJs who spin every Monday and Thursday. The ambience at the Baltic Room is low-key romantic. You'll find some great Brit pop here along with an Anglophile wait staff. The signature cocktail is a Baltic Butterfly, made with Absolut Mandarin, Absolut Citron, Campari, triple sec, cranberry and orange.

Oliver's

Mayflower Park Hotel, 405 Olive Way

If you think mid-afternoon Martinis are a thing of the past, think again. This charming, European-style bar in the Mayflower Park Hotel – with waiters in tuxedos, sparkling chandeliers, 20-foot-high ceilings and huge windows – takes you back to the elegant but unpretentious cocktail hour of a more glamorous era. This downtown Seattle landmark, Frasier's favorite nightspot in the eponymous sitcom, features the Classic Martini, voted the city's best since 1993, famous for its vermouth-soaked olives and how vigorously it is shaken.

Cha Cha Lounge

506 E. Pine Street

A flashy, over-the-top Mexican atmosphere (booths decorated with Mexican wrestlers and sombreros), employees who double as musicians in favorite local bands and strong, cheap drinks create a fast, smoky, loud, adrenaline-filled scene in the Capitol Hill district. In case you're worried you'll miss out on the Seattle experience with this south-of-the-border style, Cha Cha is teeming over with punk and indie rockers, and their grunge counterparts, still kicking around, nearly a decade after the grunge movement came to a close for the rest of the country.

Tucson

Kon Tiki Lounge

4625 E. Broadway

Frat boys and anyone looking for a good time flock to this spot, especially on weekends. Everything about it is wonderfully unchic: you need a bright cocktail full of vodka and blue curaçao to match the awful shirt you bought that day for just such a bar. It also does a fairly great Cantaloupe Martini and a mean Scorpion Bowl.

The Shelter

4155 E. Grant Road

This Shelter presents the world's best collection of everything to do with President John F. Kennedy. You can also knock back tasty Singapore Slings in the best retro dive around town. Instead of sports, the televisions show classic movies. The bartenders are pleasant and know their drinks.

Washington, D.C.

Home

99 F Street N.W.

A late-night place on five levels featuring bars and dance floors. It's the velvet rope scene to get in, but after that it's all groovy.

Zola

800 F Street N.W.

The bar at Zola is next to the International Spy Museum, so you can imagine the clientele. Bar stools are chic beige, the countertop gleams and the shelves for liquor bottles are mirrored, adding to the special effects. (Spies say it's all done with mirrors!)

Chi-Cha Lounge

624 U Street

Sample spicy herbal cocktails at Chi-Cha Lounge, aka Latin music central. It has velvet sofas and water pipes are available for the occasional smoke.

Hotel Helix

Logan Circle area

When you consider that the hotel has a glitter-covered driveway, you know the Helix Lounge is going to be cool. Try not to jump out of the ottoman you first sink into as it lights up, because that is exactly what is supposed to happen. A 63-seat bar and cafe has a snazzy lighting system. A riot of color, and the cocktails match the mood.

MCCXXIII

1223 Connecticut Avenue N.W.

An ultra-exclusive champagne and caviar club, it is worth the effort to get in, whether by dropping the right names or appearing in the latest creations. The luxurious cream couches must be reserved, but once inside even the VIP Lounge is accessible. The cocktail menu at MCCXXIII – or twelve-twenty-three – is vast and the drinks are just magnificent.

Lulus Club Mardi Gras

22 & M Streets N.W.

With ten bars and two dance floors, Lulus Club Mardi Gras in Northwest Washington – a short walk from Dupont Circle – provides nonstop activity. There are events or specials almost every night. Lulus biggest claim to fame is the March 4 Mardi Gras, which is billed as "the largest Mardi Gras party in the country outside New Orleans."

Bossa

2463 18th Street N.W.

A cozy, candlelit place serving up organic food and even organic ale for the health conscious, increasingly gentrified crowd. In the heart of the hip Adam's Morgan, Bossa features occasional live music and rotating art/photography exhibits.

Rest of America
Atlantic City
Atlantic City Bar & Grill

104 S. Raleigh Avenue

Though Atlantic City is no longer the glittering spectacle it was in the city's heyday, you can still stroll along the magnificent Boardwalk with an ice cream or hot dog, and gamble to your heart's content. The Atlantic City Bar & Grill still attracts stars from stage and screen and it was featured in the TV series *City Confidential*. "Thirsty Thursdays" are the drink special nights. The bar is known for the Crab Mary, like a Bloody Mary but made with Clamato Juice and served with crab claws as a garnish and crab seasoning around the rim. They also serve great Apple Martinis, Chocolate Martinis and Espresso Martinis.

Baltimore
The Owl Bar

1 E. Chase Street

Inside the Belvedere – a hotel built in 1903 – the Owl Bar boasts a double-size Martini! The walls are adorned, surprise, surprise, with stuffed owls.

Daytona Beach
The Boot Hill Saloon

Main Street

The Boot Hill Saloon is the traditional "first stop" on arriving in Daytona Beach, as it is the town's meeting place. The official deeds go back to the 1800s,

Student body right and left: Daytona Beach is one of the top resorts during spring break

when it was built. It was three buildings in one, one side a church, the middle section a "watering hole," better known as a bar by many, and the third portion a barbershop. Looking around the Saloon you might still spot the old church pew which remains from earlier times. At the back of the barbershop was a smoking room. The site was originally called the Kit Kat Club, and it was one of Daytona Beach's hottest spots in the early 1900s when it was booming as a resort town. Walking into Boot Hill is like walking into a time warp, with ornate chandeliers hanging from the ceiling. Looking at the memorabilia on the walls, ceiling, tables and bar will keep you intrigued for hours. The clientele may be students on spring break, hard-looking bikers or glamorous beach babes, so why not follow the bar's slogan, "Order a Drink and Have a Seat, You're Better Off Here Than Across the Street." Mind you, it is a cemetery.

Orlando

The Blue Room

17 W. Pine Street

The "pioneer of Orlando nightlife," The Blue Room features the work of local artists, which adorns the walls in this favorite of downtown clubbers. With an open bar for ladies on weekend nights until midnight, resident DJ spins jazz-influenced trance every Saturday night. They also bring in local and international DJs. You may come to Orlando for the rides, but you'll stay to dance the night away and lose yourself in The Blue Room.

Palm Springs

Casablanca Lounge

The Ingleside Inn, 200 W. Ramon Road

Better known as Melvyn's, after legendary owner Mel Haber, this is where Frank Sinatra perched on a bar stool more than a few times over the decades. The Casablanca Lounge, at the Ingleside Inn, is a classic bar, full of charm and 1950s style. Pull up a seat at the long bar, and ask nicely for possibly the best Martinis in this sunny town from a bartender who reminds you of serious boys from *The Sopranos*.

Phoenix

Chez Nous

675 W. Indian School Road (corner 7th Avenue)

A fixture of the Phoenix scene for 40 years, the award-winning Chez Nous is a lounge and cabaret bar with music and dancing.

Raleigh

Playmakers

3801 Hillsborough Street

They won't be showing cricket on any of the eight giant television screens at this favorite sports bar in the college town of Raleigh, but it's standing room only during basketball and football season, especially if Duke or the University of North Carolina makes it to the Final Four. Two of the more popular specials are a shooter Brass Balls – made with Grand Marnier and Peach Schnapps – and the Creamsicle – made with Stoli Orange and Stoli Vanilla. In the summertime, stop by for karaoke and live music out on the patio.

St. Louis

Absolutli Goosed

3196 South Grand

Absolutli Goosed stands proud in the city of the Busch brewing empire as a haven for lovers of a Martini. There are more than 60 varieties to choose from.

Scottsdale

Lateral Hazard

4341 N. 75 Street

The bartenders at Lateral Hazard actually refresh your Martini in a fresh ice-cold glass when it starts to thaw. Yeah.

Not all Mickey Mouse: Orlando and Disney may be synonymous but there are bars too

Britain and Ireland

Belfast

The Apartment

2–6 Donegal Square East

A busy and loud bar, but the compensation comes with some great views of the city.

Bar Red

Ten Square Hotel, 1 Linenhall Street

Bar Red adjoins the swank Ten Square Hotel, just behind City Hall. Although it has an impressive range of vodkas, the bar's theme is Japanese and the selection of sake and sushi is excellent.

Bittles Bar

Victoria Square

This is a gorgeous old bar that gets very lively as the night goes on.

The Fly Bar

5–6 Lower Crescent

You may need to jostle for space at the bar on some nights, but it is well worth the inconvenience.

Irene & Nan's

12 Brunswick Street

Named, it's said, for a couple of would-be glamor queens who frequented a local pub, Irene & Nan's is full of glamorous 1950s retro chic, including an unusual cocktail menu.

Northern Whig

2–10 Bridge Street

A Communist-themed bar, with uniformed bar staff who serve a large selection of cocktails.

Opium Bar

Upstairs, 3 Skipper Street

As the name suggests, the Opium has an Oriental theme and serves imaginative cocktails.

Shu

253 Lisburn Road

The cocktails at Shu have won awards but beware: they can be pricey.

Ta Tu

701 Lisburn Road

Ta Tu hosts a fashionable, good-looking crowd who partake of a large cocktail menu.

Birmingham

Carpe Diem

48 Charles Street, Queensway

Unimpressive from the outside – the windows are blacked out – walking through Carpe Diem's large front doors reveals a grand, up-market library bar with well-mixed cocktails.

Brighton rocks: The bars aren't quite this grand

52 Degrees North

Arcadian Centre, Hurst Street

52 Degrees North has stunning décor, including a glass bar that's over 50 feet long. The bartenders know their stuff and make high-quality cocktails.

Bacchus

Burlington Hotel, Burlington Arcade, New Street

Located in the basement of a plush four-star hotel, Bacchus displays the decadence of ancient times updated for the Birmingham of today. The drinks aren't cheap, but the range is excellent.

Bar Coast

Arcadian Centre, Hurst Street

Reasonably priced, but not a wave in sight! More importantly the cocktails, and the food, are excellent.

Cellar Bar & Bubble Lounge

Hotel du Vin, Church Street

There are two bars in this hotel. The Cellar Bar, with an adjacent cigar room, Cigar du Vin, specializes in rum- and tequila-based cocktails. The Bubble Lounge has nearly 70 champagnes to choose from.

Brighton

Hotel Seattle

Brighton Marina

The Seattle is sumptuously decorated with vintage décor (perspex chairs, space-age floorlamps) and Lambrettas in the foyer adding a touch of rock 'n roll. There's a restaurant bar and a chilled saloon area where you can hang in 1960s bucket chairs. A sun deck overlooks the marina, while the Black and White Bar, with Beatles memorabilia on the walls, has leather loungers and mirrored tables. Cool!

Hotel du Vin

Ship Street

This hotel is a great addition to Brighton's bars. It is dark and mysterious, with exposed beams, leather bar stools, chairs and sofas, with an upstairs pool table for ultra-hip chicks and guys. The bar is to one end of a vaulted room and its mezzanine level. There is a substantial cocktail list and wine is served by the glass straight from the bottle. It is busy at weekends with out-of-towners you might recognize.

The Grand Hotel

Kings Road, The Seafront

All the grandeur of days of old and the odd celebrity to spot, but pricey.

Bristol

Arnolfini

Narrow Quay

Great for pre-theater cocktails, Arnolfini is just the place for star gazing or, if you prefer, talent hunting.

Nocturne

1 Unity Street

A basement cocktail club, Nocturne offers table service for your cocktails. This is one place to dress to impress.

Byzantium

Portwall Lane, Redcliffe

Luxurious 1930s-inspired décor, and a favorite for romantic couples, Byzantium gives a real feel for Turkish delight, right down to tarot readings and the occasional belly dancer!

Ether

2 Trenchard Street

Ether offers futuristic décor and quite possibly the most comfortable seating at any cocktail bar in the city. More importantly, the cocktails are pretty much out in the ether too.

Severnshed

The Grove, City Docks

A riverside bar, Severnshed is great for summer cocktails where drinking and dining on the outdoor terrace is a special treat. The restrooms are well worth a visit, even if you don't need to powder your nose.

Riverstation

The Grove

So chic it's hard to believe that Riverstation used to be a river police station. The transformation is amazing: from a place where the locals certainly didn't want to go, to one where people spotting is just part of the fun.

Bohemia

Blackboy Hill, Clifton Road

Inventive cocktails in a maze of a venue that was a rather dingy pub dating back to Victorian times.

Bar Humbug

89 Whiteladies Road

Good looking clientele and colorful décor are features of Bar Humbug. The cocktails are good too.

Cambridge

Venue

Upstairs, 66 Regent Street

Dress to impress and you'll be able to sample from the finest cocktails in town.

Cardiff

Incognito

29 Park Place, City Centre

Relaxed clientele and cocktails that pack a wallop, so the comfortable seating is handy. From the outside, it's a solid Georgian house; inside, the décor is modern and very cool.

Via Fossa

Mermaid Quay, Stuart Street

New to the Cardiff Bay scene, Via Fossa is a great place for afternoon cocktails. The mermaid hasn't been spotted yet, but perhaps after a few drinks …

Metropolis

60 Charles Street

Stylish and potent cocktails match the bar's design. Metropolis specializes in different types of vodkas.

Bar 38

Mermaid Quay, Cardiff Bay

Overlooking Cardiff Bay, Bar 38 boasts décor as beautiful as the clientele, all of whom enjoy hip cocktails. The bartenders know their stuff and mix lovely drinks. Even the washrooms merit a mention with ornate fountains serving as sinks.

Dublin

The Bailey

Duke Street, Off Grafton Street

Dress in at least one designer label and come here to be seen drinking one of their cocktail creations. If the heat radiating from all the brilliance gets too much, the outdoor terrace is heated.

The Morrison Hotel

North Quay

Professional clientele enjoys well-mixed drinks while settled on snug sofas. The dark oak and cream décor suggests calm and that's exactly what you'll find.

The Chocolate Bar

Upper Hatch Street

The Chocolate Bar has steel everywhere, even in the restrooms. However, you'll be served some of the best cocktails in Dublin and they're a steal.

Octagon Bar

The Clarence, 6–8 Wellington Quay

Cocktails at the Octagon Bar are crafted with the utmost of care, so patience is required. But, as your mother always said, patience is a virtue, for which you will definitely be rewarded. (If you have more than one of their Long Island Iced Teas, you may well be punished the following day!) The décor is New York in style, but the clientele is from all over the world. It is a great place for a quiet drink before dining out at one of the many nearby restaurants.

Still waters: The bars of O'Connell Street are just a short stroll from Dublin's Ha-Penny Bridge

Cocoon

Unit 2, Royal Hiberian Way, Dawson Street

Cocoon has an all-embracing cocktail menu and lavish décor. The eponymous house special cocktail is just that, but the recipe is so secret bartenders have been known to pocket huge tips and still not divulged their secret.

Inn on the Green

The Fitzwilliam Hotel, St. Stephens Green

Although Sir Terence Conran is behind the design of this designer bar, it still retains a hint of its Irish identity. Inn on the Green attracts a stylish crowd every night of the week, although it's not a place for late-night drinking as it closes at 11 p.m. The cocktails are pricey, but extremely tasty, and served by friendly, proficient staff.

The Merrion Hotel

Merrion Street

A Georgian townhouse filled with modern Irish art. Classic-style murals mount the stairwell and works by Jack B. Yeats, the poet's brother, hang in Bar 23, the Cellar Bar and the lobby. Irish whiskeys and a weekly featured cocktail are bar highlights.

Nancy Hands

30–32 Parkgate Street

Rumor has it that the namesake of this bar ran, shall we say, a house of ill repute – not what you'd normally expect in a country like Ireland. While not in the heart of the city, it doesn't need to be when it's located close to the main gate at Phoenix Park on the banks of River Liffey. Nancy Hands is renôwned for its array of vodkas, yet champagne cocktails are the bar's real forte, with no fewer than 14 varieties from which to choose.

Edinburgh

399 Bar

The Scotsman Hotel, 20 North Bridge

This is one bar that did not get its name from its address (as so many bars do). The reason for the name is that 399 is the exact number of malts that this bar serves. Prices vary, yet accordingly you get the feeling that you're paying for the drink in your hand, not the privilege of drinking in the establishment. Decked out like a gentlemen's club of yesteryear, complete with resplendent wood paneling, this is a place for decided malt liquor drinkers and deal makers. Subtle jazz provides the soundtrack while you pore over a sophisticated cocktail menu and catch a great view over Edinburgh. And for the historians: 399 was once the hub of *The Scotsman* newspaper.

Rick's

55a Frederick Street

Although a tiny, hip hotel is connected to Rick's, in many ways you could argue that the rooms are an after-thought to the bar. New York inspired, in name and nature, Rick's is a cocktail bar where the stylish international professional is seen. When you order a cocktail here you can be assured that they are using top shelf spirits in every case, and sampling staples such as the Cosmopolitan and Rick's Martini is mandatory. Situate yourself towards the back of the bar in summer to take advantage of the glass roof and extended daylight hours. It's easy to see why this is a multi-award-winning establishment.

EH1 Bar and Brasserie

197 High Street

EH1 is a great place for people watching and enjoying well-mixed drinks before embarking on a big night out.

Looking down: Edinburgh Castle sits high above Princes Street, *the* place to be on New Year's Eve

Dome

14 George Street

Home of an authentic 1930s cocktail bar with a distinguished feel to the place. Dome is built on the site of a bank's headquarters building. The opulence remains, so sit back, relax and enjoy the sense of luxury.

Monboddo

Point Hotel, 34 36 Broad Street

A stylish glass fronted bar in the trendy Point Hotel, Monboddo provides professionals with a choice of affordable drinks.

Opal Lounge

51 George Street

Award-winning staff serves imaginative cocktails to a mixed crowd in one of Edinburgh's biggest bars.

Glasgow

Air Organic

36 Kelvingrove Street

Air Organic exhibits a strange dichotomy: the bar has an outer space theme, and heating is provided by a coal fire which warms you to the very soul, but owes its origins to a very different age; and upstairs is a great organic restaurant, very much a modern phenomenon. Apart from the outside needing a coat or two of paint, it is hard to find anything to criticize in this wonderful bar.

Bar 10

10 Mitchell Lane

Brilliant cocktails by day, however, it attracts a younger, pre-club crowd at night. Bar 10 is a little off the beaten track, close to the Lighthouse, but the search is worth the effort. Food is served, but not in the evening.

Bar-ce-lona

427 Sauchiehall Street

Star performer is an incredible indoor water feature and the cocktails are reasonably priced in this bar which, surprise, surprise, has a distinctly Catalan or Spanish theme. Bar-ce-lona is where Scotland and Spain meet for a fun night out.

Candy Bar

185 Hope Street

This is like a candy store for grownups, with an amazing variety of fun cocktails, such as the very sweet Afrocandy, comprising amaretto, vodka and cherry brandy.

The Corinthian

191 Ingram Street

Three different bars in one building, a piano lounge serving cocktails, a glass domed main bar with intimate booths, and a very exclusive bar upstairs, where celebrities feature prominently among the members-only clientele. The basement has a nightclub.

Groucho St. Jude's

190 Bath Street

Great cocktails served in a luxurious and friendly atmosphere. Groucho Marx once said, "I don't care to belong to a club that accepts people like me as members." He obviously hadn't been to Glasgow!

Rogano

11 Exchange Place

Styled like a bar on 1920s ocean liner, this is the perfect place to sip classic cocktails.

Spy Bar & Grill

153 Bath Street

Spy Bar & Grill is a must-see for all James Bond lovers, especially those who preferred Sean Connery to Roger Moore.

Leeds

Babylon

10 York Place

With its unprecedented design, Babylon has a reputation for great for pre-dinner drinks. There is a fine restaurant in its own right in the basement.

Bar 38

The Headrow

Classy venue and clientele, but be prepared for unisex toilets which are becoming popular these days.

brb

37 Call Lane

brb is a colorful bar with a good selection of cocktails, although cocktail purists might not be too impressed with beer on tap. On Mondays you can catch a movie at the bar, and the food is definitely above average.

Milo Cocktail Bar

Upstairs, 10–12 Call Lane

Varied musical selection, laid-back crowd and a selection of North African bar snacks make Milo a fine bar to visit. It isn't particularly large, but it is both trendy and friendly at the same time.

Mojo

Merrion Street

Bartenders here know their trade; however, it can be hard to hear over the music at times.

Oporto

31–33 Call Lane

Bar staff are extremely affable and experts when it comes to the classics. It gets really lively as the night wears on.

Sutra

75–76 Kirkgate

Formerly known as the Players Bar, the redesigned Sutra offers a refined atmosphere with an interesting and diverse drinks menu and table service. Although the bar has a capacity of more than 200, the waitresses stiill manage to provide a personal touch.

Townhouse

First Floor Cocktail Bar, Assembly Street

The Townhouse is an upmarket, chic designer bar with a strict door policy. However, it does get very busy on weekends. Spectacular eye candy makes this an attractive proposition.

Liverpool

Baa Bar

43–45 Fleet Street

Something of a Liverpool institution now, the Baa Bar is revered by music-loving locals but it can be rowdy at night.

The Blue Bar and Grill

Edward Pavilion, Albert Dock

Colossal concrete bar dominates the room, and it also has some of the best views in Liverpool. Upstairs, the restaurant is more than accommodating.

Revolution

18 Wood Street

Revolution has more than 60 premium vodkas on offer. Quiet in the early evening, it does get very busy as the night progresses.

The Living Room

Victoria Buildings, 15 Victoria Street

Popular bar with cocktails that cater to those with a sweet tooth and for lovers of ice cream too. There are also some yogurt cocktails for the really daring. However, if yogurt is meant to be low calorie, doesn't the Bugged Out cocktail – with Malibu, Midori, banana liqueur, toffee yogurt, fresh banana and butterscotch sauce – miss the point?

Modo

23–25 Fleet Street

Laid back by day, but dynamic once the sun goes down. The plush sofas instill a mood of relaxation, with a long drink the perfect complement.

Platinum Lounge

1 Beetham Plaza

The ultimate bar. The cocktail menu is outstanding, the range of spirits, wines and champagnes is superb and the food is not only diverse, but also presented beautifully.

London

LAB Bar

12 Old Compton Street, Soho

World renowned for its cocktails, apparently a staggering 10,000 menus are stolen from LAB annually. It has set a high benchmark for cocktail bars not only in London, but also the world over. Founders Douglas Ankrah and Richard Hargroves are the men behind both the bar and the London Academy of Bartenders, so it's hoped that LAB Bar is the way of the future for global cocktail culture. As it is extremely popular, it can get a little cramped and it might take a while to get served, but hey, they didn't build Rome in a day! And despite the hard work they have to do, especially during peak times, the staff are charming. All cocktails are a cut above the rest, however the Dekamron and Black Star Liner are fabulous. The décor celebrates 1970s kitsch and the food available is as exciting as the cocktails.

The Player

8 Broadwick Street, Soho

You'd be well advised to reserve a table in advance at The Player, to avoid being bitterly disappointed as this is a cosy and excellent basement bar. Just as important, make sure you get there early on in the evening as it has a members-only policy after 11 p.m. Although you don't have to dress to the nines, you should look as if you know a thing or two about fashion to guarantee entry. The crowd is siphoned from the local fashion, film and music industries, but that still makes for a pretty diverse clientele. The groovy interior epitomizes "Lounge Chic" (as does the table service), favoring 1970s wood paneling, rich leather and subdued lighting. The courteous bartenders are eager to educate your palate and two of The Player's cocktails definitely worth trying are the Raspberry Collins and the rich New York Flip.

Townhouse

31 Beauchamp Place, Knightsbridge

This ultra chic bar, located just moments from Harrods, has a 26-page cocktail menu. You'd be hard-pressed not to find any cocktail you desire at Townhouse. The exotic Honey Rides Again is a kaleidoscope for taste buds and the Bon Bon is perfect for sweet-toothed drinkers. Co-owner Douglas Ankrah established the London Academy of Bartending, so it's little surprise that the menu is so vast. As it is situated in a converted townhouse (hence its name), it can be easy to miss, but keep an eye out for an ivy-clad stone structure. The crowd varies in age, but you wouldn't catch anyone wearing anything that would be regarded as last season. Comfortable, adjustable leather seating, ranged across the three floors, makes enjoying the sumptuous cocktails and visual delights on the plasma TV screens effortless.

Vertigo

Level 42, Tower 42, 25 Old Broad Street

If you suffer from this affliction, perhaps the best way to confront it is with a little Dutch courage, of which there is no shortage at Vertigo. Unfortunately the venue is open only Mondays through Fridays, and you must show photographic identification (for security purposes) and book ahead. All that aside, it is worth planning a visit for a unique 360-degree view of London. While it may be more of a champagne bar than a cocktail bar, there are a multitude of Champagne Cocktails and Bellinis to choose from. The décor is reminiscent of a James Bond movie set, but it is overshadowed by the magnificent views of the capital. Situated in the banking district of London, Vertigo attracts a professional crowd and, judging from the number of couples dotted amongst the place, it appears to be a popular venue for a first date where making an impression is important. This is not a bar for those on a budget trip.

Crowded house: London's Covent Garden attracts tens of thousands of visitors every day

The Library Bar

The Lanesborough Hotel, Hyde Park Corner

When sitting in this book-lined bar, which resembles a members' club, it's bewildering to think that many of the world's international stars have at some time sipped cocktails there, and more will do so, possibly later on that day. This is certainly an establishment to dress up for, with most of the crowd being wealthy travelers and professionals. More than 100 different types of cocktails are exquisitely mixed at the bar, and lovers of fine cognac will find nearly 40 varieties, headlined by the 1796 Napoléon at well over US$1,000 per single shot. You are paying for history in a glass in that instance, but you will pay more than usual for just about everything. However, you are also paying for attentive service and exclusive ambience, to the sound of a pianist tinkling on the ivories. Cigar enthusiasts are also well catered for here by bar manager Salvatore Calabrese, who never forgets a face.

Long Bar

Sanderson Hotel, 50 Berners Street, Mayfair

To reach the Long Bar you have to go through the lobby of the Sanderson, one of the most stylish hotels in Europe – watch out for the furniture designed by Salvador Dalí. The bar is 80 feet long, but despite its length, you have to get there pretty early to ensure a spot at it, and be prepared to lose it for good should you need to go off and powder your nose. There is also a courtyard. However, you will have to employ strategy to negotiate a seat here, too. The clientele includes A-listers, but it is the ultimate faux pas to look as if you care. The crowd and design of the interior do overshadow the cocktails. Although the Long Bar's recipe range is not as extensive as in other London cocktail bars, the bartenders make them with a theatrical flourish. This is definitely a place to go if you like to feel as if you're right in the middle of the London scene!

The American Bar

Savoy Hotel, Strand

Many a Martini fanatic has made a pilgrimage to The American Bar, the London home of the most famous and sophisticated cocktail ever invented. Surely, James Bond cannot be wrong! Nor can Marlene Dietrich, Ira Gershwin and F. Scott Fitzgerald, who were once patrons here. It's reputation was firmly established by bartender Harry Craddock in the 1930s and it has remained a mecca for classic cocktail lovers since. Located only a short cab ride or walk from West End theaters, it is a wonderful place to meet up before going out. Interestingly the décor marks a departure from ambient lighting and retro chic that is de rigueur among other bars. Peter Dorelli and his well-trained bar staff are efficient and courteous and the plush environment is welcoming. A word of advice, in Savoy Place – the short street off the Strand leading to the hotel – traffic goes on the wrong side of the street.

Oxo Tower

Riverside, Oxo Tower Wharf, South Bank

If there's a tall building in London, you can be almost certain that there will be a bar taking full advantage of the view from one of the higher floors, and the Oxo Tower Restaurant, Bar and Brasserie occupies this building's rooftop, benefiting from the stunning Thames-side views. You will have to be patient during busy periods, especially for their Spiced Pear & Vanilla Champagne Cocktail. Your wallet may well be significantly lighter after the experience, but your sense of taste certainly will have appreciated it. Even on a cloudy night, you'll think you're bathing in moonbeams thanks to the unusual louvered ceiling, decorated with blue neon lights. Make sure the bar arranges a cab when you want to go home because it is not easy to find one around there late at night.

Manchester

Tribeca & B.E.D.

50 Sackville Street

One wouldn't normally expect a bar this stylish to be as reasonably priced and unpretentious. Tribeca – named after the district in Manhattan – is famous for its pitchers of fruity Margaritas and Sangrias. For this reason alone it is a lounge bar best enjoyed in the company of at least two other drinking companions. It is definitely a bar in which you can relax your posture as the majority of the seating consists of couches that are very close to the ground. However, you can take your reclining one step further by visiting Tribeca's subterranean lounge bar known as B.E.D. where you are indeed served while tucked into a rather luxurious bed. Surprisingly, B.E.D. is faster paced than Tribeca, so the recommendation is that you visit B.E.D. once – if only to experience the novelty of being allowed to drink and enjoy a snack between the sheets – but to continue the serious business of drinking exquisite cocktails in more orthodox positions back upstairs at Tribeca.

Nico Central Bar & Brasserie

Midland Hotel, 16 Mount Street

If you don't feel comfortable unless you have both hands full, go to Nico Central, which, as its name suggests, is located in the middle of Manchester city. Nico Central Bar & Brasserie is actually one of the bars in the Crowne Plaza Midland Hotel and, rather confusingly, the bar address is on a different street. The bar is famous for its long list of varied Martini-style cocktails and it is also renowned for playing host to the largest cigar humidor in town. The décor is a unique mix of southern French villa with Art Deco touches, decorated with vibrant colors and substantial chandeliers. A live jazz band plays on Fridays. Tasty bar food is also served in the cocktail lounge.

United city: Manchester has become home to numerous trendy bars catering to a varied crowd

The River Bar

Lowry Hotel, Dearmans Place, Chapel Wharf, Salford

Located within the luxurious Lowry Hotel on the banks of the River Irwell, The River Bar is definitely the kind of establishment that favors a gilded credit card. Views of the river are best enjoyed in summer when you might mingle with celebrities from the music world. You won't be disappointed in the retro chic interior. It is a great bar at which to arrive fashionably early to meet up with a friend, because the modern art placed around the bar – not to mention the elegantly bound classics in the library room will keep you occupied. Alternatively you could request a song from the pianist while you sample the driest of Martinis, before settling down in one of the luxurious plump leather armchairs to enjoy your night.

Restaurant Bar and Grill

14 John Dalton Street

The rather uninspiring name does the Restaurant Bar and Grill something of a disservice, for it is sophisticated and stylish, while also being relaxed and comfortable. The inconspicuous entrance may be easy to miss, so keep an eye out for well-dressed clientele entering and leaving the establishment. The signature cocktail, the Rum Lush, is delectable, inquisitive cocktail drinkers must try the Basil Grande – but who would have thought the flavor of basil would mingle so well with that of strawberries? Polished wood and excellent lighting open up the expansive ground floor bar, which is staffed by courteous bartenders. Modern Italian fare is served in the upstairs restaurant.

Dry Bar

28–30 Oldham Street

Dry Bar is a cool, occasional live music venue, good for drinking well into the night. It is definitely a place to behave yourself, though, because the management has no qualms about ejecting and barring misbehaving patrons, even if they are international celebrities!

Kro Bar

325 Oxford Road

Notable drinks menu served in a sophisticated townhouse conversion. Kro-Bar is a translation from the Danish for drinking establishment. After a couple of cocktails, you might just need a crowbar to force you to leave the friendly and relaxed atmosphere.

Mystique

Princess Street

Over-the-top décor inspires similar cocktails at Mystique. The food is great, but the gilded bird cages, purple velvet drapes, crystal chandeliers and bearded cacti that adorn the bar will live long in the memory. The bar is worth a visit if only to see how far your jaw drops when you take everything in.

Cut to the Chase: Under one of the arches of the Tyne Bridge is the garden of the Chase

Newcastle

Barluga

35 Grey Street

Barluga is a bar-restaurant with a gentlemen's club theme. The name is play on words for beluga and Barluga sells some fine caviar and very good fish dishes to go with excellent cocktails and a wide range of champagnes. Although this is a relatively recent addition to the Newcastle drinking scene, a restaurant had been on this site before.

Chase

13 Sandhill

This is a cocktail bar with a garden that actually ends underneath one of the arches of the famous Tyne Bridge. Chase is very popular as a pre-clubbing stop-off point. It has a quirky interior, which includes fish tanks lining the walls on the way to the restrooms and blue leather window seats. Bright and colorful sums up both the décor and the cocktails. More importantly, the cocktails are pretty good.

Head of Steam

36 Lime Street

Formerly the Cluny, and now the Head of Steam, this is a riverside bar aimed at the more artistic drinker. It incorporates an art gallery, with the exhibitions changing every few weeks, and another room where new musical talent gets the chance to perform.

Centurion

Grand Central Station, Neville Street

There has been a bar on the site of the Centurion for more than a century, because every major British railway station had a bar. The modernization of the bar at Newcastle's Grand Central Station has been carried out exceptionally well and there is, once again, an air of Victorian splendor in 21st-century surroundings.

Revolution

Collingwood Street

Incredibly high-ceilinged venue with nearly 100 vodkas on offer and a sizeable cocktail menu. The far-out feeling is increased by the magnificent, ornate marble pillars and original artworks adorning the walls. The music at Revolution merely adds to the bar's growing reputation.

Stereo

Sandgate, Quayside

At Stereo you can enjoy great views of the Millennium Bridge and Baltic Museum opposite, but you may be distracted from them as the bar is also Europe's largest private art gallery. The décor is a bit retro, but the range of snacks and cocktails are served by more than competent staff. In hot summer days, the lure of the terrace simply should not be ignored.

Nottingham

Bluu

5 Broadway, Lace Market

In the heart of town, Bluu pays homage to the original in London where the Blue Note Club once was. Good cocktail and spirits selection attracts a professional crowd, while the extensive menu and wine list are also definite big city.

Brownes Bar & Kitchen

17–19 Goose Gate, Hockley

Stylish, spacious establishment with quality cocktails, Brownes Bar & Kitchen is definitely an A-list type venue for twenty- and thirtysomethings who enjoy not only fine drinks but also good food.

Synergy

Broad Street

As the name suggests, Synergy is a combination of two bars on separate floors. They work in harmony providing a regular bar, downstairs, for those moving on soon, and – for those with time on their hands – there is a lavish upstairs lounge with plush sofas. The last manager collected a Cocktail Mixer of the Year Award, which gives an idea of the quality of cocktails to be enjoyed here.

Oxford

Duke of Cambridge

Little Clarendon Street

A strange name for a bar in Oxford, given the varsity rivalry, but the Duke of Cambridge serves great cocktails at reasonable prices.

Sheffield

Sola

21–23 North Church Street

One of the more unusual bars, Sola is at the back of the cathedral. The décor is reverse futuristic, a 1960s designer's view of modern 2003 furniture. More importantly, the bar serves award-winning cocktails.

York

Bar 38

Yorkshire Herald Buildings, Coney Street

The terrace at the back of the bar offers expansive river views while, inside, you will relax in state-of-the-art décor, including some interesting light effects. Bar 38 also boasts York's first unisex restrooms.

Henry J. Bean's

1 Tower Street

Decorated and run like a 50s-style diner with a large variety of cocktails, this bar is a lot of fun! Henry J. Bean's has 11 bar-diners in the U.K., plus another 11 – in Thailand (three), China (two), Argentina (two), Dubai, Malta, Andorra and Hungary. The chain's founder was an American and the menu and service are legacies of his roots.

Sunday opening: The Minster may be the biggest tourist attraction in York, but the city has plenty of bars that are equally worth visiting

Rest of Europe

Austria
Vienna

Castillo

Biberstrasse 8

The bartenders at Castillo are specialists in whiskeys – with around 100 to choose from – and Martinis. It has Vienna's longest bar and attracts the power-dressed beautiful people.

Sky Bar

Karnerstrasse 19

Like its name suggests, great views and a starry crowd. Sky Bar has a glass window that runs the length of the bar. Across the hallway is a rooftop bar and night club.

Nightfly

Dorotheergasse 14

An American bar that has a Latin night on Sundays, and caters to a varied crowd. Nightfly's bartenders are excellent and they produce a wide range of cocktails, especially whiskey and cognac varieties.

Jenseits

Nelkengasse 3, Mariahilf 6th District

Once a gay hangout, Jenseits looks like a regular house, with a small sign the only clue to what lies inside. To enter, you have to ring a doorbell, but it is well worth it. The tiny bar screams decadence and attracts the seriously well-to-do of all persuasions.

Belguim
Antwerp

Bar Room

30 Leopold de Waelstraat, Zuid Straat

Bar Room is a lounge bar as well as a restaurant on three levels. Beautiful bartenders serve top-quality cocktails in a relaxed and friendly atmosphere.

Het Elfde Gebod

Torf Burg 10

Decorated in religious iconography this is a very unusual bar frequented by an eccentric and artistic crowd. Literally translated from Flemish, Het Elfde Gebod means "the 11th Commandment," and if the bar is to be believed, the commandment must be along the lines of "enjoy yourself at all times."

Dock's Café

7 Jordaenskaai, Scheldekaaien

Superior cocktails and Martinis are a specialty at Dock's Café, situated on the waterfront. The food – in particular oysters and seafood – is as good as the drinks here, and there can be no higher compliment than that.

Hangar 41

41 Sint-Michielskaai, Scheldekaaien

The place to be seen in Antwerp, Hangar 41 has beautiful staff serving the stiffest of cocktails.

Brussels

De Ultime Hallucinatie

Konnigstraat 316 (Rue Royale)

The name translates as "the Ultimate Hallucination," and, no, you're not imagining that giant piano by the entrance. Once inside, enjoy the lavish décor and cocktails.

Kafka

6 Rue de la Vierge Noire

Kafka has a laid-back atmosphere and clientele. This is a place to sit back and relax while sampling an excellent range of vodkas and cocktails.

Hotel Astoria

Koningsstraat 103 (Rue Royale)

The Hotel Astoria is the most famous in Brussels. Be transported back in time as you relax in antique armchairs surrounded by plush velvet curtains and deep red carpets. A classic bar offering classic service with classic cocktails.

Czech Republic
Prague

Bugsy's

PaAizska 10

You might not have the full Czech experience at Bugsy's, but if you're a long way from home and crave some interesting cocktails and an English conversation, this is the place for you. The cocktail menu is thorough and will give your taste buds and liver (but, thankfully, not your wallet) a workout.

Tretter's Cocktail Bar

V kolkovni 3

This place is home to some ingenious cocktails. Here, 100 classics share the limelight with 50 new taste sensations. The international bar staff has brought experiences from working in cocktail bars worldwide, and mixed them together with award-winning results. Oh, and if your party contains a teetotaler, order a Dr. Mattoni!

Barock

PaAizska 24

Lavish chandeliers and a stylish metal bar are the backdrop to this surprisingly peaceful watering hole. This may not be a place to feel better about yourself if you're having a bad hair day, a matter compounded by the photos of heavenly creatures that adorn the walls. And if you're there during the winter months, just make sure you order one of Barock's Mojitos – the sun will feel as if it's shining soon enough.

The Square

Malostranská namesti

Right in the middle of town, like any good town square should be. You can expect to be refreshed by carefully crafted cocktails in this stylish bar. Tap your foot to now jazz sounds and enjoy a light snack, but don't spoil your dinner.

Radost FX

Belehradska 120

Radost is Czech for "pleasure," and it sums up the bar perfectly. There is something for everyone here.

***Overleaf*. Czech it out:** Prague has a great reputation for its bars and nightlife

Denmark
Copenhagen

The Royal Bar

Radisson SAS Royal Hotel, Hammerichsgade 1

The Royal Bar is home to the world's largest (more than 2 pints [1.14 L]) and most expensive (3,000 Dkr [US$450 or £385]) cocktail, the Royal Cocktail, consisting of a bottle of Dom Perignon, 12 cl Martell Cordon Bleu, 10 cl Campari Cordial and 8 cl blue curaçao. As befits such majesty, the Royal Cocktail is served on a music box atop a four-poster cushion throne.

The Library Bar

Plaza Hotel, Bernstorffsgade 4

Luxurious cocktail bar in which you can also enjoy a vast array of cigars. You could almost feel you were in a private club by the ambience, the red carpets, walls adorned with oil paintings, shelves of leather-bound books and a choice of brandies without parallel in the city. The Plaza's restaurant isn't downmarket either.

Pussy Galore's Flying Circus

30 Saint Hans Square, Norrebro

Pussy Galore's Flying Circus is a great place for sophisticated pre-dinner (Danish) royal watching. You may not see James Bond here, but you will discover some gorgeous cocktails.

Rust

Guldbergsgade 8

Many locals think Rust is the best bar in the city. Stylish describes both the furniture, with tables lit from inside the stems, and the oh-so-cool clientele.

Finland
Helsinki

Atelier

Hotel Torni, Yrjonkatu 26

This is just perfect for afternoon cocktails in summer. However, it is something of a tourist trap and does get rather crowded. The Atelier is the highest point in Helsinki, giving some fantastic views of the city.

France
Cannes

La Chunga

24 Rue la Tour Maubourg

Reminiscent of a 1950s piano bar, La Chunga is perfect for stargazing during the festival. Music and drinks flow until the not-so-early hours of the morning.

L'Amiral

Hotel Martinez, 73 Boulevard La Croisette

In this upmarket establishment, with a live pianist and the odd film star during festival season, it is a thrill to approach the bow-tie wearing bartender and – like Bogart in *Casablanca* – order a Manhattan.

Les Coulisses

29 Rue du Commandant André

This is one bar where booking ahead is essential; so are platinum cards. Les Coulisses attracts a young, trendy and exclusive crowd, who feast on superb cocktails and excellent food.

Marseille

Le Bar du Sofitel Vieux-Port

36 Boulevard Charles Livon, 7th Arrondissement

The quality cocktails complement the views of the Old Port from the exclusive Sofitel Hotel.

Le Guépard

38A Place Thiars, 1st Arrondissement

Table service of brilliant cocktails and ice creams, too, for those hot Mediterranean summer days.

Le Café de la Plage

Escale Borély Avenue Pierre Mendés, 8th Arrondissement

Le Café de la Plage overlooks the ocean and the Prado-wearing sunbathers, making it the perfect spot for people watching. The cocktails are excellent too.

Nice

Le Ghost

3 Rue De La Barillerie, Vieux Nice

Delectable cocktails in a traditional establishment. It is decorated in blacks and reds, and the lighting is also subdued, making for a relaxed atmosphere. An interesting selection of music is guaranteed because the DJ changes daily.

Le Lafayette

64 Rue Gioffrédo

Le Lafayette has bars on two floors, both specializing in vodka-based cocktails, but the upper floor bar has

a glass and steel feature made to look a bit like the undersea world of Jacques Cousteau with a boat and two divers. There is seating outside and the fish-based menu offers superb food.

Paris

Le Plaza Athenee

25 Avenue Montaigne

Paris is about style, and so is Le Plaza Athenee. If one of the best aspects of traveling for you is people watching, then this is the place to pull up a bar stool just as you would settle into your coziest armchair at home, armed with your remote. This bar may have been serving cocktails for close to a century, but don't let that fool you — it's very now! It is also very expensive so save up for this experience.

Fu Bar

5 Rue St-Sulpice

If you prefer "mocktails" to cocktails, this definitely is not the bar for you. The delightful alcoholic infusions couldn't come any stiffer here unless they sprayed them with starch! Luckily for those whose conversational French didn't extend far beyond high school, many of the clientele speak English fairly well, which isn't to be sneezed at after two Apple Martinis.

Harry's Bar

5 Rue Daunou

Look at any cocktail menu in any bar and you'll almost certainly find a Bloody Mary on it, and Harry's Bar is no exception. What is exceptional though, is that if it weren't for this bar, no one would have ever experienced the joy that a Bloody

Mary can bring. Harry's is located down a side street off a major Paris avenue, and you almost have to knock at the door before you realize it is a bar. Patronized by Americans in Paris with a décor that doesn't seem to have changed much in the last hundred years, this place is quintessentially French. Immerse yourself and be carried away. Also famous for the creation of the Sidecar. Still in the safe hands of the McElhone family.

The Hemingway Bar

The Ritz Paris, 15 Place Vendôme

It could be argued that Ernest Hemingway was the world's most famous habitué of bars, so it is only fitting that a place he once frequented has paid homage to him. Enjoy world-class cocktails in a bar that reeks of important literary history, much of it displayed on the walls. If a cigar tickles your fancy, then make sure you stop by on a Wednesday night for tastings. Take lots of cash and credit cards.

Hotel Costes

239 Rue Saint-Honoré

Around the corner from the luxurious Place Vendôme, the brilliantly designed Hotel Costes has become a regular fixture for actors, models, interior designers and their agents – at all levels of stardom – who hold court in the plush alcoves of the lounge. There are great small tables and the opportunity for fabulous people watching is guaranteed if you can stand the pace of beautiful people.

Le Coeur Fou

55 Rue Montmartre

Your foolish heart may be stolen at Le Coeur Fou. The frozen cocktails are as attractive as the regulars and the colors of both are matched by the wall canvases that make this bar a happening place.

St. Tropez

Nikki Beach

Route de Epi, Ramatuelle

Sip cocktails with the stars in this most glitzy of French resorts. Nikki Beach doesn't limit its entry to the glamorous, so turn up and enjoy.

Life's a beach: St. Tropez takes exclusivity to new levels so make sure your plastic doesn't melt

Germany
Berlin

Green Door

Winterfeldstrasse 50, U1/15 Nolledorfplatz

Über-chic retro interior and outlandish cocktails reside behind a Green Door (speaking of which, make sure you try one of the namesake cocktails). The motto reads "the power of positive drinking" and each drink is sensibly served with a glass of mineral water, so your liver and head are treated as well as you are. That's German efficiency for you.

Windhorst

Dorotheenstrasse 65, Mitte

If you like to feel safe when you enjoy a quiet cocktail, then nowhere is more secure than Windhorst. Since it is situated at the back of the U.S. Embassy, expect to be thoroughly frisked when you enter, but once inside, you will encounter a welcoming crowd. Martinis are served as they were always meant to be – in a glass that's so cold you could get frostbite if you pick it up too soon, with your choice of twist.

Hudson Bar

Elssholzstrasse 10, Schöneberg

For some this is the best place in Berlin to find a cocktail, and it's easy to see why after perusing a menu that's more like a heavy tome than a flimsy, laminated card. There are a large number of house specialties to keep you occupied, so many that you should visit the Hudson Bar more than once. As the name suggests, you can expect an American flavor to the place, which is decorated like many bars from the early 20th century.

Victoria Bar

Potsdamer Strasse 102 (Bundesstrasse 1), Tiegarten

This may be a new bar, but it's captured the attention of a lot of people, especially after winning an award for its brilliant interior design. Generally crowded with professional clientele, the atmosphere is relaxed. The Victoria Bar serves exquisite cocktails to a soundtrack of jazz and soul, while high-quality art adorns the walls. All this makes it a great bar to start your night.

Ku'Damm 101

Kurfurstendamm 101, D-10711

Ku'Damm 101 is a modern, chic, classless hotel. However, there are spectacular views from the seventh floor lounge bar which is open until 2 a.m.

Frankfurt

Bar Oppenheimer

Oppenheimer Strasse 41, Sachsenhausen

Bar Oppenheimer is in the Sachsenhausen suburb of Frankfurt, the haunt of the young and trendy. It is small and cosy with stylish décor, good music and bar staff with excellent mixing talents.

Cantina Mescal City

Schillerstrasse 46

Cantina Mescal is a Mexican-themed cocktail bar and tequila-based cocktails are the specialties of the house.

Living XXL

Eurotower, Kaiserstrasse 29

Living XXL is at street level of the impressive Eurotower complex. It is a luxurious bar-restaurant under a glass roof. The cocktails, served by black-uniformed waiters, are exceptional.

Stars and Starlets

Friedrich-Ebert-Analge 49, Messeturm

The interior design of Stars and Starlets is so outrageous it has to be seen to be believed. But after you try the house special, it may seem normal.

Hamburg

Turm Bar

Rothenbaumchaussee 2

Close to cinemas and shops, the Turm Bar can be found in a small tower, which is not surprising, given that Turm is German for tower. Inside you will be served reasonably priced and vibrant cocktails.

The Havanna

Fischmarkt 6, St. Pauli

The Havanna is a little bit of Cuba in Germany. A large variety of cocktails are mixed with flair, such as throwing ice cubes in the air and catching them in the shakers – don't try this at home. It is a stylish bar and it attracts a young and friendly crowd.

Munich

Schumann's American Bar

Maximilianstrasse 36

Schumann's American Bar, on the über-chic Maximilianstrasse, is world famous, but bring cash – and lots of it – because credit cards aren't accepted. However, if your money runs out, you can leave your business card, and they will send you an invoice. Beware, it isn't open on Saturdays.

Pacific Times

Baaderstrasse 28

A young and trendy place to hang out, Pacific Times will have you yearning for those good old college days. Friendly staff serve a wide and interesting range of cocktails.

Greece
Athens

Deals

10 Dem Vassileiou Str, Neo Psychicko

The best place in Athens to enjoy cocktails and cigars either inside the stylish bar or on the terrace. A fine Mediterranean menu is available to diners on the upper level at Deals.

Cosmos

Ground Floor, Deste Foundation Center, 8 Omirou Str, Neo Psychicko

A very hip bar and restaurant, offering exotic cocktails to young and beautiful Athenians. The Deste Foundation Center specializes in contemporary arts and on the second floor, above Cosmos, is an exhibition that is open until midnight.

Hungary
Budapest

Incognito

Liszt Ferenc Tér 3, Oktogon

Jazz-themed bar with tasty cocktails as well as a vast selection of coffees and teas. Incognito is a cool place to go, but it is not cheap.

Club Verne

V Váci Utca 60, Ferenciek Tere

Over-the-top cocktails complement the over-the-top marine-themed décor. Jules would be impressed even if you are only one level below the street and not 20,000 leagues under the sea. The interior may resemble a submarine but if you over-indulge in the excellent range of cocktails, made by knowledgeable bartenders, you might even see some fish swimming outside.

Iceland
Reykjavik

Astro Bar

Austurstraeti 22

If you prefer a rainbow to the clinical white décor of many urban bars, you'll be doing yourself a favor by visiting the Astro Bar when in Reykjavik. The state-of-the-art lighting can emit up to 300 different colors, which means that it would be difficult to experience the exact same ambience every time you visit. It's as if the bar itself is as lively as the beautiful and stylish clientele. It can get extremely busy, so it would pay to get there early, but you need to be a bit of a night owl as it doesn't open until 11 p.m. every evening. The cocktails are more expensive than average, but it is more than a well-mixed cocktail that you'll experience here.

Bar 101

Vogamótactigur 4

The walls of Bar 101 are decorated with antiques. Light snacks complement your cocktails.

Rex Bar

Austurstraeti 9

Rex is a Conran-designed bar that attracts the odd celebrity, but head downstairs to the Mafia Room if you want to hear what your companions are saying.

Hotel Holt

Bergstadarstraeti 37101

More than 400 paintings and prints form the most important private collection of Icelandic art and some of it is in this hotel. Skalholt Bar is for drinkers of single malt whiskeys, and the Historial Library Bar is for fans of cognac and armagnac.

Italy
Florence

Dolce Vita

Piazza del Carmine, 6R

This bar is inspired by the movie of the same name, and you can expect to drink some fine cocktails amid a relaxed clientele. In keeping with the art theme, the back rooms stage concerts and exhibitions too.

Café Caracol

Via Cinori 10R

Café Caracol is a bar for those who like to sip cocktails – especially tequila-based ones – to a Latino soundtrack. The place really rocks on theme nights in the adjoining restaurant.

Milan

Yar

Via Mercalli 22

Russian bar and restaurant specializing in Russian cocktails and vodkas. Not only trendy, Yar is also a great place for people watching.

Sayonara

Via Nievo 1

Step back into the 1930s (except for the prices) and enjoy having cocktails mixed at your table. Sayonara's service is top class, and the seafood-based dishes from the menu are worth trying.

Dynamo

Upper Level, Piazza Greco 5

Classy American-themed cocktail lounge situated above a gallery. On Tuesdays and Wednesdays, jazz provides a more than acceptable complement to the drinks.

Il Volo

Viale Beatrice D'este 40

Lavishly decorated cocktail bar for a well-dressed clientele who enjoy their cocktails in the courtyard when weather permits. Inside, as you sip your drink, watch Il Volo's stream flow between the tables.

Rimini

Bar La Loggia

19 Piazza Maggiore, Mondaino

Very fashionable bar situated in a medieval castle high on a hill in Mondaino's center. Bar La Loggia also serves tasty bar snacks.

Byblos

Via P. Castello, Riccione Alta

A high-class restaurant-bar which is open only during the summer months. The views from the Riccione Alta, and the hillside climbing out of Rimini, make a trip to Byblos more than worthwhile.

Rome

Bar della Pace

3–7 Via della Pace

Somewhat pricey fashionable café and bar, it is really called Antico, but, as it is on Via Della Pace, you won't get lost. Bar della Pace is one of Rome's institutions and no trip to the Eternal City would be complete without a stop here.

Escopazzo

Via d'Aracoeli, 41 (Piazza Venezia)

Good cocktails and regular live music make Escopazzo a bar in which it is worth spending some time.

Venice

Harry's Bar

Calle Vallaresso, San Marco

Taste a Bellini at its birthplace, knowing that the likes of Byron once knocked one back here, too. It's on a side street, and you might walk right past the small door that opens into a long bar and a crowded table area. Stand at the bar and watch the world come and go. If hunger strikes, go upstairs and eat pasta. Mamma mia! Such good-looking bar staff. You know that quality comes at a price and with that philosophy the check won't be quite such a nasty suprise.

Water, water everywhere: ... But use spring, soda or tonic water when diluting your cocktails

Millionaires' playground: Monte Carlo has one of the world's wealthiest populations

Cip's Bar

Hotel Cipriani, Guidecca 10

Recently refurbished, this is one of the most luxurious hotels in the world with a bar serving cocktails to sigh for.

Vitae

San Marco 4118, Calle Sant'Antonio, Vaporetto Rialto

Off the well-beaten tourist path, Vitae stays open late and the pleasant bartenders mix fine cocktails.

Danieli

Hotel Danieli, Castello Riva degli Schiavoni 4196

Elegance abounds in both the cocktails and the décor at this luxurious hotel close to the San Marco waterfront in this most glamorous of cities.

Monte Carlo
Monaco

Zebra Square

Top Floor, Grimaldi Forum, Avenue Princesse Grace

Exquisite views and a self-possessed crowd populate this stylish bar that specializes in vodka-based cocktails. The sea views are spectacular, and so are the cocktails.

Quai des Artistes

4 Quai Antoine Ler

If you're there during the Grand Prix, don't be surprised to see a few playboys who are handy behind the wheel. When the cars going by are not Formula One type, there's always the harbor to watch from the terrace.

Netherlands
Amsterdam

Ciel Bleu Bar

23rd Floor, Hotel Okura Amsterdam
Ferdinand Bolstraat 333, 1072 LH,

The coy size of this world-class cocktail bar is soon forgotten when you are confronted with one of the best panoramic views of Amsterdam. Calm your vertigo with a classic cocktail from the menu. Since you're in Holland, try a good gin-based cocktail, such as a Classic Martini.

Scheltema

Nieuwezijds Voorburgwal 242

Quiet cocktails are the order of the day at this Amsterdam bar. The staff definitely know what they're doing so expect to see precision cocktail making rather than a mere mixed drink.

De Stil

Spuistraat 326

If whiskey is your drink of choice, then you must visit De Stil. The bar offers more than 150 different brands of whiskey, and if you visit this establishment often enough, you will even be assigned your own bottle.

De Hooiberg

Die Port Van Cleve Hotel,
N.Z. Voorburgwal 176–180

When you sip your cocktail in this cocktail bar, someone might remind you that the Die Port Van Cleve Hotel once housed the original Heineken brewery. Those not into beer can try something with a Dutch liqueur – they make some of the best in the world.

Dutch courage: Locals as well as tourists flock to Amsterdam's Leidseplein, where bars abound

Norway
Oslo

Bar & Cigar

CJ Hambros Plass 2C

Luxurious bar for lovers of cigars and fine cognacs. The attentive bartenders know their drinks – which are on the expensive side – and their tobacco.

The Bar Royal

Christiania Hotel, Biskop Gunnerius Gate 3

Swank yet laid back. Quality liquor enthusiasts are well catered to in one of the trendiest hotels in Norway. The Bar Royal attracts beautiful people.

Cosmopolitan

Sentrum, Rusellkkveien 14

Cosmopolitan's over-28 door policy is strictly enforced and it ensures a mature crowd at this up-market bar and restaurant. Set on three floors, in the top-level lounge, bartenders mix magnificent fresh fruit cocktails, while there is a restaurant on the middle floor. The ground floor is given over to a club where DJs play music from the 1970s and 80s, for an older audience.

Portugal
Lisbon

Bica do Sapato

Avenida Infante D Henrique, Santa Apolonia

A great place to imbibe some mean cocktails before dinner, Bica do Sapato is the perfect bar for

people watching. Everybody gets to show off what they're wearing and who they're with.

Resto

Rua Costa do Castelo 7

This bar is situated high above Lisbon, and you'll need a nice alcoholic refreshment after the climb. Once you've reached Resto, the views down to the city are worth the expense, and the bar isn't cheap.

Romania
Bucharest

The Fifties

Str Roma 5

The name says it all when it comes to the décor, but The Fifties has a vast selection of excellent cocktails to savor. The ambience here will make you forget all about 21st-century Romania outside.

Opium Studio

Str Horei 5 Bis

The Opium Studio is on two levels. Decorated with unusual art, it is great for cocktails, especially those made with vodka.

Basilicum Pub

B-dul Schitu Mogureanu 16

Patience is required at Basilicum, the service is slow and the locals are posy, but the dividends pay off in the form of scrumptious cocktails.

Black Russian: Lit by a full moon, St. Basil's Cathedral in Moscow is a spectacular sight

Russia
Moscow

Balaganchik

10/2 Tryokhprudny Pereulok

Great for a cocktail from the limitless menu, especially before going to the theaters nearby. Balaganchik keeps the dramatic theme when it comes to the décor. Watch out: there are some real dummies in the bar.

Pinocchio

4/2 Kutuzovsky Prospect

This is the latest bar-restaurant to open in Moscow to great acclaim. A bar-pizzeria in flavor, it has two Cuban bartenders whose specialty is the Mojito. They sing and salsa as they shake. Bar seating area is in three discreet sections, and is traditional in style, with dark wood paneling. The rest of the décor is superb. The high ceiling is dominated by a Lalique chandelier just to distract you between sips.

St. Petersburg

Senat-Bar

Galernaya 1

Architecturally eclectic, the Senat-Bar boasts an impressively modern cocktail menu. The interior design is breathtaking.

Drago

Primorsky Pr 15

The atmosphere suggests a classy restaurant, but Drago's excellent cuisine takes a back seat to some of the most complicated cocktails on offer in Russia.

Spain
Barcelona

Boadas

C/Tallers 1

This is like a satellite of Havana's El Floridita, since it was established by an ex-employee. A lot of pride is taken by the staff to create works of liquid art as exquisite as the works of the artist Miró who, incidentally, was once a regular at this haunt.

Dostrece

Calle Carme 40

If you're craving a touch of South America in Spain, Dostrece is here to satisfy it. Brazilian cocktails are the specialty and go remarkably well with the selection of delicious tapas dishes.

The Aris Bar

Hotel Rey Juan Carlos,
Avenue Diagonal 661–671

If you ever wanted to see synergy personified, you must watch the staff at the Aris Bar make cocktails – watching your drink being made is almost as enjoyable as drinking it. Attention to detail is paramount, and most bartenders could learn a thing or two from these experts. If you're a gin lover you should definitely try the Hispania Real cocktail.

Dry Martini Bar

Aribau 162

You don't have to be Einstein to figure out that possibly the best place in Barcelona to get a good Dry Martini would be at the Dry Martini Bar. A serious drink calls for a serious bar and while the clientele have a mature attitude towards their drinking, the atmosphere is by no means at all austere. Decadence doesn't necessarily have to be untidy.

Madrid

Museo Chicote

Gran Via 12

In the past you might have bumped into Grace Kelly or Ernest Hemingway in this famed cocktail bar. Now you'll hear DJs and hot music, with hip clientele enjoying the classic cocktails to the rhythm.

Bar Cock

C/de la Reina 16

Perhaps the name does lose something in the translation, but conquer your prudishness and you'll be rewarded with superior cocktails in a relaxed, yet fashionable, bar.

Valencia

Tuvalu

Ausias March 18

Polynesian-themed bar which is dedicated to constructing vibrant cocktails. The bartenders really know their drinks at Tuvalu.

Café Infanta

Plaza Tossal 3, Old Quarter

If you had to sum up this bar in a word, it would be "eclectic." But whatever your taste, it is hard to resist the vodka-based cocktails. Wednesday nights are even more special, when antiques auctions begin after midnight. The range of music is just as diverse, with everything from jazz to disco and opera to salsa. Variety really is the spice of life at Café Infanta.

Sweden
Stockholm

Eken Bar

Hilton Stockholm Slussen Hotel, 8 Guldgränd

Spectacular views provide the perfect accompaniment to sophisticated cocktails. The Eken Bar is not cheap, but then again, when are hotel bars inexpensive?

Halv Trappa Plus Gard

Upstairs, 3 Lastmakargatan

Fashionable loft bar which is renowned for serving stiff cocktails. Halv Trappa Plus Gard is inhabited by beautiful people in a great atmosphere. The restaurant downstairs has a separate entrance.

Laroy

Birger Jarlsgatan 20

Laroy may be pricey and hedonistic, but this luxuriously appointed bar is one of the places to be seen in Sweden.

Lydmar Bar

Lydmar Hotel, Sturegatan 10

Best place for enjoying the view, both of Stockholm and of the good-looking clientele. After a hard day's shopping, just sit back and relax, but don't expect a cheap night.

Rest of the World

Argentina
Buenos Aires

Voodoo Bar

Bez 340, Las Caitas

Hip, American-style bar with a sophisticated clientele. Set on two floors, the Voodoo Bar boasts one of the longest bars in the city, so getting a drink isn't a problem. The laid-back atmosphere is helped by the jazz sound.

Move

Paseo de La Infanta, Acros 14 y 15,
Avenida del Libertador 3883

Fantastic for cocktails during the day to take advantage of the brilliant views. At night, the music is turned up and Move becomes party central.

Gran Bar Danzon

Libertad y Santa F, Capital Federal

Vast array of cocktails, spirits and cigars to be enjoyed in a laid-back atmosphere, although a lack of signs makes Gran Bar Danzon a little hard to find. It is worth the effort, though, and once there, the food should also be sampled, especially the sushi.

Mundo Bizarro

Guatemala 4802, Palermo

Ultra hip bar and restaurant with arguably the friendliest bar staff and best mixed cocktails in Buenos Aires. Mundo Bizarro has restrained illumination to say the least, with candles augmenting the dim, reddish light. But it does make for a rather seductive atmosphere.

Australia
Melbourne

Misty Place

3–5 Hosier Lane

Complicated cocktails are complemented by stylish lighting, comfortable décor and inspired bar snacks. Campari lovers are especially well catered to in this chic side-street bar which attracts an artsy crowd.

Tony Starr's Kitten Club

267 Little Collins Street

Capturing the essence of opulent 1950s and 60s nightspots, this club boasts one of the most extensive cocktail menus in Melbourne. Visit the Love Lounge or Bar, with a Powder Room for the ladies reminiscent of an old-time Hollywood starlet's dream.

Bar Deco

Grand Hyatt Melbourne, 123 Collins Street

If you take your cocktails seriously, so does Bar Deco, and to prove it they have more than 100 to choose from. This award-winning bar at the Grand Hyatt Hotel lives up to its high praise and quietly takes pride in its achievements.

Mink

Basement, Prince of Wales Hotel, 2b Aceland Street

Mink is definitely an "after dark" cocktail bar where you will find dim lighting, unimposing music and discreet seating decked out in sexy velvet. This bar has an enormous selection of spirits.

Perth

B Bar

The Colonnade, 388 Hay Street, Subiaco

A vast selection of cocktails can be enjoyed in any one of the five lounge areas. It is a perfect meeting place, as there is dancing, dining and drinking available. As well as great cocktails, there is a superb selection of cognacs and cigars.

C Lounge

Levels 33–34, St. Martins Tower, 44 St. Georges Terrace

Enjoy classic cocktails with or without cigars while enjoying the revolving 360-degree views of Perth and the surrounding regions from more than 30 floors into the sky. The views are improved by the floor-to-ceiling windows all around. Classic Martinis and Manhattans are specialties of the house. There is a restaurant on the lower level and after the meal a visit to the Cigar Lounge will round off the night.

Office Bar

The Sebel of Perth, 37 Pier Street

Located in one of the top hotels in Perth, the Office Bar is a quiet venue, open from mid-afternoon till late, and it is perfect for intimate cocktails. It has tab views of the Sebel's tropical gardens.

Culture vulture: Sydney's Opera House satisfies a thirst for culture, and many bars slake the thirst for drink

Sydney

Aqua Luna Bar

5–7 Macquarie Street

The Aqua Luna Bar is located on the hip stretch of East Circular Quay leading to Sydney's famous Opera House, and you can enjoy cocktails from a vast menu. Perfect for long summer evenings.

Horizons Bar

36th Floor, ANA Hotel, 176 Cumberland Street

Remember you're paying for the view as much as for the cocktails and both are worth every cent. No international traveler could possibly justify not paying a visit to one of Australia's most famous cocktail bars.

The Dugout Bar

Downstairs, 2 Oxford Street, Darlinghurst
(enter via Liverpool Street)

Coy and dimly lit, this subterranean gem can trick you into thinking Humphrey Bogart might wander in. And if he does, get to know him better over an exquisite cocktail in the adjoining Cigar Lounge.

Orbit Lounge Bar

The Summit, Level 47, Australia Square,
George Street

What could possibly be better than a 360-degree view of Sydney while you've got a cocktail in your hand? Quite simply, the Orbit Lounge Bar, because it also revolves, giving you virtually uninterrupted views of one of the world's most beautiful harbor cities. It would be easy for a bar like this to sit back and rely on the view it offers, but Orbit's bar menu includes such delicacies as Rose Petal Martini, which could tempt even the sweetest palate. The futuristic décor,

reminiscent of furniture in scenes from Stanley Kubrick's movie *2001*, is also worth a visit.

Fix

Kirketon Hotel, 229 Darlinghurst Road

You can get your fix of great cocktails, beautiful people and fine cigars at Fix, located in a top hotel, which also has a super restaurant, Salt, on the site.

Sand Bar

111 Sussex Street

Just one facet of the something-for-everyone Slip Inn, the Sand Bar's atmosphere is as cool as its sandstone walls on a hot summer night. They have some fascinating house cocktails, but know how to do a classic with finesse.

Brazil
Rio de Janeiro

Bardot

247 Rua Dias Ferreira, Leblon

In the heart of the exclusive Leblon area, this stylish bar attracts a similarly chic clientele. It has an up-market bohemian vibe and even if you're a wallflower, the salsa is fun to watch.

Academia da Cachaca

26 Rua Conde de Bernadotte, Leblon

With no fewer than 500 different types of cachaça on offer, this is a bar you may have to return to more than once to taste the whole menu. If a straight glass scares you, there is a vast menu of Caipirinhas to test them out in.

Fat Tuesday: Rio de Janeiro's Mardi Gras Carnival is the world's largest street party

Garota de Ipanema

Rua Vinicius de Moraes 49, Ipanema

This is a must-see for fans of 1960s music. Translated, this bar is "the girl from Ipenama," one the most famous lounge bar tunes, and the street has been renamed in honor of Vinicius de Moraes, who composed the song with Tom Jobin. Garota de Ipanema – formerly the Velloso Bar – is also the bar at which the Cosmopolitan is rumored to have originated. A must for any woman from New York.

Lobby Bar

Hotel Inter-Continental, Avenida Prefeito Mendes de Morais, 222 São Conrado

The Lobby Bar is cozy and laid back, and those with an adventurous palate will be well served by the cocktail menu. You'll find yourself mingling with a professional crowd that has come to unwind.

São Paulo

Bar Galeria e Cigar Club

Avenida das Nacoes Unidas 12559, Brooklin

Bar with a strong Cuban theme, especially when it comes to cigars, of which there are over 100 varieties available. The cocktail list continues the Cuban feel, but Bar Galeria e Cigar Club also has a wide variety of brandies and whiskeys available.

Apollinari

1206 Rua Oscar Freire, Jardim Paulista

Not a cheap night out, but certainly a tasty one. This is a very sophisticated lounge bar-cum-club and the interior design comes from some of Brazil's top people. You may have to pay a hefty entrance fee for the pleasure of spending a lot of money on quality drinks.

Grazie a Dio

Rua Girassol 67

Grazie a Dio is great if you love live jazz and fresh and fruity cocktails. The restaurant is top-notch too, serving Mediterranean-style food in candle-lit surroundings.

Canada
Montreal

Altitude 737

1 Place Ville-Marie, Niveau PH2, Suite 4340

You'll feel on top of the world in this pricey, ultramodern bar, disco and restaurant, which occupies the top three stories of Montreal's tallest building. It's worth it, if only for the stunning views.

The Typhoon Lounge

5752 Monkland Avenue, NDG

If you are adventurous with your Martinis and your whiskeys, you'll be in your element at The Typhoon Lounge, where they serve a wide range of both. The music varies from day to day.

Whisky Café

5800 St. Laurent Boulevard, North Montreal

The name says it all, with more than 100 single malts on offer. The Whisky Café's excellent service includes some unusual extras: spirit tastings, and a driver service to take you home if you have over-indulged. The restrooms are definitely different. The Whisky Café boasts that it has Montreal's only women's urinal, though for gentlemen things will certainly go more easily with a waterfall urinal.

Jello Bar

151 Ontario East, Cnr de Bullion

Jello Bar has a reputation as one of the truly great Martini bars and it's popular with Hollywood stars when they're in town. Retro décor and warm lighting in the lounge bar prepare you for the cocktail list of Martini recipes dating back decades. Three new Martini styles are added every month. There's cool jazz music early in the week and live music on weekends.

Toronto

Amber

119 Yorkville Avenue

Despite being in a windowless basement, Amber is somehow both bright and airy. The bartenders get classic cocktails just right, while also having a flair for the inventive. The food — Oriental fused with Mediterranean — is excellent too.

Rosewater Supper Club

19 Toronto Street

This lavish establishment makes you feel as if you're stepping onto the set of *Gilda* — the only thing missing is Rita Hayworth! As well as excellent cocktails, the restaurant serves food in sumptuous surroundings.

Rain

19 Mercer Street

An extraordinary steel and concrete location with a back-lit bar, Rain is housed in a former prison. As a result the bars are now welcoming, not forbidding. There is a top restaurant here too.

Eye in the sky: At more than 1,000 feet, the viewing balcony at the CN Tower gives a great view of Toronto

Vancouver

The Cellar Jazz Café

3611 West Broadway, Kitsilano

With more than 50 Martinis to sample, you could be forgiven for not noticing the variety of live jazz music on offer too. The bartenders are experts, on the subjects of both drinks and music.

Subeez Café

891 Homer Street

Fantastic restaurant-bar with chic cocktails and great art adorning the interior. There is a good selection of West Coast wines too. Subeez Café attracts Vancouver's professionals and they mix well with the trendy bar staff, who mix the cocktails rather well too.

Locus Cafe

4121 Main Street

Locus Cafe is a restaurant-bar with intimate wooden booths at the back of a large interior. It's known for its cocktails as well as its calamari.

Chile

Santiago

Maestra Vida

Pio Nono 380, Recoleta

Maestra Vida is actually a salsa bar, but it excels at classic cocktails. Remember, you've got to burn off those calories at some point.

Le Cutton

Palena 3395, Sector Lo Cañas

Forget sleek lines and minimalist décor, Le Cutton is decorated like an old antiques shop, but the mismatched furniture doesn't detract from the deliciously fresh cocktails.

El Bosque Norte

1077, Las Candes

Experience cocktails that are as big on strength as they are on flavor in El Bosque Norte.

China
Beijing

Half Dream

Ban Meng, 5 Xingbu Yicun Xili, Chaoyang District

Half Dream is one of the trendiest bars in Beijing.

The Lobby

Palace Hotel Beijing, 8 Goldfish Lane, Wangfujing

The Lobby offers a stunning selection of cocktails in a world-class hotel bar.

Hong Kong

V-13

13 Old Bailey Street, Soho

Vodka lovers cannot afford to miss this vibrant bar. There are more than 100 to choose from in V-13.

Alibi

73 Wyndham Street, Central

Put on your Sunday best or you'll look shabby next to all the supermodels, and you can get a manicure while you're sipping at Alibi.

Post 97

Cosmos Building, 9–11 Lan Kwai Fong

This is the perfect place for those who just don't know when to call it a night – Post 97 is open 24 hours a day over the weekend.

Felix

The Peninsula Hong Kong, Salisbury Road

With an unrivaled view and uniquely segregated dance floor, Felix is one of the world's most stylish bars and famous for its cocktails. Men must visit the bathroom.

Shanghai

The Glamour Bar

7/F, 5 The Bund

Where do Shanghai's in-the-know night owls head for classic cocktails, good company, great music and dramatic views? The answer is the stunning Glamour Bar, a 21st-century impression of a 1930s Hollywood movie set, which has single-handedly revived the elegant tradition of sophisticated drinks and after-dinner music in Shanghai. The warm and elegant ambience created by silver, crystal and mellow lighting makes everyone feel comfortable – and the carefully selected music gets the crowd in the right mood. Expertly crafted drinks in the classic style help with attitude adjustment as well. It's getting harder and harder to find classically trained bartenders, so it's a pleasant surprise indeed to meet the smooth and knowledgeable guys behind the Glamour Bar. Try the house special, the Glamour Cocktail, containing vodka, cherry brandy, blood orange and splashes of lime cordial. They like a laugh too, because the menu also includes a joke cocktail in Sex on the Bund, which comes with the warning, "Doesn't exist, not permitted."

Top of the World

The Regal Stadium Hotel, Tian Yao Qiao Lu

A sports bar overlooking the Shanghai Stadium, so you can drink and watch the games at the same time in the stadium, or enjoy a selection of bar games. Televisions allow the sports mad to catch up on the latest in U.S. sport from ESPN. Top of the World has special deals during the week.

Penthouse Bar

Hilton Shanghai, 250 Hua Shan Lu

The band Peru recently flew directly into this top-floor hotel bar. Sadly, the Penthouse Bar's juggling cocktail shaker has been replaced by Jennifer, but it remains a classy cocktail hangout. There is live music every day except Sunday, with each act having a residency of a few months..

Goya

357 Xin Hua Lu (by Pan Yu Road)

Goya is in an old country house and it attracts the oh-so-beautiful crowd. The owners are Shanghai natives who returned home after spending time in New York. Maybe that's why the bartenders specialize in Martinis. At last count, there were more than 30 varieties on offer

The only way is up: Skyscrapers appear to rise out of the South China Sea in Hong Kong

Groove

380 Hua Shan Lu

Discreet alcoves furnished with soft sofas invite you to relax and check out the dance floor. Chill out downstairs at Groove with top cocktails. If the garden is open, it is a super place in summer.

Tou Ming Si Kao

Unit 2, House 11, North Lane, Xintiandi, Lane 181, Tai Lang Lu

Cocktails here almost take second place to the bar, which is made entirely of ornate glass. The owner, a former actress, also runs a store specializing in glassware. The colored-glass theme continues with the cocktails, which arrive in frosted glasses of different hues. TMSK, as Tou Ming Si Karo is affectionately known, is a must-visit bar.

Havana Nirvana

210 Retail Plaza, 1376 Nanjing Road

Although this bar specializes in cigars and fine malts, cocktails are not overlooked and the Mojitos and Martinis are made with care and not a little flair. Hotel Nirvana is a haven for ex-pats from many nations working in the local offices.

Cloud 9

87th Floor, Grand Hyatt Hotel Shanghai, Jin Mao Tower, 88 Century Boulevard

Cloud 9 is the world's highest bar, in the world's tallest hotel – the Grand Hyatt Shanghai – with 360-degree views of Shanghai. However, you must expect to pay for this privilege. The bar is on the 87th floor, but drinks can be taken up to the Sky Lounge, one story higher. If that is too high for you, then there are two other great bars in the hotel, on the 53rd and 56th floors.

Cuba
Havana

La Bodeguita del Medio

Empedrado No. 206, Cuba y San Ignacio, Havana Vieja

Fidel Castro, Che Guevara, Nat King Cole. The photos of past guests at this famous bar capture history as much as glamor. A muse must inhabit this bar for it inspired both the Mojito and some of Hemingway's greatest works.

El Floridita

Obispo No. 557, esquina a Monserrate, Havana Vieja

Is there a Cuban bar Hemingway didn't make his own? Here he celebrated the Frozen Daiquiri in its birthplace. No trip to Havana would be complete without paying your respects. The Daiquiris are second to none, and the frozen versions are simply the best.

La Mina Terraza

Obispo 109, Equina Oficios, Plaza de Armas, Havana Vieja

If they bottled Cuba, you could buy it at La Mina Terraza. It is just perfect for a laid-back afternoon, followed by some great Cuban music and rum.

Hotel Havana

21 y O, Vedado, Havana

The garden terrace makes it easier to rehydrate while you work on a holiday tan. And if you like to strut, you'll have competition from the mingling peacocks. Rum lovers will be in heaven here.

Libre Cuba: Havana's streets are busy all day

India
Mumbai

Indigo

Upstairs, 4 Mandlik Road, Colaba

Catch a glimpse of the occasional Bollywood starlet while enjoying a fine cocktail in the well-stocked Cigar Lounge. Downstairs you will find one of the world's best restaurants.

Olive Bar & Kitchen

14 Union Park, Khar

Although valet parking is offered, you'd be well advised to leave the car at the hotel as the cocktail menu here could tempt even the strongest willed.

Athena

41–44 Minoo Desai Marg, Colaba

Athena specializes in champagne and cigars. You will be greeted by a younger, designer-clad crowd. The prices at this bar are exorbitant by Indian standards.

Harbour Bar

Taj Mahal Hotel, Apollo Bunder

Outstanding works of art hang in the lobby for you to ogle as you pass by to find the Harbour Bar, the oldest bar in Mumbai, in an exquisite hotel celebrating its centenary in 2003.

Copacabana

Dariya Vihar, Chowpatty Seaface

A Mexican-type bar, Copacabana specializes in Margaritas and tequila-based cocktails.

Japan
Hiroshima

As Time

Hondori L Building, 2F, 2–3 Hondori, Naka-ku

Stylish yet welcoming café bar where the bartenders mix a mean cocktail – at a price – while offering a large selection of wines. Pick your time to visit As Time, because by day it is pretty much like an ordinary café. But by night it is something special.

D Bar: Donbei Island

2–8 Fukuro-machi, Naka-ku

D Bar is an elegant and hip bar, offering any cocktail your heart desires and the range of spirits and liqueurs is truly exceptional. The elegance is reflected in the prices, but then again, where else are you served by waiters wearing white aprons over black dinner suits?

Harry's Bar

B1, Apple 2 Building, 3–15 Ebisu-cho

Up to the same standards as any of the world-renowned Harry's Bars, even though this one can't boast being the home of a classic. The standard of cocktails is, of course, world class.

Qoo

Manzoku-ya Building 2F, 5–6 Horikawa-machi, Naka-ku

Qoo's ultra stylish clientele fall over themselves to sip cocktails in the downstairs cocktail lounge. It is the place in Hiroshima to see and be seen although the prices are not for the budget conscious. This is eye-candy central.

Kyoto

Bar Fakers

47–2 Okubo-cho Tanaka, Sakyo-ku

Bar Fakers is the real thing, entertaining a strange mix of professionals and young hipsters. The bartenders are specialists in vodka-based cocktails. The prices are a very pleasant surprise and it isn't because the staff skimp on the spirits.

Orizzonte Sky Lounge

17th Floor, Kyoto Hotel Okura, Kawaramachi-Oike

Sitting in the Orizzonte Sky Lounge of this luxury Kyoto hotel – the city's tallest building – you'll get the best view of Kyoto. Everything around you, including the cocktails, suggests luxury.

Nagasaki

Cocktail Bar Joy

Nagasaki Building 7F, 10–21 Hamano-machi

Even the pickiest vodka and gin drinkers will be satisfied by Cocktail Bar Joy as there are more than 500 varieties to choose from. The bartenders know how to mix their drinks too. The clientele includes the young and the beautiful and not all of them arrive with partners.

Bar Soda

Hotel Victoria Ship 4F, 5–16 Kosone-machi

Enjoy cocktails in a modified, multi-roomed floating hotel, thankfully permanently moored in Nagasaki Harbor. Bar Soda has large windows on both port and starboard, so there are excellent views of either the ocean or the harbor.

Bar Sweet Box

Dohbiya Building 3F, 8–12 Dohza-machi

Ignoring political correctness, Bar Sweet Box was named, allegedly, because "women tend to like sweet drinks." Nevertheless, a sweet tooth will be satisfied here by more than 200 sweet cocktails.

Tokyo

Ten

B1F, 4-6-5 Higashi, Shibuya-ku

Chandeliers dominate the aristocratic décor here, but in an original way. Only the freshest ingredients are used, so if your favorite fruit cocktail isn't in season, make sure to have a substitute in mind.

New York Bar

52nd Floor, Park Hyatt Hotel, Nishi-Shinjuku 3-7-1

With skyscraper-high views of Tokyo, an occasional glimpse of Mount Fujiyama tips you off that you're not in Manhattan. The Cosmopolitans are not to be missed, making the New York Bar a home away from home for many a New Yorker in Tokyo.

Cay Bar

Spiral B1, 5-6-23, Minami Aoyama, Minatoku

Graffiti generally gets cleaned from bar walls, except when the culprits are the likes of Yoko Ono and Basquiat – try to find their artistic wall scrawls among those by other celebrities. The vast number of spirits is surpassed only by the number of cocktails in this sexy red bar.

***Overleaf*. Rising Sun:** Tokyo's great bars are the epitome of Japan's work hard, play hard ethic

John Henry's Study

Murata Building, 2–210 Kichijoji Honcho, Musashino-shi

Don't be fooled by the scholarly décor: this is one of Tokyo's finest bars, not a library. Their cocktail list reads like a catalog of obscure literary works, punctuated with classics such as Martinis, for which they certainly deserve an A+.

Low

5-46-14 Jingumae, Shibuya-ku

Wasabi cocktail shots at this basement bar at the Sputnik store are the tops.

La Fabrique

B1F Zerogate 16–9 Udagawa

The Mojitos at La Fabrique, a French-themed bar and night club, are chilling. Live bands play at the club regularly.

Shunju

27F 2-11-1 Nagatacho

A stylish bar on the 27th floor of Sanno Park Tower serves stylish cocktails. Shunju has a very wide range of whiskeys available and there is a cigar lounge adjoining the bar, but the glass partition means that the smoke is not going to be an inconvenience for non-smokers.

Republica

6-4-6 Minami-Aoyama, Raika Annexe Building

Part of the Kubakan Restaurant, Republica serves high-quality cocktails to a sophisticated clientele. If you are hoping to get away with a cheap evening, it isn't going to happen here.

Korea
Seoul

Once in a Blue Moon

85–1 Cheongdam-dong, Gangnam-gu

They take their jazz very seriously at Once in a Blue Moon – even the special house cocktails are named after jazz greats.

Mafia Bar

Apku-Jong Dong

Cocktails here are as mean as a New York Don! However, at the Mafia Bar, the well-heeled clientele's money is unlikely to have come from illegal means.

Mexico
Acapulco

Zapata Villa y Compañia

Hyatt Regency Acapulco,
Avenida Costera Miguel Aleman 1

Zapata Villa y Compañia, in the glamorous Hyatt Regency Hotel, boasts the largest collection of tequilas in the world. Try the house specialty, the not-so-quaintly named Hangman's Drink, but don't choke on it.

Tabachin

Hotel Fairmont Pierre Marques, Playa Revolcadero

Tequila lovers will be spoiled by the collection of specialized cocktails at Tabachin, the bar and restaurant at this exclusive hotel.

Cancun

Lorenzillo's Sunset Pier

Kukulcan Boulevard, Km 10.5

Lorenzillo's Sunset Pier is great for tropical cocktails at sunset out on the deck, with live jazz toward the end of the week.

Pat O'Brian's

Plaza Flamingo, Paseo Kukulkan Km 11

If you like your cocktails on the larger side, you won't be disappointed at Pat O'Brian's, a Cancun offshoot of the New Orleans bar. It features great live music and a restaurant serving Mexican and American food.

Mexico City

Area Bar & Terrace

6th Floor, Hotel Habita,
Avenida Presidente Masaryk 201, Colonia Planco

This bar just oozes style, with patrons as tasty as the cocktails.

El Estribo

Hacienda de los Morales, Vazquez de Mella 525, Col. Del Bosque, Polanco

The interior is decked out like the bar of an old world Spanish conquistador, and you won't be able to avoid a dash of tequila given that this bar has over 300 on the shelves.

Viva Acapulco: It is hard to find a blue curaçao that matches the deep blue of the water in Acapulco

Cosmo

Avenida Presidente Masaryk 410,
Colonia Polanco

Cosmo by name, Cosmo by nature, this bar caters to an older crowd, especially those wearing top Western designer labels. Although it is a little pretentious, the bar staff is very good and Martinis are the cocktails of choice here. The music and lighting blend together well to make for a good atmosphere.

La Opera Bar

Avenida Cinco de Mayo 10

An old-fashioned bar that has changed little since it was opened in 1870 but has a great elegant ambience.

New Zealand
Auckland

Green Room

Princes Wharf

The décor in the Green Room is retro funky, with a long central table inside and an outdoor area with chairs and loungers for the afternoon and early evening cocktail sippers. It is a sunny spot on the harborside with great service.

Mo's Bar

Federal Street

A small (holds about 20 people) swing and jazz bar with 1950s vinyl décor and wall-to-wall concertina windows opening onto the street. Mo's Bar is a great champagne bar and has a cigar wall.

Lime Bar

Ponsonby

A tiny bar with a huge selection of vodkas and mighty cocktails. It is standing room only inside Lime Bar as there are only a few barstools, but there is a small outdoor area. It has the best 1980s music in town. Almost an Auckland institution, it's popular with middle-agers who recall the heyday of the 80s. The trained bar staff is keen to mix what you want with style.

Rouge

Ponsonby

Under a French restaurant called Provence, Rouge employs awesome bar staff. Big cast-concrete central tables are located indoors and out. Awesome also covers the wine and cocktail lists. The atmosphere is distinctly French, unusual for a New Zealand town. You could spend the night there without too much trouble.

Chandelier

Ponsonby

A new bar entered through extravagant velvet curtains into a world inspired by the movie *Moulin Rouge*. At Chandelier, decadence rules, OK!

Christchurch

The Boulevard

Cnr Oxford Terrace & Hereford Street

Enjoy spectacular fruit cocktails in a European-styled bar-restaurant. The staff is much more friendly than in the average European bar. The Boulevard has a discount card for regular visitors.

XO Club

128 Oxford Terrace

Conscientious and friendly bar staff at the XO Club mixes cocktails with pizzazz. Enjoy your drinks on the most comfortable of leather couches.

Queenstown

The Cigar Bar

Steamer Wharf

Enter into the spirit and enjoy sophisticated cocktails while listening to live jazz at the Cigar Bar.

The Bunker

Cow Lane

The Bunker is a treasure that is hard to find, but the hunt becomes all the more rewarding when you succeed.

Bardeaux

Eureka Arcade

A vampish crowd enjoys the vast cocktail list and wine selections. Bardeaux is distinctly up-market and the eye candy — male and female — adds to the attraction.

Boardwalk

Steamer Wharf

The likes of Bill Clinton have enjoyed the lake views from Boardwalk despite the fact that they don't specialize in cigars. The cocktails of choice are Martinis and Manhattans, while the seafood restaurant is top class.

Wellington

Concrete Lounge

Cable Car Lane, Lambton Quay

Magnificent ocean views can distract you from the enormous cocktail menu at the Concrete Lounge, but not for too long. The cocktails are worth equal consideration.

Amba

21 Blair Street, Central City

Exotic vodkas, intoxicating cocktails and inventive shots attract a hip, jazz-loving crowd to Amba.

Motel Bar

Forresters Lane

Unusual spirits are combined to create unique concoctions in this bar that is more like an American jazz club of the 1950s than a roadside motel.

Singapore
Singapore

BLU

Shangri-La Hotel Singapore,
22 Orange Grove Road

BLU offers one of the most impressive views in Singapore by night. This stylish cocktail bar offers unsurpassed service to the tune of live jazz.

***Overleaf*: Singapore Sling:** The Raffles Hotel is the birthplace of the Sling and the Long Bar is one of the world's most famous bars

Long Bar

Raffles Hotel, 1 Beach Road

Outside of New York, there are probably no cocktail bars with more of a history than those at the Raffles Hotel in Singapore and, to millions, even the Big Apple has to take a knee to the British Colonial bar which was birthplace of the Singapore Sling. Named for Sir Stanford Raffles, the founder of Singapore, the Raffles Hotel has been the base for the great and the good traveling across Asia since the 1880s. The Long Bar, built on two levels, opened in the 1920s and is based on Malayan plantations, with carved wooden paneling everywhere. It is rightly famous for the Singapore Sling, but the bar also boasts that the knowledgeable staff can create any cocktail imaginable. And remember, it's tradition to throw your used peanut shells on the floor, so don't be shy! Don't expect a cheap night out, however: somebody has to pay for the history. Among the other bars in the hotel are the Bar & Billiard Room, which has a couple of tables from the turn of the 20th century; the Courtyard Bar, which has an alfresco kitchen and tables under the palm trees; and the Writer's Bar, which pays homage to the famous authors who have stayed at the hotel. A selection of restaurants makes this possibly the single most important watering hole in the world.

Bar

11 Unity Street, 01-23/24 Robertson Walk

Perfect for professionals who are serious about their shots, but rum and vodka concoctions are also a Bar specialty.

Ritz-Carlton Millenia

7 Raffles Avenue

Gaze at the art by Andy Warhol, David Hockney, Frank Stella and more, as you enter the lobby and

then get a cocktail in the bar. Order something shimmery like the yellow glass spiral work, *Sunrise*, by American glassmaker Dale Chihuly.

South Africa
Cape Town

The Space

Cnr Main & Boyes Roads, Kalk Bay

The Space is situated atop Table Mountain, which overlooks Cape Town. It is worth making the long climb just to reach the bar, with the views being matched only by the quality of the cocktails.

Fez

38 Hout Street

Fez is decorated like a Middle Eastern harem's headquarters, and the bartenders serve classic cocktails with precision and finesse.

The LAB

19 Dorp Street, Gardens

Established by the same people who are behind London's LAB, expect nothing less than over 100 expertly mixed cocktails. This is a place where the beautiful people of Cape Town hang out.

Johannesburg

Ritrovo

Michelangelo Hotel, Sandton Square, West Street

Ritrovo, a luxurious Italian-style bar in a city-center hotel, attracts professionals and politicians.

Drink in the view: The Space is on top of Cape Town's Table Mountain looking down on the city

Buzz 9

7th Street, Melville

There is a wide-ranging cocktail selection at Buzz 9 with yogurt-infused house specialties.

Katzy's

The Firs, Oxford Road, Rosebank

The sophisticated clientele indulges in the extensive selection of whiskeys, cognacs and cigars available at Katzy's.

Thailand
Bangkok

Compass Rose

59th Floor, Banyan Tree Bangkok Hotel, 21/100 South Sathorn Road

Undoubtedly the best views of Bangkok in a sophisticated cocktail environment.

Bed Supper Club

26 Sukhumvit Soi 11

Futuristic interior design with the theme carried on by uniformed staff offering table and divan service.

Bamboo Bar

The Oriental Hotel, 48 Oriental Avenue

Historic live jazz bar decked out like a jungle bar, serviced by an ex–Harry's Bar bartender.

Venezuela
Caracas

Citron Café

Mall Sambil, Plaza Central

Afternoon cocktails can be enjoyed here with a designer crowd.

Barrock

4A Transversal

Sophisticated piano lounge with private rooms available to sample colorful cocktails.

The Well-Stocked Bar

Every professional or home bar requires a basic collection of spirits before interesting mixed drinks and cocktails can be made. Always buy the best quality brands to be assured of the purest taste. As with most things, good quality can be found at reasonable prices.

Ice

Ice cools the spirit as it is poured into a glass. All ice must be fresh. Only filtered, or even bottled, water should be used to make ice. There are four types of ice used in cocktails: crushed, shaved, cracked or cubed. Ice can be used in a blender, a shaker, a mixing glass or directly in a glass, but cubes should not be served in a cocktail glass. Cracked and shaved ice are more watery than cubes and they dilute the spirit more quickly than cubes. Use cubes in a shaker and crushed ice in a blender. Don't put ice from a blender into the glass.

Bar necessities

Spirits	Liqueurs	Wines	Extras
Bourbon	Amaretto	Champagne (or	Coconut cream
Brandy	Bailey's Irish Cream	sparkling wine)	Cream, heavy
Gin	Cointreau	Vermouths, dry and	Egg-white powder*
Pimm's No. 1 Cup	Crème de menthe	sweet	Pepper
Rum, light and dark	(white and green)	Wine, red and white	Salt
Tequila, white (silver)	Crème de cacao		Sugar, superfine
and gold	(white and brown)	**Bitters**	Tabasco sauce
Vodka	Curaçao, blue	Angostura	Worcestershire sauce
Whiskey	Grand Marnier		
			Syrups
* Use instead of fresh			Gomme syrup
egg white if preferred.			Grenadine

Spoiling yourself: At home your cocktail menu can be as adventurous or conservative as you like

Whiskey

How do you like your whiskey? Scotch, American, Canadian or Irish? With a few pretenders in between, there is an incredible choice of types, blended or malts. Each method of distillation is just different enough to ensure that the taste experience is always varied.

Scotch whisky is brewed in the northern, eastern, western and central Highlands regions of Scotland, in Speyside (a premier malt whisky region on its own) and on the islands off the mainland, including Islay, Mull, Jura and the Orkneys. The Lowlands and Campbeltown also produce whisky. In the U.S., it centers on the Southern states of Kentucky and Tennessee.

Whiskey is made from grain, water and yeast. The difference in taste and color come from the distillation methods employed by the producer. Some of the variations are: pot still or patent still; types of yeast; the kinds of wood used for aging, and the size of the barrel; how long the spirit is in the barrel; the source of the pure water; the type of cereal grains used (barley, corn, wheat, rye or oats). Flavor and its amber color are added during the maturation process when the liquid is placed in wood (usually oak) vats or casks.

Scotch must be aged a minimum of three years. In the U.S., federal law states that bourbon must be aged for at least two years.

What do you look for in a whiskey? Purity. Color ranges from light amber to honey and a deeper chestnut brown. Malts are paler versions, whereas bourbons are darker, almost reddish. Kentucky bourbons and Tennessee whiskeys are generally sweeter than Scotch; Irish whiskeys are like a light Scotch; and Canadian types, produced in Ottawa and Montreal, are easy-drinking, probably because the majority of the grain is corn. Japan is also a big producer of whiskey, but mainly for domestic consumption.

Deer friend: The Glenfiddich stag is one of the best-known Scotch whisky labels.

Rum

The light rum industry is almost as large as, if not equal to, the vodka industry. Rum is a great mixer, the taste behind great cocktails filled with fresh fruit juices. Without rum we would have no Daiquiri, Pina Colada or Rum Punch, and the world would be an even sadder place than it is.

Rum is, along with tourism, a major industry in the Caribbean. This time-honored nectar is made from sugarcane, and it has been a favorite drink of sailors for centuries. Islands in the Caribbean are dotted with vast plantations growing sugarcane to meet the demands of distilleries. Rum is produced from molasses, and is the byproduct of manufacturing raw sugar from sugarcane. The molasses is turned into alcohol by the process of fermentation. The alcohol is then distilled and becomes clear and colorless.

The spirit is aged in small oak barrels, whether the resulting rum is white or dark. Wood is porous and lets the rum spirit breathe, and with each breath, oxidation takes place. Light rum is matured in pale ash-wood barrels for one year only and then it is transferred to steel vats where it is left to age longer. Dark rum types are in the barrel for three years and longer (some for up to 20 years), after which, distillers believe, they start to lose flavor.

Most rums are blended from a selection of aged rums and from different styles of rum. How much caramel and flavoring, and which spices are to be added, are up to the blender. Once the mix has been ordained, it is diluted with water to the required bottling strength.

Rum is made all over the world. But it should not be confused with cachaça. This is a spirit distilled in Brazil, made from molasses, sugarcane juice or a combination of both. Cachaça is probably best known as the spirit underlying the delicious **Caipirinha** (see pp. 220–21).

Ready for a caning: Molasses and raw sugar come from the cane, and from molasses comes rum

Rum types

White Also known as silver or light, it is clear and light, and has a dry flavor.

Gold Also oro or ambré, it is sweeter, with the color gained from the oak cask or sometimes from the addition of caramel coloring.

Dark Also black, this type has been aged in a charred barrel.

Premium Aged/Añejo/Rhum Vieux Valued by connoisseurs, these are the pick-of-the-crop mature rums.

Flavored and Spiced These types are served with fruit juice or a mixer.

Overproof The white types are used for blending.

Single Marks These are rare, unblended rums produced by individual distilleries and are sought after. You don't often see them on top shelves.

Gin

Gin, known as "Mother's Ruin" in England, has been produced since the 1600s, when the Dutch first produced this full-flavored spirit. Then it was a distilled grain spirit flavored with juniper berries, which were thought to have beneficial effects on problems with the kidney and the bladder.

Early gins, such as Old Tom, were more like sweet cordial-type spirits. But, in Britain, over many decades it lost its sweetness to become London Dry in style. Gin was introduced to Britain when British soldiers returned from the series of wars on the European mainland.

In the 17th and 18th centuries gin was so popular that the government was forced to take control of its production by legislation – the streets and public houses were full of too many gin-soaked people. In 1736 the distilleries were taxed; they, in turn, raised the price for drinkers; 20 years later they outlawed the distillation of corn, and a series of riots ensued. It took until 1760 for the laws to be repealed. Gin was not a respectable drink at that time, and it took decades for it to gain respectability in high society. It's a different matter these days.

The best gin is recognized as that made from a grain – preferably corn – spirit and contains very few impurities. Any gin made with a molasses spirit will taste slightly sweeter. Most gin is made in a continuous still to produce the 96 percent alcohol by volume ratio required. Once this is achieved, the spirit is redistilled. The second distillation involves the spirit being distilled along with natural botanicals to produce a subtle premium gin.

When you pour a measure of gin, you get a whiff of the aroma instantly. Gin has a neutral-grain base and it is the addition of botanicals that gives gin its character. Each of the contemporary brands is blended to produce an individual taste.

If you have a refined palate, you might taste some of the following herbs in the gin: aniseed, angelica, coriander seeds, juniper berries, ginger, almonds, orange rind, cardamom, cinnamon or licorice root. For example, extra-dry gins usually contain more angelica or licorice, whereas gins with a dominant citrus flavor have more orange or lemon peel. The gin is then reduced to bottling strength, 75-proof in America and 35 per cent alcohol by volume (ABV) in Europe.

Many of the best-known classic cocktails are made with gin: the original **Martini**, **Gibson**, **Pink Gin**, **Singapore Sling** and **White Lady**.

Basically, there are four types of gin: Dry gin (unsweetened), London dry gin (unsweetened), Old Tom gin (slightly sweetened), and Plymouth gin (slightly sweetened). Although you may have to search liquor stores for Old Tom gin, the other types are generally available.

Ruined reputation: The nature of gin may have changed, but it remains a classic cocktail base spirit

Vodka

According to Pablo Picasso in 1950, "The three most astonishing things in the past half-century have been the blues, cubism and Polish vodka." He may well have been right. Vodka, Polish or otherwise, is the perfect base spirit for a cocktail because it is colorless, tasteless and odorless.

Pass someone an orange drink and they'd never know that underneath this colorful exterior lies the world's "most drunk" spirit. Nearly everybody in the world of drinking age has had a sip of vodka and many of today's drinkers are brand loyal, preferring the flavor and style of one vodka over any other.

Vodka first came into America's consciousness after World War II when Heublein began to distribute Smirnoff vodka (see **Moscow Mule**, pp. 234–5). Its advertising played up vodka's very tastelessness and, before you knew it, the classic **Martini** kissed gin goodbye and became a vodka-based cocktail. We have Ian Fleming's charismatic character, James Bond, to thank for that. Yet, the **Bloody Mary** (with or without the celery) was born using vodka, just as the ubiquitous **Harvey Wallbanger** and the **Screwdriver** (oh, those memories of drunken high school parties).

The name "vodka" derives from the Russian word for water, *voda*. There is a long history associated with this spirit, allegedly born in Russia. Or was it? Scandinavians and Poles claim vodka was made as early as, or even earlier than, the era claimed by the Russians – the 14th century.

As a general rule, spirit production uses starchy (potatoes and grains such as rye, wheat, barley, millet or corn) and sugary (molasses, sugar beets, fruit) materials. However, vodka made in America is pure grain neutral spirit distilled from fermented corn, rye or wheat, which is distilled in a continuous still. Charcoal filtration results in a clear and clean-tasting product. All three

European countries use rye grain as a main ingredient.

New vodkas, aimed at the connoisseur in the same way as armagnac, cognac and whiskey, are distilled up to three times, and then a trace of a separately distilled, lower-strength spirit may be added for character. These types are best taken from a shot glass.

Flavored vodkas are also creating an interest. Blackcurrant, cherry, pineapple, lemon, orange, peach and pepper are just some of the flavors on offer. Flavoring spirit can be a very simple process and distillers are secretive about the processes they use. In Poland, flavorings such as fruit and herbs are generally prepared in two ways, using either the classic maceration or the circulation method. With the classic method, ingredients are macerated in spirit which varies in strength (usually 40–60 percent ABV), according to the type and ripeness of the ingredients.

After the first four weeks, the spirit is drained (and reserved), with another batch of spirit added for a further three-week maceration. These two liquids are blended, together with a residual liquid pressed from the macerated ingredients. All three "spirits" are then adjusted to a standard alcoholic strength, prior to bottling.

The circulation method uses ingredients such as bison grass spread across a sieve inside a stainless steel vat. The alcohol circulating in the tank passes through the sieve twice every eight hours, usually over a period of four to seven days, according to the ripeness and type of ingredients.

Vodka producers have jumped on the health bandwagon with products such as Poland's Korzen Zycia. It is the world's newest version of an ancient ginseng vodka produced by Lancut Distillery, which has mastered the secrets of its production and obtained access to genuine red ginseng. Lancut is the only maker of red ginseng liquor outside of Asia. It is produced in the time-honored Korean way, with red ginseng extract and a red ginseng root in every bottle.

Note: Vodka should be served chilled, between 2°C and 6°C, never higher than 10°C. Because the aroma of vodka is not perceptible when chilled, distillers put the greatest emphasis on taste.

Brandy

The category "brandy" encompasses perhaps the widest selection in the spirit world. The choice of flavors, textures, aromas and appearances is unique in the world of distilled spirits. At the top of the range, there is probably no more exclusive a drink than cognac.

There is French brandy, including armagnac and cognac, and brandies made in other parts of France; there is Spanish brandy (Brandy de Jérez); Italian types, including grappa; South African, Mexican and American; and pisco from South America. Then there are eaux-de-vie and liqueur brandies. Statistics reveal that two-thirds of the brandy for the American market comes from California, center of the nation's wine industry.

So, what are you buying when you ask for a drink? "Brandy" is a generic term for a spirit distilled from the fermented juice of fruit. The name itself, brandy, is from the Dutch word *brandewijn* – literally "burnt wine" – and from the perspective of history, the creation of brandy was due almost entirely to Dutch traders who traveled the coastal ports of France and Spain in search of wine for their sailors.

The Dutch demand eventually forced the French to change the way they shipped wine to Holland, where it was used as a raw material in *wijnbranders* ("wineburners"). Distilled spirit was cheaper than wine to ship (it was less bulk), so the French began to use the technique and equipment, introduced by the Dutch for distillation, particularly in the Charente region.

In the modern world, brandy is made from grapes that have been distilled in either a small copper-pot still (called an alembic), or a continuous still, then transferred to age in oak barrels. After this period of maturation they are allowed to age further in glass jars.

South American brandy is called pisco and hails from Peru and Chile. Made from Muscat grapes, distilled and then aged in oak or in clay jars, pisco is the base spirit of a famous **Pisco Sour** cocktail.

Cognac

Grapes from vineyards of the Charente–Maritime area in France are used to make cognac. Grown in six regions, Grande Champagne, Petite Champagne, Les Borderies, Fins Bois, Bons Bois and Bois Ordinaires, the Ugni Blanc, Folle Blanche and Colombard grapes are distilled and then matured only in oak casks from the Limousin or Troncais forests.

All cognac is a blend of cognacs from different houses and vintages, as is most whiskey. Any details on a bottle's label refer to the number of years the youngest cognac in the blend has been in the cask. Three Star/V.S. is the youngest at three years; V.S.O.P., V.O. (Very Old), Very Special (or Superior) Old Pale has a four-and-a-half-year-old as the youngest; and XO, Extra, Napoleon, Vieille Réserve has, as its youngest, a six-year-old. The actual aging is generally longer. When it is aged between 40 and 60 years old, it is considered excellent quality.

Armagnac is the second French region that comes to mind when brandy is mentioned. A relatively small player on the scene, rivalry between the two regions is great, each claiming and counter-claiming the benefits of its style of brandy. Armagnaçais producers claim single distillation gives their brandy the edge whereas the Cognaçais dismiss talk of vintages for distilled wines.

Centuries prior to cognac's production, grapes were being distilled by Spaniards in Andalucia, who had learnt distillation from the Moors who occupied Spain for over seven centuries. Generally, these are robust, perhaps sweeter (they are aged in former sherry casks) and simple brandies. Now, no country produces more brandy than Spain.

What should brandy taste like? You should be able to taste several layers, with sweet, woody and fruity flavors on the tongue. If it burns your throat, try another type. A brandy should make your throat feel warm, but it should not feel harsh and raw.

Tequila

To write of tequila is to write about the true spirit of Mexico, and to recall those nights when the moon shone brightly as you licked the salt, sipped the tequila shot and bit the lemon. The moon shone brighter after that. Oh, by the way, it's the spirit base of a Margarita. But you probably knew that.

Tequila is an unusual distilled spirit produced from the fermented juice of the swollen stem of the blue agave, a flowering succulent plant found all over the Mexico. Tequila is a specific mescal and is not to be confused with the drink with the worm in it. This is mescal made from a different variety of the agave.

By law, tequila can be produced only in Mexico (in the same way that cognac can come only from Cognac) and is produced in designated regions, mostly in Jalisco, but also in designated villages within four states: Guanajuato, Nayarit and Tamaulipas.

Types of Tequila

There are two basic types of tequila: 100 percent agave and tequila mixed with other sugars (mixto). Read the label. If it does not say 100 percent agave, it is mixto.

Tequila and cocktails go together like sex and the city. Well-known tequila cocktails include **Margarita**, **Tequila Sunrise** and **Tequila Mockingbird**. Each of these exotic names reminds the drinker of vacations in the sun, of lazy days and haunting evenings.

Seasoned drinkers claim it's harder to get a hangover from drinking a 100 percent agave than with a mixto. Purity excels! At the bar, if you're set for an evening of tequila, it is preferable to ask for a blanco, a pure agave tequila, regardless of what you mix it with. At least the spirit remains untouched by added chemicals.

Tequila

Before the Spanish conquest in 1521, Mexico was home to ancient American cultures which regarded the agave as a "gift of the gods" because it was useful in a variety of ways. (Aztecs painted many of their writings on agave fiber.) According to Bob Emmons in his fascinating account, *The Book of Tequila*, the alcoholic properties of the plant were discovered before the rise of the Aztecs. The discovery of the liquid known as *pulque* supplied a means of relaxation. The Aztecs also consumed it as a narcotic during the rather less palatable rites of human sacrifice.

In 1792 Ferdinand IV lifted the ban on spirit production in Mexico and in 1795 he granted a license to one Jose Maria Guadalupe Cuervo, a Spaniard who set up a distillery in Tequila, Mexico, using cultivated, as opposed to wild, agave to produce the spirit. Now there are over 65 distilleries producing tequila for consumption at home and abroad. And, by the way, the U.S. consumes more tequila than the rest of the world.

What should tequila taste like? Connoisseurs speak of fine tequilas in much the same way as experts in cognac and fine wine drinkers describe their favorite drinks. For instance, of a Tequila Herradura blanco, one expert waxed lyrical with, "Dry complexity to the nose with floral overtones, good herbaceousness and smooth alcohol."

That's before you suck the lemon.

Tequila types

Blanco or plata (white or silver):	Reposado (rested):	Anejo (aged):	Joven abocado (often called gold):
Clear in color, and bottled immediately after distillation. Can be left for no longer than 60 days in stainless steel tanks before bottling. It may be 100 percent agave or mixto.	Aged for not less than two months in wooden vats or oak barrels. Can be 100 percent agave or mixto.	Produced from 100 percent agave and must be left for a year or more in wooden barrels. Either 100 percent agave or mixto. The very best are seldom left in the barrel for more than four years.	Unaged tequila with the characteristics of an aged tequila, but the golden color is produced by an additive such as caramel. A mixto variety, it can taste more mellow than the usual mixto.

Liqueurs

It's all sweetness or creaminess in the liqueur business. Coffee, banana, chocolate, strawberry and raspberry flavors abound in delicious mixtures that swirl into the glass in an appealing way. And the colors can be as vivid as those of an artist's palette or as muted as a warm summer's evening.

Let's get this straight. A liqueur is not a cordial; we're talking true distilled liqueur. The word "liqueur" comes from the Latin word *liquefacere*, to melt or dissolve. Centuries ago, liqueurs were distilled from recipes by monks and apothecaries whose main task was to cure ailments.

Dutchman Lucas Bols is responsible for the start of the modern liqueur industry. Back in the 16th century Bols knew that caraway was good for the digestion, and he created kümmel. Benedictine has been made since 1510, and Chartreuse had been made for the brothers at an abbey in France long before it became available in 1848.

Spirits including brandy, cognac, whiskey and rum are used as the base for liqueurs. Fruits, plants, fruit skins and/or roots are steeped in alcohol in a still, heated, and the vapors are condensed to produce the spirit. Maceration is used only for fruit with pulp – raspberries, blackcurrants and aromatic plants, such as tea. The picked fruit is put into vats with alcohol and an infusion occurs.

A crème, such as crème de menthe, is a sweet and thick liqueur with 28 percent sugar content. A cream, such as Baileys Irish Cream, is a combination of alcohol and dairy cream.

If you are serving a liqueur straight, do so at room temperature and in a small liqueur glass. It should be sipped and savored, not gulped down, like a shot, in a single swallow. Liqueurs are usually served after a meal, without ice, to get the full flavor without it being diluted.

Patience is a virtue: Monks have been making Chartreuse for centuries; the recipe remains a secret

Champagne

Ask any champagne producer when is the best time to drink champagne and he will tell you "any time of the day or night." There is a magic about sipping champagne before lunch to which it never quite aspires in the late afternoon or evening. Champagne is also possibly the best aperitif.

The famous British wartime leader Winston Churchill, a great champagne drinker (mainly Pol Roger), called for it as he settled into his seat for a Clipper flight to America, much to the consternation of a colleague.

Many people who have been swilling champagne for a lifetime don't know it is made predominantly from the juice of red grapes. The proportion of juice from white grapes is usually around one-third. Another interesting fact is that a bottle of the best champagne may contain the juice from 15 different vineyards; some superb champagnes have juice from more than 30 vineyards.

Champagne is produced in an appellation controllée region in France. Only wine from this region can be labeled "champagne." Wine labeled "Méthode Champenoise" is made by a similar method, but outside the Champagne region.

Styles

Brut A tiny amount of sweetening is added. **Demi-sec** Sweet champagne. **Extra Sec** Dry champagne.	**Non-vintage** Any champagne made using grapes from different years. A non-vintage champagne (NV) is not necessarily of lesser quality.	**Rosé** Made with some of the still red wine of the Champagne region with white wine. **Sec** Medium-sweet champagne.	**Vintage** A "vintage year" is declared by the authorities when weather conditions have been superb. A bottle of vintage champagne is one for which all the grapes were harvested in the same year.

Champagne moment: Bottles of champagne in their final stage of maturation

Mixers and Garnishes

Not every ingredient in a cocktail contains alcohol. Indeed there is probably no more refreshing a drink than a St. Clement's, made with fresh orange juice and bitter lemon. And without grapefruit and cranberry juice a Sea Breeze becomes a straight vodka.

Mixers

Ginger ale (punches)
Lemon-lime soda
Soda water
Spring water, still and sparkling
Tonic water

Juices

Cranberry
Grapefruit, white and pink
Orange
Pineapple
Tomato

Garnishes

Garnishes provide the finishing touch to a cocktail. To choose the right garnish, think about the dominant flavor and color of the cocktail and choose a fruit or leaf that will go with it. Add a piece of fruit that's in proportion to the glass. Don't add a garish touch.

Strawberries are versatile as a garnish added to the drink, particularly in a champagne cocktail, or placed on the rim. Cut out the green stem, make a slit in the bottom of the strawberry and place it over the rim.

Bar craft

Citrus fruit spiral
Press a zester firmly into the rind of a lemon/lime/orange, starting from the top. Carefully cut around the fruit, making a long spiral as you go. Add it to the cocktail.

Twist
Cut a 1- to 2-inch wide piece of rind from a lemon or orange. Place it on a cutting board, pith down. With a sharp knife, trim a thin strip, about 2 inches long, from the wider piece. Hold it over the glass and twist the ends so that the juice from the rind falls into the drink.

Fruit

blackberries (nonalcoholic drinks)

celery sticks
  (optional for Bloody Mary)

cherries, maraschino
  (cocktail cherries)

cucumber peel (for punches, Pimm's)

lemons

limes

mint, fresh

green olives (for a Martini)

oranges

pineapples

raspberries

strawberries
    (for champagne and punches)

Above: **A touch of zest:** The versatile lemon is a cocktail staple as a base ingredient or as a garnish

Left: **Berry nice:** As well has having medicinal properties, cranberries are popular in modern cocktails

Glasses

Clear glasses are ideal for cocktails. Since the beginning of the cocktail craze, each type of drink has had a shape specifically for it. For example, a Martini is served in a martini cocktail glass. Common sense dictates a liqueur should be sipped from a small glass because it is so sweet.

Main Glass Types and Sizes

Most glasses come in regular sizes as an industry standard, but there are some different shaped and sized glasses, particularly double cocktail glasses. This list should provide a useful guide. It should give an indication of the amount of drink required for a party. Smaller glasses mean less drink is consumed … unless the guests are very thirsty.

Glass type	Capacity	Characteristics
A) Cocktail	4 oz. (120 ml)	Popular for any cocktail served without ice
B) Flute	6–8 oz. (180–240 ml)	For champagne and champagne cocktails
C) Highball	10 oz. (300 ml)	Ideal for long drinks filled with ice cubes
D) Irish Coffee	8–10 oz. (240 300 ml)	Developed not to break with the warmth of coffee and spirit
Liqueur	2–3 oz. (60–90 ml)	A tiny glass for sipping after-dinner cocktails or a straight liqueur
E) Old-fashioned	5–6 oz. (150–180 ml)	A short glass with a heavy base
Saucer	5–7 oz. (150–210 ml)	By legend the shape was modeled on the bust of Empress Josephine, but champagne goes flatter more quickly than in a flute
F) Shot	2–3 oz. (60–90 ml)	Small glass to hold a measure of spirit that will be thrown down the throat
Toddy	8–10 oz. (240–300 ml)	Has a handle and can withstand hot drinks
Wine	4–9 oz. (120–270 ml)	For a drink not suited to a cocktail glass but too small for a highball

Bar craft

Glass cleaning
Clean the glass with a lint-free towel before pouring a drink. Do not wash with soapy liquids because these can leave a residue on the glass.

Shakers

The shaker is the most important tool for making great cocktails. As a rule, any recipe with a spirit, a juice and cream is shaken. Most bars have a different type of shaker than those on sale in a regular store. The professionals' Boston shaker is a two-piece unit: one metal, the other clear glass.

The ingredients are poured into the glass section, and the ice is added. The metal part is placed over the glass, sealing the two sections. Turn the shaker upside down. Shake the drink and let it settle before separating the sections. To serve, pour the cocktail through a bar strainer into a glass.

The shaker available in most stores consists of a base, a small lid with a fitted strainer, and a solid cap. When shaking, always hold the lid down firmly. If it becomes stuck, ease the lid up with two thumbs to loosen the vacuum. There's nothing worse than a lid coming loose and having the precious cocktail go everywhere but into the glass.

Cocktail shakers have also become collector's items and can sell at auction for considerable sums. One of the most popular antique shakers is the Penguin, dated circa 1936. It has a hinged beak that lifts to reveal a spout for pouring.

A search of the U.S. Patent Office files disclosed that applications for "an apparatus to mix drinks" were filed in the 1870s. By the late 19th century novelty cocktail shakers were all the rage. They included a lighthouse, buoy, skyscraper, golf bag and even a teapot!

Early shakers were made of silver, and as technology progressed, more were made of chrome-plated stainless steel. Today, most shakers are made of plated metal and are relatively inexpensive, but the crystal glass company William Yeoward has released a very expensive, colorful version called Lulu that, at one look, sparkles and seduces the mixer into creating the most fabulous cocktails.

Mr. Bond would approve: A Martini with a shaker, not a stirrer

Other Equipment

A basic cocktail tool kit consists of a few small but important items, listed below. Most can be found in a housewares store or in the bar accessories or kitchen department of major stores. As with all things, the cheapest is unlikely to be the best, but functional is more important than flashy.

Bar knife must be very sharp, used to slice fruit

Barspoon mixes and stirs cocktail ingredients in a mixing glass or a shaker

Blender blends spirits, juice, fruit and crushed ice, especially for frozen cocktails

Champagne stopper keeps the champagne bubbly once opened

Cocktail sticks spears bits of fruit and cherries as garnish

Corkscrew opens wine bottles; the best is a waiter's friend

Cutting board hard, flat surface on which to chop mint, dice garnishes, slice fruit

Dash pourer adds drops and dashes of other spirits and liqueurs

Ice bucket saves regular trips to the freezer

Ice crusher takes cubes and crushes them

Ice scoop to add ice to a shaker or blender

Ice tongs picking up ice cubes hastens the melting process

Jigger obtains the correct spirit and liqueur measures for a cocktail

Juicer to make fresh lemon and lime juices

Mixing glass to mix two or more ingredients

Muddler pestle that mashes or pulps mint or fruit berries

Shaker for shaking cocktails

Stirrers and straws long cocktails should be drunk through a straw

Tea towel wipes up spills

Zester peels lemon, orange and lime rinds to make garnishes

Avoid accidents: When using a blender always remember to put the lid on

Bartending Techniques

Cocktails came back into fashion in the late 1980s and 1990s, as the bar – as opposed to club or pub – culture returned to prominence. For a while the job of bartender ranked as one of the most glamorous. But, for all the show, the art of making cocktails should not be taken lightly.

Shaking

It might look simple when the guy behind the bar starts with his act, but for a beginner who has yet to hold a shaker ... Firstly, it's very cold, wet and slippery on the outside and that makes it hard to handle. Grip it firmly in both hands, with one hand under the base and the other firmly holding the top while, simultaneously, you splay the fingers around the sides.

Now here's the groovy bit. Move only the wrists, not the arms and shoulders. Flick it with finesse, hard, not half-heartedly. The aim is to combine the ingredients inside and chill them as they are swished back and forth over the ice. After about 20 attempts, a personal style will develop. Good bartenders have a personal rhythm to their shake and this is what novices should aspire to.

Using a mixing glass

Cocktails with ingredients that need mixing, and are served chilled, are mixed in a mixing glass, then poured through a bar strainer into an old-fashioned glass or a cocktail glass. Place the ice cubes into the mixing glass and stir the ice around with a barspoon so that it chills the glass. Add the spirits and stir, then strain into a glass. Use a tall glass with a solid base – or a large medicine beaker – if a proper mixing glass isn't available.

In the glass: Tom Cruise shows how it is done but, without practice, the chances are you'll miss

Muddling

Muddling is an action that requires a bit of strength in the wrist. And it requires a muddler. Some barspoons have a section on the end that can act as a muddler, but usually they are made of fine wood or marble (as in a pestle and mortar).

Many younger bartenders use muddling to great effect in their new cocktails. The item is placed in the bottom of a shaker/mixing glass/highball/old-fashioned glass and mashed to release its color, juice and flavor. A Mint Julep is made with mint muddled in the bottom of a glass. It is imperative to use a glass with a heavy base.

Layering/Floating

Layered drinks look superb. They're impressive, and everyone wonders how it is done. In fact, it's easy. Each spirit in a recipe weighs more or less than the others. Start with the heaviest, then add the second heaviest, and work up to the top until the lightest is floated as a finishing touch.

Usually, layered drinks are made in small glasses such as a shot or liqueur glass. A steady hand is needed, although a barspoon or a small teaspoon may be used to float each liquid over the one already in the glass.

If there are five ingredients in a recipe, begin with the first ingredient in the recipe, because it ought to be the heaviest. To pour, place the spoon on the edge of the first layer in the glass, with the back of the barspoon facing you. Pour the next spirit slowly over the spoon, and watch as it creates a second layer. Repeat the action until each ingredient in the recipe has been used.

Blending

Blended cocktails have a smooth, fruity texture and are a delicious summer drink. It's an unwritten rule that cocktails whose ingredients contain cream, fruit and crushed ice should be blended. With blended drinks, it is possible to make two or three drinks at a time, which is especially useful if there are a few people around for a pool party.

Wash any pieces of fruit before adding them to the blender. Follow instructions for dicing, too. If there isn't enough liquid in the blender when the fruit has been put in, add a teaspoon of water to aid the blades. For a really smooth result, pour the blended mixture through a strainer, and mash the mixture thoroughly, forcing the liquid through into the glass below.

Make this type of drink immediately and serve in a suitable glass, such as a wine goblet, a colada glass or even a margarita glass. Here's a tip. Add the ice at the last minute and blend again to chill the drink.

Chilling a glass

Professional bartenders always chill cocktail glasses and champagne flutes before pouring in any liquid. The opaque glass effect makes a drink look mysterious and as it fades, the drinker is left watching the cocktail itself emerge. Alternatively, place a few glasses in the freezer compartment for about half an hour before guests arrive. If that is impractical, the same effect can be achieved by putting crushed ice in the glass while the cocktail is being shaken or mixed. Remove the ice before pouring in the mixed drink.

Crusting a rim

For many drinkers, licking the rim of a Margarita, before sipping the drink, is the most pleasurable part of the whole experience. Many classic cocktails were born with a crusting and have remained that way ever since. Crusting a glass is a very simple task.

A wedge of lime is rubbed around the rim of a glass. Then the glass is turned upside down and, held by the stem, the rim is twirled around a saucer filled with fine salt. Make sure the salt sticks to the rim. If a more crusty effect is required, use slightly crushed sea salt. And, for a very special effect, salt only one half of the glass.

If the recipe requires a sugared rim, the method is exactly the same. Different and colorful effects can also be achieved by using chocolate or cocoa powder or a food coloring in sugar to give an exotic alternative.

Cocktails by Type

Cobbler: A traditional drink, it is a mixture of a spirit, fruit juice and mixed berries with mint as the garnish. Serve it with a straw.

Collins: This traditional drink was formerly served in a collins glass, but usually a highball is used. It's long and refreshing, and made with lots of ice. There are many versions of Collins, depending on the base spirit: Tom (gin), Colonel (bourbon), Pierre (cognac), Joe/John (vodka).

Cooler: Contains soda or ginger ale, perhaps bitters or grenadine, with a peel of citrus spiral hanging from the rim. The name has become misused.

Cup: When someone was drunk, people used to say that the drunk was "in his cups." The origin of this amusing phrase is this type of drink, which is traditionally British. It is a wine-based drink ideal for quenching thirsts in hot weather. The most famous cup is, of course, Pimm's No. 1 Cup, served with lots of mint and fruit slices.

Fizz: Like its name suggests, this drink is always shaken and usually served in a highball, complete with two long straws.

Flip: Of the same genre as an eggnog, a flip contains a fresh egg yolk, but no milk. It is a creamy drink sipped from a small wine glass.

Julep: A perennial favorite, it's a tall thirst-quencher made with fresh mint and bourbon. (A Mojito is a Julep made with rum, not bourbon.)

Punch: Traditionally rum and water, hot or iced, with sugar and orange or lemon juice. Now made with spirits, mixers, orange and lemon slices.

Rickey: A mixture of spirit, lime juice and soda water, dating back to 1893. More sour than sweet.

Sling: A drink made with a spirit, citrus juice and soda water, served in a highball with ice. The most famous sling is a Singapore Sling.

Drink me: Long, cool, refreshing, summer drinks. Is there a better way to relax on a hot afternoon?

Hangover Cures

How many times have you groaned, held your thumping head in your hands and wished you could sleep this off over the next few days? You feel lethargic, your head throbs, your eyes are bloodshot, your liver is damaged and the rest of your body aches. What will make you feel better?

Some people swear by the "hair of the dog" as an alcoholic remedy. In medieval times, if someone was bitten by a dog, the village medic cleaned out the wound, and added a hair from the dog that had bitten them. However, this shouldn't be tried at home!

The "hair of the dog" concept has remained a popular hangover cure in drinking culture. Why do people recommend drinking more of the same? Adding more alcohol to a system already overwhelmed by it can only make matters worse. It's a myth that drinking more of what was drunk the night before helps. In reality, it only prolongs the moment before the hangover kicks in.

Cures

Downing a vodka-based Bloody Mary, though, provides the beneficial effects of tomatoes, high in vitamin C and potassium. Pure organic tomato juice is best.

Others swear by nonalcoholic remedies, energy sources full of natural vitamins and minerals, and water. In fact, water is the one and only liquid that will help cure a hangover. It gives the kiss of life to a body suffering from severe dehydration, which is the prime cause of a hangover.

Coffee, containing caffeine, is not a good thing to drink. It doesn't sober you up because it doesn't decrease the amount of alcohol in the bloodstream.

Effervescence: Some people swear by hangover tablets, but water rehydrates the hungover body

Caffeine is a diuretic and dehydrates you even more. It is much better to start the day with peppermint or camomile tea, both of which are mild on the stomach.

Another good thing to drink is freshly made carrot juice. Vegetables such as carrots are full of vitamin A, and support the liver and stimulate urine flow! Rich in carotene, which is converted to vitamin A by the liver, they are invaluable as detoxifiers. There are also commercial preparations, such as Berocca, a concoction of multivitamins, that come in a single tablet that is dropped into a glass of water and drunk.

Bartenders keep a bottle of either Underberg or Fernet Branca, or both, behind the bar for themselves and other staff. Both are bitter liqueurs and, although they taste horrible when taken straight, they work wonders on the stomach and the head.

As for eating, imagine what grease does to one's already delicate insides. Bacon causes acid to flow into the stomach and causes indigestion. Sausages bring on a second acid attack. Fried eggs are also not a good idea, so try milder poached or scrambled eggs. Eggs are also found in the Prairie Oyster, Eggnog and a Polish hangover cure of raw egg yolk, vodka and a dash of black pepper. Eat plain, dry toast without butter. Generally, it is far better to eat bland foods such as rice and a scoop of apple sauce.

Prevention

Fats and carbohydrates are best for slowing alcohol absorption, and sugar intake prevents hangovers. Eating a few small snacks throughout the evening, while drinking, will help to absorb the alcohol.

Drink a glass of milk before embarking on a drinking session. Milk lines the stomach and thus allegedly protects the lining from any alcohol damage. There's no scientific evidence that this helps, but it's a good idea. Instead of milk, try drinking a tablespoon of olive oil. It also lines the stomach.

It is recommended that you drink one glass of water for every glass of wine or strong spirit consumed. This slows down the number of drinks you can consume, and also gives the kidneys and liver a break from alcohol.

This may sound sexist, but women shouldn't try to keep up with men. They just don't have the built-in tolerance for alcohol that men do, even when they are the same size. For men, the standard is two drinks per evening. For women, it ought to be one drink for smaller women (weighing in at less than 120 lbs. [55 kg]) and one and a half for the remainder. (A drink is defined as one mixed drink, 4 oz. (120 ml) of wine or 12 oz. (355 ml) of beer. A "half drink" is a light beer, or a wine cooler.)

Eat sugar. This also helps, because alcohol breaks down sugar stored in the liver and that needs to be replaced. Some people recommend drinking energy drinks such as Gatorade, or similar sports drinks, before going to bed. Honey is good. It contains fructose, fruit syrup which helps the body rid itself of alcohol, and helps balance the blood sugar level, which is low the morning after.

A holistic solution

There is one other thing to try: Massage. A masseur or masseuse releases tension. Fingertips will encourage toxins out of the body's cells and the patient will feel better in an hour, if not from the massage itself, then from the fact that they have survived an hour of the day without being ill.

A–Z of Bars

For ease of reference, bars with identical or similar-sounding names have the city and country listed.

Guide to Ingredients

Some ingredients may be unfamiliar, so here are brief descriptions. If you can't find the exact ingredient, this may help you find the closest substitutes.

Absinthe:	Bitter-tasting liqueur, once banned around the world because of its reputed ability to cause dementia, made from wormwood, which contains Thujone – a mild hallucinogen – and herbs, mainly anise
Advocaat:	Dutch liqueur made from eggs and honey, normally with brandy base
Alizé Gold Passion:	Passion fruit-flavored liqueur, made with cognac
Amaretto:	Almond-flavored liqueur
Amer Picon:	A bitter orange-flavored liqueur/cordial
Anisette:	Aniseed-flavored liqueur
Baileys Irish Cream:	A rich, creamy liqueur, orginally from Ireland. It is now one of the world's top 10 drinks
Benedictine:	An ancient French liqueur with a citrus and herb flavor
Bitters:	A staple of cocktail making, the best known bitters are Angostura (a mix of herbs and spices), peach, orange and Peychaud's (another mix of herbs and spices)
Calvados:	Apple brandy
Campari:	An aperitif or cocktail mixer made from herbs and spices, originally from Italy
Chambord:	Raspberry-flavored liqueur
Chartreuse:	One of the oldest liqueurs in the world, it is made by Carthusian monks in France. There are two variations: green Chartreuse, with chlorophyll added, is stronger than the yellow variety, which has honey and saffron added

Guide to Ingredients

Cherry Heering:	Cherry-flavored liqueur
Clamato:	Mixture of tomato juice and clam, used in variations of Bloody Mary cocktails. Nonalcoholic
Cointreau:	Bitter orange liqueur with a brandy base
Crème de ... :	Liqueur flavored with a variety of ingredients; some of the most popular are: banane (banana), cacao (chocolate), cassis (blackcurrant), fraises (strawberry), framboise (raspberry), menthe (mint), mure (blackberry)
Curaçao:	Orange-flavored liqueur very popular in cocktails, especially as a mixer. It comes in five colors: clear, blue, orange, green and red, although the flavor and strength remain identical
Drambuie:	Scotch-whisky-based liqueur, flavored with honey and herbs
Dubonnet:	French – often red – wine aperitif made from fortified wine, spices and a hint of quinine, occasionally used as a cocktail ingredient
Eggnog:	This is a blend of light cream or milk, eggs and sugar, flavored with nutmeg and liquor (originally rum but now whiskey and brandy are used)
Fernet Branca:	A bitter herb-and-spice-flavored liqueur
Frangelico:	Hazelnut-flavored liqueur
Galliano:	Italian herb-flavored liqueur
Ginger ale:	Carbonated soda drink with slight ginger flavor. Nonalcoholic
Ginger beer:	Carbonated soda drink with a ginger flavor between ginger ale and ginger wine. Can be alcoholic or nonalcoholic
Ginger wine:	A great mixer for a cold spell, ginger wine can be drunk neat, but it has a very sharp aftertaste
Gomme syrup:	Sugar syrup used to sweeten various cocktails. *Gomme* is a French word and the same product may be found as gum syrup. Nonalcoholic
Grand Marnier:	Bitter orange liqueur

Guide to Ingredients

Grenadine: Syrup made from pomegranate, this is a very popular mixer in cocktails. Nonalcoholic

Hpnotiq: A fruit-flavored, vodka-spiked cognac liqueur in a bright blue bottle

Jägermeister: A bitter liqueur from Germany containing more than 50 herbs, fruits and spices. Jägermeister means "hunt master" in German

Kahlua: Chocolate-flavored liqueur

Kirsch: Cherry-flavored liqueur

Kümmel: Colorless liqueur flavored with caraway, cumin and fennel

Lillet: A French aperitif made from wine, brandy, fruits and herbs, it can be either red or white, depending on the base wine

Limoncello: Lemon-flavored liqueur

Madeira: A dark fortified wine

Malibu: Coconut-flavored liqueur

Mandarine Napoléon: Tangerine-flavored liqueur with a cognac or brandy base

Mescal: Almost identical to tequila, but made outside the tequila-making region

Midori: Melon-flavored liqueur

Opal Nera: Black sambuca, a darker version of sambuca, an anise-flavored liqueur from Italy

Orgeat: Almond-based syrup used to sweeten cocktails. As well as almonds, orgeat contains sugar and either rosewater or orange-blossom water. Nonalcoholic

Ouzo: An aniseed-flavored liqueur, it goes cloudy when mixed with water, giving a cocktail an immediate air of mystery

Parfait Amour: Violet-colored liqueur, with a flavor of rose and vanilla

Pastis: Aniseed-flavored liqueur from France

Guide to Ingredients

Pernod: Aniseed-flavored liqueur

Poire William: Pear-flavored liqueur, normally with a brandy base

Prosecco: A sparkling Italian wine, it makes a nice alternative to champagne

Prunelle: Wild plum-flavored liqueur with a brandy base

Sambuca: An anise-flavored liqueur from Italy, slightly sweeter than other anise liqueurs

Schnapps: Clear liqueur, originally from Germany, that is frequently flavored with different fruits, the most of popular of which are peach, peppermint and cherry

Shrub: An unusual cocktail mixer, it is a concentrated acid fruit drink, made with fresh fruit vinegars, unbleached cane sugar, honey and spices. Nonalcoholic

Sour mix: A cocktail ingredient made from lemon or lime juice and sugar syrup (gomme), it is also known as sweet and sour mix or bar mix. Nonalcoholic

Southern Comfort: Peach-flavored bourbon liqueur

Strega: Liqueur with a herb flavor

Tabasco: Hot peppery sauce used to give an extra kick to cocktails, especially those with tomato juice. Nonalcoholic

Tia Maria: Coffee-flavored liqueur

Tonic water: Originally manufactured as a malaria cure by a Dutchman, Dr. Jakob Schweppe, the tonic was almost undrinkable and gin was added to make it palatable. Nonalcoholic

Triple sec: Very popular mixer with a bitter orange flavor

Vermouth: Wine, normally from Italy or France, infused with alcohol, herbs and other ingredients, which can be either an aperitif or cocktail mixer. There are two main types: dry, which is the stronger, and sweet, which, in turn, can be either red (rosso or rouge) or white (bianco or blanc)

Worcestershire sauce: A hot sauce that adds spice to cocktails in the Bloody Mary family. Nonalcoholic

General Index

Numbers in italics refer to picture captions.

Acknowledgments

In addition to Jordan Spence, the publishers would like to thank the following people for their contributions to the project: Chris Edwardes for providing many of the traditional cocktail recipes; David Ballheimer for indexing and for other editorial services; Rachel Federman for research work; Karl Adamson for the special photography; Bartok Borkowski for mixing drinks and Jowita Margula for her efficient help.

Picture Credits